The Politics of East Asia

The Politics of East Asia: China, Japan, Korea

John E. Endicott
and William R. Heaton

Westview Press / Boulder, Colorado

The views and conclusions expressed by the authors are their own and do not necessarily reflect those of the USAF Academy, the Department of Defense, or the U.S. government.

Copyright © 1978 by Westview Press, Inc.

Published in 1978 in the United States of America by
  Westview Press, Inc.
  5500 Central Avenue
  Boulder, Colorado 80301
  Frederick A. Praeger, Publisher

Library of Congress Cataloging in Publication Data
Endicott, John E.
  The politics of east Asia.
  Bibliography: p.
  Includes index.
  1. East Asia—Politics and government. I. Heaton, William R., joint author. II. Title.
DS518.1.E52   320.9′5   77-1346
ISBN 0-89158-127-8
ISBN 0-89158-128-6 pbk.

Printed and bound in the United States of America

About the Book and Authors

The Politics of East Asia:
China, Japan, Korea
John E. Endicott and William P. Heaton

This is the first undergraduate text on the politics of East Asia to be published since 1970. Looking at both domestic and international politics, the authors discuss the political systems of China, Japan, and Korea within the context of environmental factors, culture, society, the economy, geography, language, historical and political traditions, etc. The People's Republic of China is presented as a country with strong traditions, committed to rapid development under frequently changing ideological auspices. Its two governmental apparatuses—the party and the bureaucracy—sometimes act in unison, sometimes are locked in fierce struggles, and often are motivated by differing ideologies and administrative dynamics. Japan is seen as a mature society and a developed economy with functioning democratic institutions and a strong party system, but, like the PRC, subject to powerful traditions and influenced by radical ideologies. Both North and South Korea are discussed, with a comparison and contrast of the authoritarian-democratic system in the South, where a basically democratic parliament finds itself in conflict with a quasi-dictatorial regime and an all-powerful president.

The book is completely up to date. The section on China takes into account the major developments of the post-Mao period, including the accession of Hua Kuo-feng and the struggle against the Shanghai faction. The discussion of Japanese politics covers the 1976 elections, and the creation of the Shin Jiyu club in the developing thrust away from factional politics to an issue-oriented electorate.

Lt. Col. John E. Endicott is a member of the Pentagon Air Staff. He received a Ph.D. from the Fletcher School of Law and Diplomacy. Capt. William R. Heaton holds a Ph.D. from the University of California, Berkeley. He is currently a research fellow at the National Defense University. Both authors were formerly professors of political science at the U.S. Air Force Academy.

Contents

Figures, Tables, and Maps

Maps

Preface

There are a number of East Asian politics texts on the market that contain valuable insights into the various countries. However, they tend to quickly become outdated because of the rapid changes taking place in this part of the world. We feel that our book can help to bridge the gap because of what it does and does not try to do. It is designed for introductory undergraduate level courses and does not attempt to explore every issue in depth; nor does it attempt to present the final word on anything. Rather, it outlines the politics and important issues of three East Asian countries, with special attention directed to China and Japan.

We have found it most effective to teach the countries separately using a common methodology, and tying them together at the end of the semester. By staying on a very general level we have been able to incorporate current scholarly articles that illustrate and update certain points; our lectures fill out the discussions.

Instructional emphasis can take two directions. One is to expand the number of countries to include, for example, Mongolia, Taiwan, or perhaps Southeast Asia. The other is to explore topics in depth through special readings. For example, when we teach the portion on China, we direct students to current topics of interest like the Tangshan earthquake, the purge of the "Gang of Four," and changes in economic policy since the death of Mao. For Japan we look into topical issues like the defense budget, the Lockheed scandal, and airline hijackings. We feel that this approach enables our students to correlate the basic information in the text with ongoing business.

We have divided the major country studies into four subtopics: historical background, the nature of society, political institutions and decision making, and contemporary problems. The three countries we examine share geographic proximity and historic cultural ties, but their political systems have many differences. We have selected the factors we believe are most important for understanding contemporary politics. For example, in the chapter on society in China we discuss the efforts of the regime to mobilize and transform the society. In the chapter on Japanese society we discuss voter attitudes and how they have affected elections. The two chapters are related but obviously very different, covering the elements most important to the political culture in the respective countries.

We must also mention our sources. Although we are familiar with primary source materials, we have avoided citing them and have used translations wherever possible. Undergraduate students are often turned off by long romanizations of primary source materials that they cannot read. Most of the sources we cite are readily available in most undergraduate libraries. We also frequently cite interesting English language publications from the countries being studied (e.g., *Peking Review, China Reconstructs, Japan Echo*).

In essence, our purpose is to give beginning students a good solid background in East Asian politics and to expose them to the literature that will become more important as they advance in their studies of the region. We have tested this approach with our students at the USAF Academy and feel it has been highly successful. We wish to thank our cadets in Political Science 473, The Politics of East Asia, who read our drafts and assisted us in revising our material. We would also like to thank our colleagues at the Air Force Academy who supported us in a variety of ways. We are grateful to our typists, our bosses, our wives, and our publisher, all of whom were patient with us throughout this enterprise. To them goes much of the credit for this production although we, of course, remain ultimately responsible for the contents.

John E. Endicott
William R. Heaton

The Politics of East Asia

PART ONE

CHINA

CHAPTER ONE

The Revolution in Historical Perspective

A revolution is not a dinner party, or writing an essay, or painting a picture, or doing embroidery; it cannot be so refined, so leisurely and gentle, so temperate, kind, courteous, restrained and magnanimous. A revolution is an insurrection, an act of violence by which one class overthrows another.

—*Mao Tse-tung*[1]

There are a number of approaches to Chinese politics. Some scholars prefer to compare and contrast the China of today with yesterday's China, observing continuity and change. Others describe political institutions and functions, while still others examine China as a communist totalitarian system. The Chinese Communists themselves view China's politics as an ongoing process of revolution which leads to a certain, if distant, future.

All of these approaches have made contributions to this book. We recognize the importance of Chinese history, language, culture, and geography as the environmental setting for contemporary politics. We realize the importance of ideology and institutions; most importantly, we recognize that the Chinese political scene is dynamic, that it involves conflict and struggle. We hope to achieve a balanced view by combining contemporary social science analysis with the Chinese emphasis on revolutionary change.

WHAT IS REVOLUTION?

In the words of Mao, revolution is not a dinner party. It involves violence and struggle. Indeed, one need only review Chinese history over the past century to recognize that violence and struggle are an integral part of political life. Yet revolution is not merely violence and struggle. Chalmers Johnson points out that revolution consists of changes in both the value system and the structural features of a society brought about by violence.[2]

People's Republic of China

UNION OF SOVIET SOCIALIST REPUBLICS

HEILUNGKIANG

MONGOLIA

SINKIANG UIGHUR A R

TIBETAN A R

TSINGHAI

KANSU

NINGHSIA HUI A R

SHENSI

SZECHWAN

YUNNAN

KWEICHOW

KWANGSI CHUANG A R

KWANGTUNG

HUNAN

KIANGSI

HUPEH

HONAN

ANHWEI

SHANTUNG

SHANSI

HOPEH

PEKING MUNICIPALITY

TIENTSIN MUNICIPALITY

INNER MONGOLIAN A R

LIAONING

KIRIN

NORTH KOREA

SOUTH KOREA

KIANGSU

CHEKIANG

FUKIEN

SHANGHAI MUNICIPALITY

TAIWAN

HAINAN

AFGHANISTAN

JAMMU AND KASHMIR

INDIA

NEPAL

SIKKIM

BHUTAN

BURMA

THAILAND

LAOS

NORTH VIETNAM

PHILIPPINES

YELLOW SEA

EAST CHINA SEA

SOUTH CHINA SEA

FORMOSA STRAIT

Harbin

Chang chun

Shen yang

Antung

Dairen

Shih chia chuang

Tsinan

Tsingtao

Tientsin

Taiyuan

Cheng chou

Ho fei

Nanking

Shanghai

Hangchow

Nan chang

Foochow

Canton

HONG KONG

U K

MACAO

Port.

Nan ning

Kun ming

Kuei yang

Chung king

Cheng tu

Wu chang

Chang sha

Lan chou

Yin chuan

Hu ho hao t

Si an

Hsi ning

Ho ning

Urumchi

Lhasa

Mekong River

KEY

International boundary

Province boundary

A R Autonomous region

0   200   400

MILES

48

36

24

72   84   96   108   120   132

Applied to China, Johnson's concept gives insight into what happened. The social order of traditional China was unable to adapt to external and internal pressures. The ultimate result was "disequilibrium" between values and social structure. For a hundred years this disequilibrium was manifested in rebellion, foreign conquest, war, and turmoil. It eventually culminated in the civil wars of the 1930s and 1940s which brought the Chinese Communists to power. The Chinese Communists have sought to achieve radical changes in both values and social structure; struggle and violence have characterized this process up to the present.

As we shall see in subsequent chapters, the new social structure envisioned for China is based on a class analysis of Chinese society based on Marxist-Leninist theory as modified by Mao Tse-tung's thought. Mao's ideas also constitute the basis of the new system of values being propagated by the Chinese Communists. To the Chinese the most basic ingredient of Chinese politics is the concept of struggle—the struggle between the old and the new which leads to the establishment of socialist society.

SOURCES OF REVOLUTION IN CHINA

By the mid-nineteenth century a number of factors had combined to bring about instability in China. One of the most important elements was the decline of the ruling Manchu (Ch'ing) dynasty. Established in 1644, the 200-year-old dynasty was plagued by ineffective administration and fragmented leadership. The empire was confronted by a number of serious rebellions and was embarrassed and threatened by Western imperialism; all of these placed severe strain on the financial, military, and administrative capabilities of the dynasty. There were some attempts to reform and revitalize the dynasty in the late 1800s, but they were ineffective. The Manchu dynasty literally collapsed in 1911.

Another source of instability was rapid population increase. Between 1700 and 1800 China's population doubled from about 150 million to 300 million. This high rate of increase created pressure on the land and contributed to a lowering of the standard of living for many Chinese; it also aggravated the problem of famine.

Still another source was the challenge to traditional social structures brought by Western-style capitalism. China had remained an agrarian society while Europe was being industrialized. European commercialists introduced industrialization in the treaty ports; the degree of industrialization remained small, but it had significant

impact on China's internal trade. Urban centers such as Canton,
Shanghai, and Tientsin witnessed the growth of a small but
important working class.

While administrative decline, population pressure, the introduction of industry, and other factors challenged the social order, there
were also challenges to China's value system. The impact of the West
was perhaps even more significant in this process. With Western
money and gunboats came Western ideas. In late Ch'ing various
reformers had sought for methods by which China could adjust to
Western technology while maintaining the vitality of Chinese
tradition and culture. For one reason or another these efforts failed,
yet the influence of Western ideas carried to a new generation of
Chinese. The values associated with Confucianism were increasingly
discredited.[3]

Western concepts which appealed to the Chinese included
nationalism, democracy, and the need for scientific and technological
modernization. None of these concepts are neatly unified so it is not
surprising that their articulation in China resulted in the formation
of disparate groups, all seeking national salvation. Group conflict
further exacerbated social disequilibrium.

By the turn of the century, China was in a revolutionary situation.
Social structures were unable to change rapidly to adjust to the
onslaught of administrative decline, population pressure, and
technology and industry. Similarly, Confucianism, the glue of
China's social fabric, was less acceptable to a modernizing
generation. The indicators of disequilibrium—war, rebellion,
administrative decline, and political turmoil—were constantly to be
seen. Under such circumstances China entered revolution.

THE REVOLUTIONARY PROCESS: BEGINNINGS

While the roots of China's modern revolution run deep in China's
history, it is useful to begin with the "century of humiliation"
introduced by the Opium War of 1839-42. Prior to the Opium War
China had been able to remain aloof from the machinations of
Western imperialism, but the superior military technology of various
European countries, the United States, and eventually Japan enabled
these countries to gain inroads. For the West, both trade and
Christianity were motivating factors in the desire to "open" China.
Ch'ing authorities were generally reluctant to accept either,
consequently conflict was inevitable. The Opium War resulted in
humiliating defeat for China, and the treaties of Nanking in 1842 and

Tientsin in 1858 ushered in an era of Chinese subjugation to the West.

These treaties along with many other "unequal" treaties concluded with Western nations and Japan challenged China's sovereignty. Franklin Houn has listed several types of concessions and privileges extracted from China by the West under these treaties. Some of them included territorial control, trading rights such as the "most favored nation" clause, control of Chinese government agencies, right to send missionaries anywhere in China, right to extract minerals and to build factories and railroads, and extraterritoriality.[4]

The many concessions made by the Chinese in these treaties served as symbols to Chinese modernizers and nationalists, reminding them of the necessity of achieving self-determination and national power. John K. Fairbank has pointed out that not all of the results of the treaty system were negative for China.[5] The system of foreign trade was not as exploitative as has sometimes been alleged; Chinese urban merchants profited as much as did the foreigners and in some cases internal trade was benefited. Christian missionaries, while gaining fewer than 60,000 converts in China, brought many ideas through schools, hospitals, and other social services. It is small wonder that many of China's revolutionaries came from a background of education in a missionary institution. Scholars continue to disagree over the precise impact of Western imperialism in China and how good or bad that impact was. The issue cannot be resolved in this short space even if all the evidence were available. It is sufficient to repeat that the interaction of the West with China at this time helped to stimulate the forces of revolution.

Corresponding with the increased presence and pressure of the West was a series of internal revolts which exacerbated social conditions. The Taiping Rebellion (1850-64) is now hailed by the Chinese Communists as a progressive movement, but it resulted in great destruction and the death of millions. It was followed by the Nien Rebellion (1848-68), the Miao Rebellion (1855-72), a Muslim Rebellion in Yunnan (1855-73), and another Islamic rebellion in the Northwest from 1861 to 1878. Reformers such as K'ang Yu-wei and Liang Ch'i-ch'ao sought to reform the Manchu dynasty and strengthen it. They were willing to accept foreign aid and advice; however they were resisted by the Ch'ing dictator, the Empress Dowager Tz'u-hsi, and their programs were only briefly put into operation. The end result was further weakening of the dynasty.

The Boxer Rebellion (1900-1902) demonstrated the inability of the government to cope with internal disorder which only invited even greater foreign intervention. Meanwhile, several reformist and revolutionary organizations grew in strength. The most prominent of these was the *t'ung-meng-hui* (Alliance Society) led by Dr. Sun Yat-sen. Sun, a Western educated physician, sought the overthrow of the Manchus and fundamental changes in China's society and government. His *san-min chu-i* (Three People's Principles) advocated nationalism and self-determination, democratic political institutions, and a kind of economic socialism for China. These principles subsequently became the official program of the Kuomintang (Chinese Nationalist Party) which Sun later founded in 1922.

When the Ch'ing dynasty collapsed in 1911, Sun was called from his travels abroad to return to China to form a government. However, the fragmentation of his movement and lack of military support prevented him from consolidating power. Yuan Shih-k'ai, a commander in the imperial army, gained the presidency of the newly formed republic and planned to restore the monarchy with himself as ruler. Yuan died in 1916 before realizing his ambition. Meanwhile, China drifted into a period of warlordism. A number of warlords with private armies ruling various regions of China competed with each other for control of a powerless central government.

In spite of the turbulent situation at home, the Chinese government joined the Allied cause in World War I in the hope of regaining German acquisitions in Shantung. When these holdings were handed over to Japan during the Versailles negotiations, the nadir of China's humiliation was reached. The Peking government remained powerless to respond to this indignity, although massive demonstrations erupted in China's major cities. Students, intellectuals, and other Chinese joined in an overwhelming show of discontent. The May Fourth movement, as these activities were collectively called, symbolized the rapid growth of nationalist sentiment in China. This movement caused intellectuals to form new organizations which could mobilize other groups in society.

The May Fourth movement also stimulated interest in Marxism. Chinese intellectuals were impressed with the revolution in Russia and the implications the Bolshevik movement might have for China. Furthermore, the Soviet government had repudiated Tsarist unequal treaties with China. An organization devoted to the study of Marxism at Peking University became the nucleus of the Chinese Communist Party (CCP), which was organized with *Comintern* assistance in Shanghai in 1921. Ch'en Tu-hsiu, a philosophy professor at Peking University, became its first chairman. Mao Tse-tung, a librarian's assistant at the university, became an early member.

Sun Yat-sen had moved to Canton and sought the formation of a new government. He also received support from Comintern agents in the creation of the Kuomintang (KMT) in 1922. Soviet advisors urged a united front with the Chinese Communists so the organizations formed an alliance. From 1924 to 1926 Communists held positions in the KMT and worked together with the Nationalists to consolidate and expand the new government.

THE CHINESE CIVIL WAR

After the death of Sun Yat-sen in 1926, a struggle for power within the KMT developed. Chiang K'ai-shek, a commander of the newly formed and trained army, was able to consolidate his position as leader in spite of Soviet opposition. Chiang planned and prepared the Northern Campaign by which he hoped to unify China and was supported by the Chinese Communists until 1927 when, for a variety of reasons, he turned against them. Communists were expelled from the KMT and many were imprisoned or killed. The Communists, at Stalin's behest, also tried to sustain peasant uprisings in various parts of China, but these were quickly suppressed.

The failure of the united front left the Communists on the verge of extinction; nevertheless, Mao Tse-tung, who had been involved in organizing peasants in Hunan, and a small number of followers escaped to Ching-kang-shan. In this remote area of Kiangsu Province, the Communists organized a soviet, or council, and gradually developed their strength. Under the leadership of Mao and Chu Teh, an insurgency was planned. There was competition for leadership of the CCP, and it changed several times during this period. Generally speaking, Soviet-supported leadership controlled the Party until 1935 when Mao was able to consolidate his power on the eve of the Long March.

While the Communists organized in the wilderness, Chiang K'ai-shek proceeded on his Northern Campaign and succeeded in defeating some warlords and forming alliances with others. The Nationalists formed a government, established a capital at Nanking, and obtained foreign recognition and assistance. The KMT sponsored political reforms, advanced industrialization, and improved education and health. In spite of certain KMT weakness, it launched ambitious programs for social change. Unfortunately for the Nationalists, many of these ambitious programs were never accomplished. Those groups most desirous of change were grouped with the Communists. Furthermore, the requirements of foreign financial support and maintaining alliances with warlords precluded

"Moving Toward Victory," an oil painting by Peng Pin, depicts Mao's ascendancy to power at the Tsunyi conference in 1955 during the Long March.

Soldiers of the Communist Fourth Front Army in north Shensi at the end of the Long March.

significant changes in many areas.

It is easy to criticize the KMT from hindsight, but it must be realized that serious problems continued to plague the Nationalists. The Communist insurgency in the South and Japanese machinations in the Northeast preoccupied Chiang and caused him to emphasize military solutions. He was most concerned with the Communists and mounted five major extermination campaigns against them in the early 1930s. In the final campaign in 1934, the Nationalists, supported by German advisors, surrounded the Communists and nearly defeated them. However, the Communists broke through the encirclement and embarked on the Long March which finally ended in Yenan in early 1936. The hardships of the Long March cost the Communists thousands of lives but helped to develop a solid core of strongly disciplined cadres and soldiers, as well as the talented leadership which would become the foundation of the People's Republic years later.

During the Long March the Communists changed from a policy of direct confrontation with Chiang K'ai-shek to one which called for a new united front against the Japanese. In Yenan the Communists propagandized that Chinese should not fight Chinese while the Japanese were invading. This propaganda campaign began to have an effect although Chiang remained determined to eliminate the "red menace" before turning attention to Japan. Chiang was forced to change his policy after the famous Sian incident in which he was kidnapped by one of the warlord generals on Christmas Day of 1936 while on a visit to the anti-Communist front. The Communists and the Nationalists concluded a new united front directed against Japan. Japan began an all-out war against China in 1937, but in spite of this threat, the new united front was never viable.

Most of the Nationalist armies were defeated quickly by the Japanese, and the government moved inland to Chungking. The Communists remained behind Japanese lines and expanded their insurgency. During World War II, or the War of Resistance against Japan as it is known by the Chinese, the Communists effectively combined patriotic appeal with social reform to consolidate and expand their power. While the Nationalists became increasingly bogged down in a swamp of corruption, debt, and lack of will, the Communists became more confident of achieving victory. In the early 1940s the Communists conducted a *cheng-feng*, or rectification campaign, designed to purify the Party by heightening ideological knowledge and commitment to the overall policy of the Party. The rectification campaign enabled the Party to develop the administrative infrastructure required for eventual establishment of a national government.

A civil war between the Communists and the Nationalists developed as they fought the Japanese and after the defeat of Japan it quickly erupted in serious engagements. At first the Nationalists appeared to have the upper hand inasmuch as they had superiority in manpower and weaponry, as well as foreign support. The Communists, however, had superiority in will and morale. The United States sent several representatives including George C. Marshall to attempt to arrange an end to the civil war, but in spite of various agreements, the negotiations were never fruitful, and full scale war continued. In 1948 and 1949, the Nationalist armies suffered defeat, and the KMT government was forced to flee to Taiwan. The KMT established the government of the Republic of China, which continues to claim to be the legitimate government of all China though it effectively rules only Taiwan. The victorious Communists moved quickly to consolidate power. On October 1, 1949, Mao Tsetung stood at Tienanmen in Peking to proclaim the establishment of the People's Republic of China and said, "The Chinese people have stood up."

In retrospect the Communist victory appears to have come not because of support from the USSR or because of failure of the United States to support the Nationalists at critical junctures. Rather, the reasons for Communist victory are to be found in the goals and purposes being articulated by all revolutionary political groups in China, including the Nationalists. The Chinese people increasingly demanded the establishment of unity, self-determination, national pride and power, and socio-economic reform. The Communists won because they were able to articulate these types of goals effectively and to organize and mobilize people better than other movements. This was the source of their appeal and their power.

THE REVOLUTIONARY PROCESS AND CONTEMPORARY POLITICS

The preceding historical synopsis of how the Communists came to power sets the stage for a discussion of the issues debated by students of Chinese politics. One of the most important of these issues is the role of Mao in the Chinese revolution. Edgar Snow's biography of Mao, written shortly after the Long March, revealed Mao's life to have been a microcosm of the revolution. Robert Lifton and Richard Solomon, among others, have examined the development of Mao's personality during the Communist rise to account for policy options in China today. Lifton argued that the Cultural Revolution was based on Mao's psychological desire to achieve "revolutionary immortality," while Solomon related the psychology of Mao to the development of ideology.[6] Scholars such as Benjamin Schwartz, Stuart Schram, and Frederick Wakeman have provided insights into the development of Mao's thought and his contributions to Marxism-Leninism during this period.[7]

While Mao has occupied a singularly important role in Chinese politics, it must be remembered that for many years he was not in the mainstream of CCP affairs. Earlier leaders of the CCP are now officially condemned as "right" or "left" deviationists, just as have many who have been closely associated with Mao in the exercise of power since 1949. Movements such as the Cultural Revolution are more clearly understood when Mao's uphill battle to gain control of the Party in the 1930s is recognized. Men such as Chu Teh, Liu Shao-ch'i, Chou En-lai, and many others also contributed significantly to the Communist success. To focus exclusively on Mao would be a mistake.

Another issue has to do with precisely how the Chinese Communists were able to appeal to the masses to strengthen themselves during the anti-Japanese and civil wars. Chalmers Johnson has presented a strong argument that the Communist program rested primarily on anti-Japanese nationalism; the Chinese

Communists achieved social mobilization among the peasantry through patriotic propaganda and harnessed peasant nationalism through effective organization.[8] Mark Seldon, on the other hand, argues that the social and organizational reforms achieved by the CCP were the primary source of their power.[9] Other scholars have also contributed to this ongoing debate. For our purposes, it is instructive to point out that both nationalism and social reform were significant elements of the CCP's appeal.

Still another issue has to do with foreign support. Chiang K'ai-shek's book *Soviet Russia in China* argued that the victory of the CCP was little more than the Soviet conquest of China. Scholars have challenged this argument, though some have stressed the importance of Soviet aid to the Chinese.[10] Interestingly, the "revisionist" scholarship now prevalent in the USSR argues that Mao was a fascist from the beginning, a reactionary militarist who sided with the Soviet Union only temporarily for convenience but then showed his true colors after consolidating power. In the Soviet view, the USSR gave significant support to the Chinese revolution, yet Mao betrayed his own party and the revolution; therefore, Mao's opponents are the true revolutionaries.[11]

As Soviet support for the CCP is a topic of debate, so is the role of the United States in China. During the early 1950s, the issue of "who lost China" resulted in considerable political recrimination, particularly against those State Department officials who served in China during the war and sometimes presented a favorable impression of the Yenan government. In the early 1970s, just as most scholars were coming around to the view that China was never anyone's to lose, the debate heated up with Anthony Kubek's introduction to a series of documents on that period. Kubek again charged that officials of the U.S. State Department bore much of the responsibility for the fall of China to Communism.[12] Kubek's charges produced a burst of new scholarship including a response by John S. Service, a principal in the event, who completely discredited Kubek's account.[13] A host of new research on this period and the American role has hence been forthcoming.[14]

The Chinese revolution is being reexamined by scholars from various countries. Much of the current research has increased our understanding of the period, yet few issues of the type we have raised here have been resolved. The Chinese revolution has been a highly complex movement, and it is likely that new interpretations will continue to be forthcoming. With these complexities in mind, it is useful to compare and contrast the revolutionary programs of the Chinese Communists with the social and political milieu in China as they came to power.

REVOLUTION AND TRADITION IN CHINESE POLITICS

Franz Schurmann has pointed out that a revolution does not immediately sweep away the values and structures of a society and replace them with new ones.[15] Rather, aspects of the prerevolutionary society and the newly articulated values and structures exist side by side for a time. Certain facets of China's political heritage seem to have been especially significant in influencing present political values and structures.

One of the most important of these is related to the goal of territorial unification mentioned earlier. Historical precedent demonstrated that strong dynasties sought to consolidate China's frontiers. This territorial consolidation was symbolic of dynastic strength and vitality as well as necessary for national defense. It is not surprising that the Chinese Communists at the outset sought to reclaim territories such as Inner Mongolia, Sinkiang, and Tibet, which were traditionally part of China but which had experienced moves for autonomy and independence during the late Ch'ing and early Republican periods. The Chinese Communists did not hesitate to use military force to maintain control of these areas when necessary. Indeed, the territorial question continues to influence China's relations with the USSR, India, Vietnam, and other countries on its periphery.

Another aspect has to do with the relationship between ideology and governmental institutions. Many historians have maintained that dynastic China found a synthesis between Confucian values and the legalist state.[16] China is familiar with authoritarian-style political structures. Thus, it is really not much of a change for the Chinese to be under a Communist rule which is also authoritarian. Some scholars have gone so far as to portray the present regime as a dynasty.[17]

We should be quick to point out, however, that there are fundamental distinctions between Confucianism and Maoism. John Starr has pointed out that Maoism has served many of the same functions for Chinese society as did Confucianism, yet, the two concepts are basically opposed.[18] Confucianism, for example, emphasizes harmonious relationships whereas the thought of Mao

Tse-tung stresses contradictions and struggle between social classes. The thought of Mao is rooted in the Marxian concept of dialectical materialism while Confucianism makes no assumptions about the forward momentum of history. Confucianism was elitist while Maoism is strongly egalitarian. There are numerous other differences in philosophical content; consequently, it is no surprise that the Communists have thoroughly repudiated Confucianism in their attempt to transform society through political socialization of the masses.

The contemporary effort to achieve the "correct" socialization of the Chinese people far exceeds anything attempted in the past. In traditional China, Confucianism was largely the property of the ruling groups while only a watered-down version, usually mixed with local religious preferences, filtered to the masses. Presently, a large propaganda apparatus is maintained by the state to facilitate the fostering of correct political attitudes. This has implied much greater linkage between the state and society today than ever existed in China past. In this respect, the power of political institutions is much greater now. The Party is much more concerned with the thought and conduct of the masses, and the masses are much more aware of the policies of the state. This process of social mobilization is continuing.

Another important aspect of China's heritage relevant to the present has to do with the economy. Before the CCP came to power, China already had considerable internal trade based on standard marketing areas.[19] At the same time, concepts of personal property were never highly developed in China.[20] Consequently, the efforts toward collectivization of property by the Chinese Communists are not really outside the realm of historical patterns and may actually have been facilitated by traditional values and structures.

We have noted only some of the most salient aspects of China's heritage which are relevant to the contemporary political system. In subsequent chapters we will deal much more thoroughly with the issues of revolutionary change in values and structures. The purpose of this section has been to introduce the proposition that while the Communists are promoting revolutionary change, there are still many elements of China's past which have import for the establishment of the new society.

THE REVOLUTIONARY REGIME: AN OVERVIEW

Since the establishment of the People's Republic in 1949, the regime has gone through several phases. This section will give a brief

On October 1, 1949, Mao Tse-tung proclaimed the establishment of the People's Republic of China stating, "The Chinese people, comprising one quarter of humanity, have now stood up."

overview of these phases. The first period was that of reconstruction
which extended from 1949 to 1952. During this period the Chinese
Communists consolidated political authority and began the economic reconstruction of the country. Initially, political administration was in the hands of the People's Liberation Army (PLA), which
established Military Control Commissions to govern various regions
as they were "liberated" from Nationalist control. The PLA was
responsible for mopping-up operations against pockets of Kuomintang or bandit resistance and for establishing civil authority. As
authority was consolidated, areas were gradually returned to civilian
control; however, the five field armies were assigned various
geographic regions and remained in the background. In establishing
civil administration the Chinese Communists sometimes utilized
former KMT bureaucrats until a sufficient number of cadres could be
recruited and trained to fill positions.

A number of mass movements were launched to begin the
transformation of the society. The most important was land reform,
accomplished by acts of violence that symbolically rejected the
traditional social structure and were extremely important in enabling
the Communists to continue the process of transforming the loyalties
of the people.[21] In urban areas a campaign was begun, to place large
industrial enterprises under the control of the state. Almost
surprisingly, the Communist reforms were accomplished with few
economic dislocations. China's economy had been so ravaged by
years of war that it was possible to undertake substantial change
without creating disaster. Through land reform and the various
urban campaigns, the CCP was able to gain the upper hand over
problems—particularly inflation and corruption—that had undermined the Nationalists. Public confidence in the regime was thereby
stimulated.

In foreign policy, China formed an alliance with the Soviet Union
and entered the Korean War. China's involvement in Korea, although
extremely costly (the United Nations command estimated that China
sustained over 900,000 casualties) proved that the regime would
uphold its pledge to "stand up" to foreign aggression.[22] The
movement to "Resist America, Aid Korea," that swept China
demonstrated the great sacrifices the people were willing to make to
support the "People's Volunteers." This movement furthered
linkages between the government and the people and enabled the
regime to increase its legitimacy.

Though some of the campaigns resulted in much violence and
personal suffering, the overall effect was to establish the new

government on a sound footing. A new corps of politically motivated administrators was being created, the economy was improving, and most importantly, the masses were being mobilized in pursuit of the new goals articulated by the CCP. These successes encouraged the Communists to begin a new phase of broader social change.

The second period, from 1953 to 1957, coincided roughly with China's First Five-Year Plan. The treaty with the Soviet Union provided for Soviet aid and advisors for China's industrialization. Industrial growth was predicated on a Soviet model, which was successful in rapidly improving production in key sectors. In 1949 the gross value of industrial output (GVIO) was 14,020 million *yuan*, and by 1957 it had increased to 78,390 million *yuan*, or about 5½ times the 1949 figure. However, there were imbalances; many Chinese leaders felt that agriculture, in particular, was being neglected. Furthermore, the interest on Soviet loans was high, and the Soviets had demanded concessions, such as military bases in China, that the Chinese were unwilling to make. By the end of 1957, the Chinese Communists were becoming increasingly dissatisfied with the Soviet model.

In agriculture, China began a process of gradual collectivization. Peasants were encouraged to join Mutual Assistance Teams on a seasonal basis. As their economic situation improved, they were urged to form Agricultural Producers' Cooperatives (APCs).[23] These changes were accompanied by rural economic improvement, though rural development was greatly outdistanced by industrial development.

The development of industry and the collectivization of agriculture also produced changes in the social landscape. Industrialization meant the rapid growth of urban areas and implied an educational system geared toward training skilled workers. Collectivization of agriculture set the stage for specialization in peasant work and made possible the expansion of mechanization, rural electrification, rural public works, and reclamation projects. Great strides in health care and education were also made during this period.

In political affairs, a constitution for the PRC was promulgated in 1954 after delegates to the National People's Congress were chosen in elections held throughout China. People were mobilized to participate in the elections—to support candidates already chosen by the party. In 1954-1955 there was some unrest within the Party as Kao Kang and Jao Shu-shih challenged Mao's leadership; they failed and were purged. In 1957 the short-lived Hundred Flowers movement gave rise to much criticism of the regime on the part of intellectuals. Initially the criticism was encouraged by Mao, but when it proved to be more than Party leaders anticipated, they moved quickly to silence the critics.[24] According to Mao, the situation in Hungary warned the Chinese leaders to take steps to stifle dissent before counterrevolutionary forces could cause serious trouble. Since 1957 the intellectuals have not mounted a serious challenge to the regime, though they have been frequently and persistently criticized.

In foreign policy, China continued to adhere to its alliance with the USSR even though political and ideological disagreements were beginning. The decision of Khrushchev to repudiate Stalin in 1956 contributed to the rift, although the rift was not obvious to outsiders at the time. China ushered in a period of appeal to nonaligned countries though "Bandung diplomacy." Chou En-lai articulated the "Five Points of Peaceful Coexistence" as a standard for mutual relations between countries. China participated at the Geneva Conference on Indochina that produced a French withdrawal. In short, although China's relations with the Soviet Union were beginning to show signs of strain, China's relations with many other countries were improving.

The third period—that of the Great Leap Forward—extended from 1958 to 1960. During the Great Leap the Communists launched an all-out effort to achieve socialist transformation of the economy and the society. Overoptimistic assumptions about past performance encouraged the authorities to organize people's communes in rural areas. The communes were to produce a combination of technological skills and rural manpower for rapid economic development. They were characterized by complete public ownership of property.

In fact, the communes never got off the ground. Faulty statistics inflated by pressures for achievement, bad weather, and natural disasters quickly turned the Great Leap into an economic fiasco. The consequences were severe. In 1961-62 Hong Kong witnessed the tremendous suffering of thousands of refugees who tried to escape South China. Food shortages caused serious dissatisfaction with the government, and many areas were in administrative turmoil.

By 1960 the government realized the seriousness of its errors and began a program of retrenchment. The communes were decentralized so that the production team—equivalent in size to the former APC—became the unit of production decisions. Private plots of land, fruit trees, livestock, and other personal property were permitted. Generally speaking, the programs of the Great Leap were abandoned, although there was a greater effort to coordinate agriculture and industrial production than there had been prior to the Leap.

The Great Leap was not a total failure, however. The organization of communes demonstrated the ability of the Communists to introduce changes in social structure and to mobilize the population in pursuit of social as well as economic goals. Large numbers of cadres were sent down to rural areas in a massive *hsia fang*, which greatly expanded Party membership in rural areas and contributed to leadership in these areas.

In political affairs, another major purge of leadership occurred when Marshall P'eng Teh-huai, minister of defense and commander of Chinese forces in Korea, challenged Mao's authority. P'eng was dismissed and replaced by Lin Piao; but at the same time Mao was forced to retire from his position as head of the government and was replaced by Liu Shao-ch'i. Mao retained the Party chairmanship but was removed from the process of day-to-day decisions.

In foreign affairs the disagreement with the Soviet Union became a serious rupture. The Soviet Union refused to supply nuclear weapons and technology to China, expressing concern that Chinese policy had become too adventuristic. The Soviets were concerned not only about China's domestic policies, which appeared too radical, but also with the crisis that had been developing in the Taiwan straits. Worried about the possibility of another Sino-U.S. war, the Soviets were reluctant to support China. The withdrawal of Soviet advisors began during this period and was completed by 1961.

The next period in Chinese politics, from 1961 to 1966, was characterized by economic improvement and increasing political instability. The Great Leap had addressed the problem of unbalanced growth between agriculture and industry, and the post-Leap period brought about a new synthesis between them. The Chinese Communists relied heavily on the accumulation of agricultural surplus to finance industrial development. The primary thrust of industry, however, would be to serve agriculture. The concept of self-reliance, based on the Yenan experience and the Great Leap experience, combined state planning with some degree of decentralization of production decisions. This flexibility permitted an upsurge in production. The regime also permitted an expansion of material incentives to stimulate production in both agriculture and industry.

These policies fed a growing disagreement between China's leaders. In Communist terms, the contradictions between the two lines were revealing their antagonistic character. On the one hand were those who pursued policies classically identified with modernization—bureaucratization, recruitment of technical specialists for Party and government positions, material incentives in the economy, and the expansion of foreign trade. On the other hand were those who favored an emphasis on ideological purity, political criteria in recruitment, and normative incentives. The "two-line" dichotomy is undoubtedly an oversimplification of the various forces feeding the dispute; nevertheless, it became increasingly apparent that China's leaders were in disagreement over fundamental policy questions.

In foreign affairs, the dispute with the Soviet Union became more serious. When the USSR sided with India in the border war of 1962, the split probably became irreconcilable. A series of bitter polemics between the two countries demonstrated the seriousness of the rift. China maintained that a "capitalist restoration" had occurred in the USSR and that the leaders had betrayed the revolution. The USSR made equally serious charges against the Chinese. The split between the two countries was reflected in the international Communist movement inasmuch as parties in most countries also split into pro-Soviet and pro-Peking parties.

Mao and his supporters likened what was happening in China to the revisionism of the USSR. Convinced that China must be purified of such leanings, Mao encouraged development of the Socialist Education Campaign in 1964-65, designed to overcome these revisionist tendencies. Mao's closest ally, Lin Piao, had groomed the military for such a campaign by emphasizing the study of Mao's works. The primary slogan of the Socialist Education Campaign became "Learn from the PLA." This movement only served to heighten the antagonisms between various elites, and it soon gave way to the Cultural Revolution.

The next period in China's political history was the Cultural Revolution, from 1966 to 1969, which witnessed unprecedented political upheaval. On the eve of the Cultural Revolution, China was confronted with serious policy problems, the growing rift with the USSR, increasing U.S. involvment in Vietnam, the issue of nuclear weapons and military strategy (China detonated an atomic bomb in 1964), incentives for economic development, leadership succession, and a host of other issues, both domestic and international. Resistance to the Socialist Education Campaign on the part of leading Party authorities convinced Mao that his opposition must be eliminated. In the fall of 1966, the Red Guards, sponsored by Mao's wife, Chiang Ch'ing, and his personal secretary, Ch'en Po-ta, began an attack on important Party leaders. Demonstrations and riots broke out throughout China's major cities. Not only were a large number of Party leaders purged; but both Party and state organs became incapable of performing their responsibilities. The government became virtually paralyzed.

Eventually Mao called on the military to restore order. Revolutionary Committees were established under military auspices to perform political administration. The Red Guards were disbanded; many were sent to the countryside to make revolution by integrating with the peasants. The military was able to restore order, but it took several years to reestablish Party organs in the provinces. By the spring of 1969 this work had been largely completed, and the CCP held its Ninth Party Congress. Nearly half of the members of the new Politburo were military officers; the same held true for the new Central Committee. Lin Piao was designated Mao's successor in the new Party constitution.

Despite the upheavals of the Cultural Revolution, China apparently did not sustain irreparable economic harm. The education system was shut down, and new political criteria were established for admission to higher education before the institutions reopened. There were also reports that peasants hoarded grain and did not meet state requirements. These difficulties were overcome as order was restored.

China's foreign policy was characterized by strong vocal support for People's War. All of China's ambassadors were recalled except the ambassador to Egypt. Research demonstrates that China was quite cautious in actual support for insurgency,[25] but the popular image presented was one of radical fanaticism for supporting guerrilla wars. China did become involved in serious border clashes with the USSR early in 1969, and both sides escalated military preparations along the border. Thus, the Cultural Revolution was characterized by upheaval in both domestic and foreign policy.

Between 1969 and 1975 China experienced continued turmoil; yet a gradual reestablishment of Party and state organs was achieved. Several Politburo members were purged between 1969 and 1970, including Ch'en Po-ta. In September 1971 Lin Piao supposedly organized a coup against Mao and was killed in an airplane crash along with other top military leaders when they attempted to flee China after the coup collapsed. During the Cultural Revolution, Lin had stacked the upper echelons of the Party with cronies from the 4th Field Army; after his downfall, a gradual realignment occurred that suggested a balance of power among key regional commands had been restored at the center.[26]

In August 1973 the Tenth Party Congress was held and a new constitution for the Party was promulgated. This constitution made Mao, already the Party chairman, also chairman of the Military

Commission, and named no successor. Shortly after the congress, China's regional military commanders were shifted, an unprecedented occurrence. An uncomfortable interface between political factions in China was demonstrated by a nationwide campaign to "Criticize Lin Piao and Confucius," which had overtones of a criticism against China's premier, Chou En-lai. Nevertheless, in January 1975 the long-delayed Fourth National People's Congress was convened. The congress symbolized a reconstruction of state organs on all levels; the composition of the new state leadership indicated balance among various factions.

In foreign affairs the Soviet Union became China's antagonistic contradiction, and relations with the United States improved. After initial visits by Henry Kissinger and other officials, President Nixon visited Peking in 1972. The Chinese and American governments issued the Shanghai Communique, which pledged an improvement in relations between the two nations. Since then trade and cultural relations have expanded, but full normalization of political relations has not yet been achieved, owing primarily to continued U.S. recognition of the Nationalist government on Taiwan and its defense treaty with that government. President Ford also visited Peking and met with Chinese leaders, and President Carter has pledged to continue the implementation of the Shanghai Communique. During this period, China was admitted to the United Nations as one of the five permanent members of the Security Council and has achieved full diplomatic recognition from most countries in the international community. While it pledges never to be a superpower and identifies primarily with the cause of the developing nations, China has enjoyed correct and friendly state-to-state relations with most countries outside the Soviet sphere of influence.

The most recent phase of China's political history may be termed the era of leadership transition. In late 1975 and early 1976 such important "old-guard" leaders as Chu Teh, Tung Pi-wu, Kang Sheng, and Chou En-lai died. In September 1976 Mao himself died, touching off a power struggle among his would-be successors. In April 1976, after the death of Chou En-lai, it was anticipated that Teng Hsiao-p'ing would become premier. Teng was purged shortly after giving Chou's eulogy and was replaced by a relative newcomer, Hua Kuo-feng. Hua also claimed the Party chairmanship after Mao's death, and after gaining the support of key regional military commanders, proceeded to purge four leading Politburo members including Mao's wife, Chiang Ch'ing. During 1977 Hua presided over a massive campaign against the "Gang of Four" in an effort to consolidate his position. The Eleventh CCP Congress convened in August 1977 and the Fifth National People's Congress in early 1978 confirmed the position of Hua and brought about another rehabilitation of Ten Hsiao-p'ing. These meetings also furthered a dramatic revision of Cultural Revolution policies.

While China remains committed to the goals of unity, power, and economic development, the period of leadership transition will likely be characterized by changes in policy. In the late 1970s China is turning away from the policies of the Maoist era; whether it will also depart from the political turmoil that has marked Communist rule so far remains to be seen.

SUMMARY

The purpose of this chapter has been to give insights into the historical background of the Chinese Revolution. We have given a brief account of this history and have suggested that it is related to contemporary politics. This relationship will become increasingly clear as we examine the society, ideology, political structures, decision making, and other elements of the policy process.

The main point is that for a variety of reasons China entered a revolutionary situation in the late nineteenth and early twentieth century. The Chinese Communist Party came to power as a benefactor of the situation and leader of the movement. The CCP's objective is to reorder society based on values articulated by Mao's concept of the future. In no small measure, Chinese politics is an account of struggle between China past and China future.

CHAPTER TWO

Ideology and Society

Apart from their other characteristics, the outstanding thing about China's 600 million people is that they are "poor and blank." This may seem a bad thing, but in reality it is a good thing. Poverty gives rise to the desire for change, the desire for revolution. On a blank sheet of paper free from any mark, the freshest and most beautiful characters can be written, the freshest and most beautiful pictures can be painted.

—*Mao Tse-tung*[1]

In many respects the establishment of the People's Republic of China in 1949 was only a beginning. The idea of "continuing revolution" has been frequently articulated in the various movements to mobilize and transform Chinese society. Chapter One gave insights into the roots of contemporary Chinese politics; this chapter examines the social environment of their politics. We first examine the ideological principles that are at work, and then we discuss the unique aspects of Chinese society.

IDEOLOGY

The Marxist image of society is one of coercion and struggle. According to Marx, societies evolve through various stages, activated by a dialectical process. Dialectical materialism specifies that economic relationships are the basis of social organization, that societies change as the material basis is transformed, and that consciousness is a reflection of the changing material base of society. Revolution will occur in advanced capitalist societies, the bourgeoisie, or ruling class, will be overthrown by the working class, and eventually socialism will be achieved. Lenin argued the need for a highly-organized, well-disciplined "vanguard of the proletariat," or Communist Party, and advanced the idea that imperialism could forestall revolution in advanced capitalist countries. Lenin also foresaw the rise of revolutionary movements in developing countries in response to imperialism and colonialism.

It has been argued by many that Mao added very little to the fundamental tenets of Marxist-Leninist ideology. Mao's most significant contributions are in the area of application. Franz Schurmann observes that Mao's major contribution to the world has been the creation of "practical" ideology. According to Schurmann's view, Mao has taken the "pure" ideology of Marxism-Leninism and has creatively applied it to the practical problems of China's revolution. The result is what is known in China today as the Thought of Mao Tse-tung.[2]

Precisely what constitutes the Thought of Mao Tse-tung is difficult to ascertain since there are now five volumes of his *Selected Works,* copies of numerous speeches, and even his off-the-cuff remarks at various meetings have been cited in the official media. Mao's Thought ranges all the way from quite profound theoretical works such as "On Contradictions" to such down-to-earth slogans as "Serve the People." Frederic Wakeman has demonstrated significant influence on Mao's thinking by classical Chinese and Western philosophers, as well as Marx and Lenin.[3] Now that Mao is no longer around to define correct interpretations of his thought, it is anticipated by many scholars of China that his thought will be manipulated by his successors to justify whatever policies they want to implement. The exact nature of this practical ideology may be hard to discern, but its influence on society has been quite dramatic.

Of all Mao's concepts, four appear to be most fundamental: the idea of will and struggle, the idea of self-reliance, the idea of the mass line, and the concept of contradictions. These four are constantly repeated in propaganda and would appear to constitute the basis of Mao's ideology.

Will and Struggle

A major feature of Maoist ideology is emphasis on changing the objective world through will and struggle. In essays such as "On Practice" and "Where Do Correct Ideas Come From," Mao states that experience is necessary before correct knowledge can be obtained. The purpose of correct knowledge is action—the accomplishment of revolution. Unlike Marx and Engels, who predicated ideas on objective reality, Mao believed that social consciousness could be created through education and experience. By participating in revolution the people could achieve a "revolutionary class consciousness" in spite of the backwardness of their material circumstance.

Mao's ideas clearly reflect the nature of social reality in China. In the absence of an advanced industrial base or a large proletariat, Mao saw that revolution in China had to be based on the peasantry. Yet to square the realities of China with Marxist-Leninist ideology, it was necessary for Mao to explain how a revolutionary consciousness could be created among the peasants. The idea that this consciousness could come about through involvement in revolutionary movements was based on Mao's own personal experience.

From the early days of its organization until 1935, Mao was not usually in the mainstream of Chinese Communist Party ideology. During that period the CCP experienced several major disasters, most notably the dissolution of the first united front with the Kuomintang in 1927-28 and the encirclement at Kiangsi in 1934-35. Mao believed that these failures were due as much to ideological as to other causes; the key lay in mobilizing the peasants and leading them correctly. During World War II when Chiang Kai-shek was defeated by the Japanese, Mao gained enough control of the CCP to effectively implement his ideas of mobilizing the masses. Once the masses were mobilized, sufficient political and military power was available to expand the movement, eventually bringing victory over the Nationalists and the establishment of the People's Republic.

In 1945 Mao told his cadres, "We must thoroughly clear away all ideas of winning easy victories through good luck, without hard and bitter struggle."[4] Again, Mao likened the work of the party and the masses in eliminating imperialism and feudalism to the "Foolish Old Man Who Removed the Mountains."[5] The themes of will and struggle—that people can change their objective condition through determination, hard work, patience, and sacrifice—have continued to the present. Various mass movements in China have mobilized the people to fight against everything from counterrevolutionaries to flies. During the Great Leap Forward the masses were urged to "Go all out, aim high," and during the Cultural Revolution they were urged to "Dare to swim against the tide." Individuals who are hailed in the official media for their successes reflect the values of will and struggle.

Self-Reliance

Closely related to the value of will and struggle in Maoist ideology is the value of self-reliance. Prior to 1949 the Chinese Communists were in a defensive position, usually isolated and often on the verge of extinction. Under such trying circumstances, it was necessary for the Party to not only mobilize the masses, but also to rely on them. In fact, Mao came to believe that over-reliance on outside aid could result in disaster. Only reliance on oneself could ensure success.

The concept of self-reliance is demonstrated in a variety of ways. The People's Liberation Army is expected to produce much of its own food and medicine. Communes are expected to be innovative in developing their resources rather than seek assistance from the state. The Tachai Production Brigade, for example, has been singled out as a model of self-reliance because it refused assistance in overcoming a series of natural disasters and went on to achieve a high level of production. In industry, the Taching oilfield has received similar accolades. National conferences have been held to promote the emulation of Tachai in agriculture and Taching in industry, the concept of self-reliance being fundamental to their reported successes.

The concept of self-reliance extends above the personal and regional levels to the national level. During the Cultural Revolution the slogans of self-reliance were greatly emphasized and continue to be emphasized. In trade with foreign countries, for example, China has sought to avoid indebtedness to others. For a time, China encouraged the development of wars of liberation among various countries, but it always insisted that if these countries relied on outside aid—even aid from China—their movements would fail.

The concept has undergone some modification in recent years. For example, during the Cultural Revolution, Chinese trade with foreign countries greatly declined under the doctrine of self-reliance, but recently foreign trade has been greatly expanded under the same concept. Nevertheless, self-reliance continues to be a central theme in articulated ideology. In a tour of three Northeast China provinces in May 1977, Chairman Hua praised those enterprises that demonstrated self-reliance.[6]

The Mass Line

Another important element of Maoist ideology has to do with the manner in which policies are decided upon and implemented. According to Mao, Party cadres are responsible for receiving the ideas of the people, turning them into systematic ideas in accordance with a correct ideological viewpoint, and returning them to the masses as policy. This process must be continuous.[7] Two cardinal sins are "commandism" and "tailism." Commandism exists when cadres give orders to the masses without making thorough investigations of concrete situations or without explaining policies clearly and correctly so as to gain the enthusiasm of the masses. Tailism exists when cadres fail to exert positive leadership and fall in with the "backward elements" among the people. These errors can be avoided through proper application of the mass line.

In theory, the mass line should counteract the evil of bureaucratism. As a revolutionary Mao has been consistently suspicious of institutionalization and institutions. The mass line can prevent authorities, from the lowest levels up through the upper echelons, from becoming divorced from the needs and aspirations of the people. Party officials are encouraged, sometimes even required, to participate in *hsia fang* campaigns—that is, they are sent to rural areas or industrial enterprises to engage in physical labor. Thus, they rub shoulders with the masses and become apprised of their situations.

Although the theory of mass line seems to be purposeful, various campaigns and newspaper accounts indicate that in practice it has been problematic. Cadres have been frequently criticized for failing to correctly implement the mass line. Sometimes they are accused of commandism, "mountain-topism," or tailism. Indeed, it is difficult for a cadre to popularize policies and mobilize the people in pursuit of economic and political goals decreed from higher levels. It is small wonder that many cadres meet with serious obstacles in implementing the mass line.

Contradictions

Mao's ideas on contradictions are most clearly spelled out in his two essays "On Contradiction" and "On the Correct Handling of Contradictions among the People." Following the argument of the dialectic, Mao sees all societies as containing numerous *mao dun*, or contradictions. In any given society there is likely to be one major or antagonistic contradiction and several secondary or nonantagonistic contradictions. Antagonistic contradictions must be resolved through violent struggle and opposition, whereas nonantagonistic contradictions can be resolved through criticism, study, and nonviolent struggle.

The contradictions follow a dialectical process as society is transformed. Some antagonistic contradictions will be resolved, but then previously nonantagonistic contradictions will become antagonistic ones, so the process goes on, even after the achievement of socialism and communism. Mao has analyzed the history of Chinese Communism in these terms. In current politics, the antagonistic contradiction is to be found in the incorrect political line put forward by the "Gang of Four," who are now identified as counterrevolutionaries. Nonantagonistic contradictions can be found in such things as the relationship between the Han majority and various national minorities in China, the urban-rural dichotomy, relations between cooperating classes, and differing intellectual viewpoints. In foreign policy, until 1968 the United States was perceived as the antagonistic contradiction; however, since the Soviet invasion of Czechoslovakia the Soviet Union has become the principal contradiction.

These four basic themes are constantly reiterated in the Chinese media, but interpretation is sometimes problematical. Mao is no longer present to establish genuine orthodoxy; his successors are applying his ideological principles to justify their own course of action. Thus, it would not be surprising to witness an ongoing ideological transformation in China—as with the idea of self-reliance, the slogans may remain constant, but the applications will vary. Mao himself would probably not be displeased by all this since he believed in learning and changing through practice.

The Functions of Ideology

Many scholars of traditional China have observed the relationship between Confucianism and the social structure. Confucianism explained social relationships, legitimized authority, justified rebellion when authority became illegitimate, and served as the "civil religion" of the society. The content of Maoist ideology differs considerably from Confucianism, but many of the social functions are similar. Schurmann observes that in a revolutionary situation, as values undergo rapid transformation, ideology serves as an alternative set of values for the new society. Clearly, the Thought of Mao Tse-tung offers both the goals and the means to achieve them for the New China.[8]

In traditional China the ruling class consisted of the emperor, the court, and a comparatively small number of officials (usually about 20,000 to 40,000 out of a population which numbered about 400 million by the beginning of the twentieth century) recruited from the land-owning groups. The degree holders or "gentry" acted as brokers between the central government and the people. The official ideology of those holding power was Confucianism. Today the government of China centers around the Communist Party (which numbers about 35 million in a population approaching 900 million). Those who are admitted to the Party are ostensibly representatives of the workers, peasants, and soldiers, the preferred groups in Maoist ideology. Recruitment for CCP membership is based on demonstrated knowledge about and application of Maoist ideology. Maoism justifies the rule of the Party.

Maoist ideology also posits a code of behavior for both rulers and those ruled. Officials are urged to serve the people, to avoid bureaucratism, and to lead in the development of a socialist state. The masses must sacrifice, work hard, and transform themselves to become new socialist men and women. Just as Confucianism served as a kind of civil religion in traditional China, so Maoism functions today. In more extreme times Maoism has become a cult. During the Cultural Revolution the adulation given Mao's person and portrait bordered on worship; his thoughts were believed to hold magical abilities to heal the sick, help grow larger melons, or even help discover oil. Mao rejected these more extreme forms of devotion, but the building aspects of his thought have been frequently utilized by others to mobilize and control the people.

One of the primary functions of Maoism has been to legitimize authority, but it also justifies rebellion. During the Cultural Revolution Mao's statement "to rebel is justified" was taken by the Red Guards as a key slogan in their struggle against Party and government institutions. Maoist ideology is suspicious of bureaucratic institutions, yet a large bureaucracy is necessary for transforming China into a modern socialist state. This paradox can be seen repeatedly in the political struggles that have rocked China in the past few years. In the recent struggle against the "Gang of Four" for example, the four were charged with having opposed the correct ideological line by fostering turmoil and opposing expertise in running various agencies, including the military. Only a short time earlier, those who opposed promoting revolution (or turmoil) and emphasized normalcy and expertise would have been considered the counterrevolutionaries. At times, then, Maoism has justified rule; at other times it has been used to justify those who rebel.

SOCIAL MOBILIZATION

Perhaps the most important function of ideology in China has to do with social transformation. Ideology specifies both the goals of the Chinese leadership and the manner in which these goals are to be achieved. Not the least of these goals is the transformation of China into a socialist state. In order for this to be accomplished, the people themselves must be transformed.

This process of transformation is sometimes called social mobilization. Social mobilization refers to the process by which the people's attitudes, beliefs, and values are changed so that a new culture is created. The changing of attitudes, beliefs, and values is accompanied by a change in loyalty. In traditional China basic loyalty was directed toward the family or clan. The goal of the Chinese Communists is to transform this loyalty toward the nation state and ultimately toward a socialist society. As noted earlier, classical Marxism suggests that beliefs, attitudes, and values are reflections of the economic basis of society; in order to transform them, the material base must be transformed. Maoism seeks to achieve simultaneous change in beliefs, attitudes, values and the economic base. The most important tool for this transformation is the mass campaign.[9]

Mass campaigns of varying intensity and duration have occurred repeatedly in China. Some has lasted several years and have affected the entire nation. Others have been limited in scope and have died out fairly quickly. We will touch on some of the more significant ones here.

Land Reform

Land Reform was one of the most significant of the early mass campaigns. Between 1950 and 1952 peasants throughout China were encouraged to form peasant associations, to burn the land deeds, and to struggle against the landlords and divide up the land. Land tenancy was abolished. By participating in this movement, peasants physically (and psychologically) rejected centuries of traditional social relationships. In some areas the campaign became violent and large numbers of landlords were executed. In spite of (and in some cases because of) the violence, land reform was generally popular with the peasants and helped to create support for the new regime. Land reform set the stage for future collectivization of agriculture and demonstrated the commitment of the new regime to revolutionary change. In conjunction with land reform, elections of delegates to local people's congresses were conducted. Thus, land reform had great political, economic, and social significance.

The "Resist America, Aid Korea" Campaign

During the Korean War the Chinese people were called upon to provide several hundred thousand soldiers and to participate in drives to accumulate supplies, equipment, and funds to support the war effort. This movement was conducted throughout China. Chinese involvement in Korea required sacrifice, but it helped build support for the regime; it was the first time in nearly a hundred years that a Chinese army had stood up to the West with any degree of credibility.[10] To the Chinese the Korean War was a victory, because they prevented an American invasion of China and fought the world's greatest military power to a standstill.

The Three-Anti and Five-Anti Campaign

This campaign was conducted principally in China's urban areas. Cadres were organized to reform large and small industry, to achieve state control of the banking system, to control economic planning and development, to manage internal and foreign trade, and to prepare for industrialization. Through this movement the power of the urban industrialists was largely eliminated, bribery and corruption were checked, and industry was reorganized. Inflation was controlled through government price fixing, and the currency was made stable. Though not without problems, this campaign helped create confidence in the new government (rampant inflation had been a major factor in the collapse of the Kuomintang) and it laid the foundation for future economic development. Wealthy persons were fined, jailed, or even executed, and their property expropriated. Some were made factory managers to avoid dislocations in production.

The Socialist Transformation of Agriculture

This campaign consisted of several stages. Shortly after land reform, peasants continued to own their own land and agricultural implements, but they were encouraged to share labor during planting and harvest periods by forming Mutual Aid Teams of from 5 to 20 households. The Mutual Aid Teams were to give way to Agricultural Producers' Cooperatives (APCs) of about 26 households. Featuring some joint ownership and a more systematic organization of labor, APCs were formed on a large scale throughout China during the 1954-56 period. The next stage was combining several APCs into higher APCs of about 160 households.

In theory, as the rural economy improved, larger cooperatives would be formed, the final goal being collectivization. The APCs and higher APCs were to be economically efficient (e.g., they would permit greater mechanization of farming) and were also to help transform the consciousness of the peasants so they would identify with a collective entity higher than the family and could thus achieve a higher technological knowledge through specialization. The system apparently was successful in increasing production and raising the living standard of the peasants, and for these reasons most of these reforms were welcomed.

In late 1956, in conjunction with the meeting of the Eighth CCP Congress, Mao called for a speedier formation of collectives. A big push was made throughout the country to achieve 100 percent collectivization, but the overenthusiasm and overconfidence of the move resulted in some setbacks. In some areas peasants resisted the formation of the APCs and showed their dissatisfaction by not working as hard as production goals demanded. Even so, in 1958 during the Great Leap Forward, the peasants were exhorted to form even larger production units called People's Communes.

Although not totally successful, the process of collectivization required interaction between the people and the state to an unprecedented degree. Cadres were trained and organized to work with the peasants. Collectivization altered the fundamental relationship that had existed between the peasants and the land for centuries. Private land holdings, though not completely abolished, were gradually circumscribed through the collectivization process.

The Hundred Flowers Movement[11]

In 1956 Mao Tse-tung urged intellectuals to speak more freely of their feelings toward the political system. He was probably surprised when they actually began to speak out, the trickle of criticism became a torrent. Mao, seeing a direct relationship between de-Stalinization in the USSR and the Hungarian revolt, became concerned about the security of the CCP in China. In 1957 a "Campaign against Counterrevolutionaries" was launched. This campaign resulted in the destruction of intellectual opposition to the regime. Since 1957 there has been little open criticism of the CCP from within China. The Chinese intellectual, never highly regarded by Mao, has generally been either supportive of, or silent toward, the Chinese Communists. This is in stark contrast to the USSR, which has witnessed increased public dissidence over the past few years. In 1976-77 it appeared that some kinds of criticism might be more openly aired in China, but it remains uncertain whether the Communists will significantly alter their controls on intellectuals.

The Great Leap Forward

By 1957 the Chinese Communists had become increasingly dissatisfied with the Soviet model for economic development. In the Chinese view, major accomplishments had been achieved in industrial development, but agricultural production was lagging. Mao and his supporters within the CCP leadership called for a new mass movement to rapidly develop agriculture as well as industry while also hastening the achievement of socialism.

In rural areas the cadres were instructed to form People's Communes of 5,000 households with public ownership of property. Several higher APCs were to be combined; there would be public facilities like nurseries and dining halls to free men and women, young and old alike, for productive work. The communes were organized on paper almost overnight, but many of the public facilities were never completed. Nonetheless, an attempt was made to mobilize the peasants to participate in these units, which numbered nearly 24,000 throughout China.

The Great Leap also envisioned the spread of technology. The "backyard steel furnaces" associated with the Great Leap were part of China's effort to overtake Britain in steel production in fifteen years and were indicative of the determined effort directed toward faster industrialization. Education was also to be rapidly expanded, and by 1960 China was claiming that illiteracy had been eliminated.

The Great Leap is now largely remembered for its economic failure. Some natural disasters combined with poor planning and the lack of an economic infrastructure undermined the aims of the Leap. In fact, China entered several years of depression. There were some accomplishments; peasants were mobilized at unprecedented levels to participate in regime-directed programs, and some achievements in construction and reclamation were made. Most importantly, China signaled to the Soviet Union that it would no longer rely on the Soviet model—that China must make its own road to socialism.

The economic failures resulted in a reversal of Leap policies. By 1960 communes had been decentralized as production units. The production team (roughly equivalent to the lower APC of earlier years) became the primary unit of production, and the brigade (an intermediate unit between commune and production team) became the unit for financial accounting. Communes continue to exist in China, but they are somewhat smaller than the original communes and more numerous, having increased to about 74,000. According to research by William Skinner, they now approximate the standard marketing areas of traditional China in size and geography.[12] Urban communes were rapidly abandoned. The Great Leap Forward had envisioned some decentralization in economic management— communes were to become self-sufficient as circumstances would permit in all areas of production—but by 1960 control was returning to the state bureaucracy.

The Socialist Education Campaign

In the early 1960s, while the economy was recovering from the Great Leap, Mao and his supporters became concerned that bureaucratism would again raise its ugly head. The Socialist Education movement was designed to repudiate revisionist influence in China. The Soviet Union was said to have experienced a capitalist restoration, and China needed to take steps to avoid a similar fate. A campaign to learn from Chairman Mao's teachings was conducted within the People's Liberation Army, and the society was then instructed to learn from the PLA. This campaign, intended to continue the class struggle and advance the revolution, soon gave way to the Cultural Revolution.[13]

The Cultural Revolution

The Cultural Revolution is generally remembered because of the violence and turmoil it produced.[14] It was one of the most complex campaigns China has witnessed, but it did begin with certain goals. By 1966 it had become clear to Mao that key elements within the Party and government bureaucracy were resisting the Socialist Education movement. Many officials genuinely feared that Great-Leap-style campaigns could only damage the good of the nation; furthermore, their own positions were threatened by such antibureaucratic movements. Resistance to Mao's leadership was subtle but real. Mao was not without support, however. Some key leaders, including his wife, Chiang Ch'ing, and Defense Minister Lin Piao supported his position. Moreover, Mao acknowledged a readily tappable source of discontent in China—young people who made up the educated unemployed of China's cities. These youths were unable to find jobs commensurate with their education or to gain admission to the Party and government bureaucracies. Mao's supporters used this group of discontented youths to form the Red Guards, who in August 1966 began a series of attacks on officials opposed to Mao's policies.

Wholesale purges occurred at the highest levels of Party and government structures, and the bureaucracy rapidly fell into disarray. The Red Guards, drunk with initial success, quickly tried to expand their movement, but the result was confusion and chaos. The Red Guards split into numerous warring parties, and by mid-1967 China was nearing a state of anarchy. Mao called on the PLA to restore order. The army, albeit reluctantly, responded and in 1967-68 formed revolutionary committees in various provinces consisting of PLA officers, Red Guards, and remnants of former officials deemed to be politically reliable. In most areas, political administration relied heavily on the PLA.

By 1969 the Cultural Revolution was officially ended, but aftershocks have continued to the present day. The education system underwent considerable transformation. Many former cadres who were purged then are only now being rehabilitated. The reforms of the Cultural Revolution have become the object of debate in recent campaigns, as in the recent campaign to repudiate the influence of the "Gang of Four." The facade of unity that had characterized CCP leadership up until the mid-1960s was firmly broken, and many scholars now emphasize the role of factions in CCP leadership. The PLA gradually reduced its role in political administration, but it remains important, particularly in the higher levels of the Party. Consequently, the influence of the Cultural Revolution is still very much present in China.

The Campaign to Repudiate Lin Piao and Confucius

During the Cultural Revolution, Defense Minister Lin Piao was regarded as "Chairman Mao's closest comrade-in-arms" and was named as Mao's successor in the 1969 Party constitution. In 1971, however, when Lin was accused of having plotted a coup against Mao and was reported killed in an airplane crash in an attempt to escape to the USSR, he became the object of a repudiation campaign.[15] Many of Lin's associates were purged along with him, causing more tremors in China's upper echelons of power.

This campaign against Lin was linked with a campaign to criticize Confucius. Confucius was deemed to be a reactionary who tried to maintain the slave-owning system during the onset of feudalism in China. Lin Piao was said to have admired Confucius, thereby demonstrating that one reactionary can draw folly from another. The criticism of Confucius was directed primarily at intellectuals, and prominent scholars like Feng Yu-lan who had once praised Confucius were forced to recant.[16]

More recently, it has been said that this campaign was an effort by Mao's wife and other "Shanghai radicals" to discredit Chou En-lai. Historical analogy has been an important feature of many Chinese campaigns. In this case Chou was cast in the role of pragmatic compromiser, an opportunist not unlike Confucius. Unfortunately for Chou's detractors, he was able to ride out the storm of criticism and even turned the campaign to his advantage.

Struggling against the "Gang of Four"

After the death of Mao in September 1976, conflict over the succession immediately erupted. With support from the military and the police Hua Kuo-feng moved to consolidate his power by having Chiang Ch'ing, Wang Hung-wen, Chang Ch'un-ch'iao, and Yao Wen-yuan arrested. These "Shanghai radicals," referred to as the "Gang of Four" in the Chinese press, were accused of having formed a

Workers at Taching oil refinery rally to criticize the "Gang of Four." Taching is China's national industrial model.

clique in opposition to Mao's instructions and of conspiring to seize power upon his death. During the year following Mao's death, a nationwide campaign to repudiate the "gang" was conducted.[17] Local supporters of the "gang" have also been exposed and purged. Although these purges resulted in significant changes in the leadership of some provinces, the influence of the "gang" remains strong in other areas. The four were dismissed from all positions by the third plenum of the Tenth Central Committee in July 1977 but the struggle against them goes on. They are accused of being counterrevolutionaries and of having sabotaged China's economy, education system, scientific development, art, and culture. The ongoing struggle was evidenced by postponement of the Fifth National People's Congress from the fall of 1977 to the spring of 1978.

In fact, the purge of the "gang" is associated with a more general move to moderate some past policies. China has increased wages for urban workers, expanded foreign trade, and even indicated a willingness to purchase military technology from abroad. These policies apparently contradict the position taken by the "Gang of Four" on how economic development in China should be achieved.

The Movements to Learn from Taching and Tachai

In recent years the Tachai production brigade in Shansi Province and the Taching oil refinery have become the national models for agricultural and industrial production, respectively. According to official accounts, the Tachai brigade is located in an area almost hostile to agriculture. It repeatedly suffered from the effects of floods, droughts, and other natural problems. However, through self-reliance and hard work the people were able to overcome these difficulties and increase production. They built terraces and improved irrigation so that farming became successful. They have become a model of political correctness. In the mid-1960s Mao himself called on the nation to learn from the example of Tachai. The leader of Tachai, Ch'en Yung-kuei, subsequently became a member of the CCP Politburo. China now holds annual conferences in which representatives from around the nation gather to discuss the campaign to "learn from Tachai." Each county and province sets goals to achieve a certain number of "Tachai-type" brigades annually. Although the entire nation has been mobilized in this campaign, official accounts indicate that results are not as good as the authorities had hoped. Many areas are falling short of achieving the desired number of Tachai-type counties.[18]

In April 1977 a national conference on learning from Taching was

Chen Yung-kuei, now a member of the CCP Politburo, chats with members of the Tachai production brigade. The brigade, formerly headed by Chen, is the national model for agricultural development.

conducted on site with important leaders in attendance. Hua Kuo-feng delivered the keynote address and called on industries throughout China to continue to emulate Taching. At the Fourth National People's Congress in January 1975, Premier Chou En-lai had stated that China's goal would be to achieve overall modernization on a level with advanced Western countries by the turn of the century. Hua restated this goal, saying that emulation of Taching would be a significant factor in its achievement.[19] Emulation of Taching involves learning from the wage system, political motivation, production, and other achievements. During 1977 every province conducted a "learn from Taching" conference.

The Dynamics of a Campaign: A Case Study[20]

We have presented a brief discussion of some of the major mobilization campaigns in China; we will now examine a specific campaign in greater detail to illustrate how they work. Each campaign has unique features, but there are also interesting similarities. We have selected the recent campaign to criticize Teng Hsiao-p'ing as our example. In early 1976, after the death of Chou En-lai, it was widely anticipated that Teng would succeed as premier. Teng had served as general secretary of the CCP until his purge during the Cultural Revolution; he was then rehabilitated after the Tenth CCP Congress in late 1973. He rose to become a CCP vice-chairman, vice-premier of the State Council, and chief of staff of the PLA.

In late 1975 a debate arose at Tsinghua, Peking, and other universities over a reported effort by "revisionists" to implement an adverse current in education during the previous summer. The revisionists reportedly wanted to overcome reforms made in the educational system during the Cultural Revolution, particularly the system of worker-peasant-soldier colleges geared to give preference in admission to those of correct background rather than proven ability. The debate continued in wall posters until the death of Chou En-lai on January 8, 1976. Within two weeks of Chou's death, the movement had spread throughout China's educational system. On January 18 some students at the Chekiang College of Fine Arts posted a wall poster denouncing "the right deviationist wind to reverse past verdicts," a phrase which became prominent throughout the campaign. By the end of January, nearly every province had reported the debate in an educational institution or in Communist Youth League conferences being held throughout China.

The timing of the campaign is interesting, in that it spread so rapidly immediately after Chou's death. Some reports indicate that during meetings of the Central Committee of the CCP shortly after the funeral Teng proposed a new five-year plan, which was severely criticized by Yao Wen-yuan and Chang Chun-chiao. This incident, if true, may have led to the heightened factional conflict that ultimately resulted in Teng's ouster. Just how quickly Teng was singled out as a target is unclear, since the campaign proceeded from the general to the specific over the next few weeks.

The campaign entered a new phase on February 6 when the *People's Daily* issued an editorial entitled, "The Continuation and Deepening of the Great Proletarian Cultural Revolution—Gratified to See the Mass Debate on Education Revolution at Tsinghua University Advancing against the Waves." The editorial praised Tsinghua faculty, students, staff, and workers for launching a counterattack against the revisionist line put forward at the university the previous summer. The editorial stated: "The bourgeois representatives blowing the right deviationist wind to reverse previous verdicts are primarily those capitalist roaders who have been criticized and exposed during the Great Proletarian Cultural Revolution but have refused to repent."

On February 7, the day after the editorial appeared, it was learned that Hua Kuo-feng had been appointed acting premier. There was speculation that Teng might be in trouble, but the use of the plural "roaders" suggested more than one target. Almost immediately, the provincial media in Shanghai and Chekiang reported attacks on capitalist roaders who had refused to repent; other provinces came later so that by February 14, every province was reporting denunciations of unspecified capitalist roaders in the Party.

On February 19 Yao Wen-yuan met with a visiting Japanese delegation and explained the necessity of the campaign which was designed, he indicated, to eliminate revisionists and their influence in China. The following day, wall posters in Hangchow attacked Teng personally. On February 25, former President Nixon was taken to Tsinghua University and shown the wall posters, some of which were clearly attacks on Teng. Two days later on February 27 Teng was denounced by name for the first time in public Peking wall posters, and on the next day the *People's Daily* for the first time shifted to the singular "capitalist roader" in its editorial denunciation. Within four days all other provincial media had shifted to the singular.

By the end of February it was clear from the content of the denunciations that Teng was the major target. The criticisms spread from attacks on his position and policies toward education and science to include art and culture, health, military affairs, and other areas. Teng was frequently mentioned by name by Chinese officials in conversations with foreign newsmen as the object of the attack, yet the national and regional media used only the term "capitalist roader" in references to him.

The campaign continued in both national and provincial media, but the most virulent attacks issued from Tsinghua. In a cautionary note, the *People's Daily* editorialized on March 9:

> The struggle to repulse the right deviationist wind to reverse verdicts should be conducted under the leadership of Party committees at various

levels. No ties should be established and no fighting groups organized. . . . Leading cadres must march ahead of the movement and take the lead in studying, exposing, criticizing, and repelling the right deviationist wind to reverse previous verdicts. . . . We must remain coolheaded about this.

As the campaign against Teng mounted, other leaders were also named in wall poster attacks. Both Ch'en Hsi-lien, commander of the Peking Military Region, and Li Hsien-nien, Deputy Premier, were attacked during the course of the campaign, as were the leaders of ten provinces. Nevertheless, the official media did not pick up these attacks, and the focus of the struggle remained on Teng.

On March 20, Canton Television showed Hua Kuo-feng and Yao Wen-yuan escorting a Laotian delegation around Tsinghua University. Closeups of the wall posters showed that Teng was being attacked by name; this was the first time the national media had used or shown Teng's name in connection with public denunciations of the capitalist roader. Nevertheless, both national and regional media continued to use the term "capitalist roader" in all references, instead of Teng's name, until after the notice of dismissal on April 6.

On March 28, a *People's Daily* editorial stated that the campaign would result in production increases. One of the major topics of the campaign began to center around the issue of production. Teng was accused of having pushed "taking the three directives as the key line," rather than "taking the class struggle as the key line" as Chairman Mao had advocated. The three directives included: (1) pursuing class struggle by studying Marx's theory of the dictatorship of the proletariat; (2) practicing stability and unity; and (3) promoting the national economy. By emphasizing these, critics charged, Teng was seeking to abrogate the class struggle and pave the way for capitalist restoration. Though there had been nothing in Teng's previous public statements to substantiate this charge, his past record had indicated that he believed stability was necessary for economic improvement. At one point in his career he had stated that so long as a cat catches mice it doesn't matter whether it is a white cat or a black cat. This allegorical statement about how to develop China's economy got him in trouble during the Cultural Revolution and was resurrected by his enemies. Teng's critics charged that his failure to give proper emphasis to the class struggle would actually hinder production.

The first week of April witnessed a rapid escalation of events. On April 1, New China News Agency (NCNA) removed Teng's picture from all files. On April 4 during the celebration of the Ching Ming festival, some wall posters attacking the *Wen Hui Pao* (a Shanghai newspaper noted for its radical editorial position) and other antiradical wall posters were put up alongside wreaths and portraits honoring Chou En-lai. These wall posters and the wreaths were removed that evening. The next morning demonstrations and even rioting erupted in Tienanmen square, with cars overturned and burned and some buildings damaged and ransacked. By the evening of the fifth the mayor of Peking, Wu Teh, had appealed for calm, claiming that those who instigated the demonstrations were counterrevolutionaries. On April 6, a resolution in the name of the Central Committee dismissed Teng from all positions, but allowed him to retain his Party membership so that he might have the opportunity to repent. On April 7, another resolution officially appointed Hua Kuo-feng premier of the State Council and first deputy chairman of the CCP. On April 8 hundreds of thousands demonstrated in Peking to support the resolutions dismissing Teng and appointing Hua. Within the next few days every major city and provincial capital held a rally to support the Central Committee decisions.

It was subsequently reported that counterrevolutionary incidents occurred in other cities as well. Though Teng was never formally charged with complicity in the riots, his influence was often blamed. The movement to criticize his influence quickly spread into factories, PLA units, communes, and other units at the regional and local levels. Meanwhile, at the center, a determined show of unity was made by members of the Politburo in a special reception for those who put down the Tienanmen incident on April 26. Again, on May 1, the Politburo members appeared together (with the exception of a few who appeared at regional rallies) during the May Day celebrations. Still, some members of the Politburo were under attack by name in wall posters, as were some regional leaders. Moreover, the Shanghai journal *Study and Criticism* and other journals at Peking and Tsing-hua Universities alleged that other top party leaders were supporting Teng and urged their overthrow, though they avoided mentioning specific names.

In contrast to these journals, an article in the June issue of *Red Flag* stated that, although the handful of class enemies should never be dealt with mercifully, caution must be exercised so as to avoid both ultrarightism and ultraleftism. The provincial media clearly were uninterested in singling out other persons for denunciation. On May 16, a joint editorial in *People's Daily, Red Flag,* and *Liberation Army Daily* entitled "The Great Cultural Revolution Will Shine Forever" was issued to commemorate the tenth anniversary of the May 16, 1966, Central Committee circular that launched the Cultural Revolution. Rallies were held in every province to celebrate the occasion. The editorials and reports of the rallies continued to attack Teng, but suggested that there were no other immediate individual targets. Rather, they stated that people must be vigilant against revisionist influence spread by Liu Shao-ch'i, Lin Piao, and Teng Hsiao-p'ing.

The campaign against Teng continued through the summer; no other major figures were purged. Individuals were criticized at all levels, but there were no major political changes—in sharp contrast to the anti–Lin Piao campaign earlier and the anti–"gang of four" campaign that came afterward. The end of the anti-Teng campaign was signaled by Hua Kuo-feng's eulogy at Mao's funeral when the movement was not mentioned. Before long, the "Gang of Four" was being blamed for many of the same crimes Teng had been accused of earlier. Teng was not immediately rehabilitated publicly but he was reported to be back at work. In July 1977 he was fully reinstated. The official announcement was accompanied by massive rallies similar to those that had, a year earlier, accompanied his downfall.

Recent campaigns, such as the one criticizing Teng, have more limited aims than broad campaigns like the Great Leap or the Cultural Revolution. The major campaigns, which have more fundamental political and social changes as goals, are usually of longer duration and involve a much greater effort in sending the cadres down to participate in mass mobilization. Major campaigns to achieve mobilization in rural areas largely ended with the Great Leap Forward, though rural areas were not totally unaffected by the Cultural Revolution. In recent years, most national campaigns appear to have had specific political objectives—to criticize Lin Piao and Confucius, to repudiate Teng Hsiao-p'ing, or to repudiate the "Gang of Four."

Each campaign has unique features, but there are also similarities. Campaigns are not always well orchestrated. They develop out of other campaigns, and they are manipulated by persons with different viewpoints. The movement to attack Teng, for example, grew out of an earlier movement in the universities to attack the "reversal of past verdicts." The campaign was used by Teng's enemies not only to get rid of him but also to attack others who favored his policies. Teng's supporters tried to direct the campaign away from individuals, and stressed the need to improve production. The outcome of a campaign often depends on who is able to secure its ultimate control. A campaign rarely has a definite, distinguishable ending; rather, it usually fades into a new campaign. The anti-Teng campaign gradually died out in the press and was ended when his chief enemies, the "Gang of Four," were themselves brought under attack.

The Impact of Campaigns: Some Observations

Research by Skinner and Winckler has shown many campaigns to be cyclical in nature.[21] Using Etzioni's model of normative, remunerative, and coercive inducement factors, they observe that the campaigns go through several stages. Often a campaign begins with a normative thrust; that is, the authorities appeal to the patriotism of the masses for support. This is replaced by coercive power if the people do not respond or if pressure is exerted through cadres to get quick results. Coercive power usually causes resentment and ultimate disruption, which eventually gives way to remunerative inducements like better wages or improved treatment. A classic example would be the formation of communes during the Great Leap. First the peasants were exhorted to organize communes, then, during the high tide of the campaign, they were coerced into organizing them. Finally, when the commune movement began to falter, private plots of land, livestock, fruit trees, and so on were restored to the peasants in order to bolster enthusiasm. Technically, each campaign should finish on a level of mobilization higher than it began. Through successive campaigns the participants should eventually have their conscious-nesses raised to the desired level. Of course, not all campaigns fit neatly into this pattern. The anti-Teng campaign was short-lived and seemed to blend various kinds of inducements. Certainly, Teng's supporters were required, at least temporarily, to support the campaign through coercion—through fear of the consequences if they did not support it.

Whether each campaign actually brings the people to a higher level of political consciousness is uncertain. In fact, the reverse may be true. There are some indications that cynicism results from frequent campaigns. This has been particularly true for political campaigns in which the targets are reversed. For example, the back and forth campaigns criticizing Lin Piao, Teng Hsiao-p'ing, and the "Gang of Four" must create some credibility gap. Chairman Mao, the great teacher, great leader, and great helmsman, apparently was not very good when it came to choosing successors. Some refugees in Hong Kong have reported disgruntlement and confusion over the shifting targets of campaigns.

Moreover, all campaigns involve unanticipated consequences. Few authorities would have predicted the strength of the adverse reaction to the formation of communes. Few could have predicted the outpouring of criticism of the regime during the Hundred Flowers movement. The classic cases are probably the ones dealing with the treatment of minorities. During the early years of CCP rule, the Party gave favorable attention to the recruitment of minorities to be trained as cadres, and special attention was given to minority languages, customs, culture, and religions. The intent was to create support among the minorities who hitherto had been antagonistic to Han Chinese rule. The campaign did have some positive results but it also created a heightened sense of separate identity among the minorities. Consequently, during the Great Leap it was decided that many of the previous policies had only fostered "local nationalism" and the regime moved to a more direct assimilation policy. This, in turn, produced backlash from many minority groups and was partly to blame for the Tibetan revolt of 1959. Unanticipated consequences in the anti-Teng campaign resulted from the purge of the "Gang of Four." It was decided that the "Gang" was really responsible for the country's problems, and that the errors of Teng were comparatively minor. An effort is now being made to rehabilitate Teng's reputation; this was clearly not the expected outcome of the original campaign.

The Political Socialization of the Chinese People

The mobilization techniques of the mass campaign are only one aspect of the socialization of the Chinese people. By political socialization we refer to the process by which political beliefs, attitudes, and values are inculcated among the people. The agents of socialization include the family, the education system, peers, and other groups. Generally, speaking, these groups and institutions are utilized by the government in the effort to encourage certain political ideas.[22]

In China, as in most societies, the primary unit of political socialization is the family. During the land reform campaign, the regime sought to break the power of the clan system, which exercised political power in many rural areas. For the most part this was achieved, although contemporary campaigns occasionally mention the continued influence of the landlord class in some rural areas. During the Great Leap Forward, the regime tried to use the communal organization to break up the family and lessen its socializing influence. Children were to be removed from the home at an early age and placed in day care centers, nurseries, and schools, and the elderly were to be placed in nursing homes. This idea was rapidly abandoned however, and today in both urban and rural areas the family is likely to consist of the nuclear family, often including grandparents as well.

The goal of the Communist authorities is to see to it that the family reinforces desirable attitudes; that is, the family should inculcate those values deemed appropriate by the state. A portrait of Chairman Mao and copies of Mao's writings can be found in most homes. Parents are expected to set a good example for children by engaging in family political discussions, by studying the Chairman's works, and by exemplifying the values of self-reliance, hard work, and struggle. For example, when young middle school graduates from urban areas are to be sent to the countryside to engage in physical labor, special meetings are convened in which parents are called upon to praise the revolutionary fervor of their sons and daughters. Parents who have reputedly sought to shelter their children by preventing them from being "sent down" will often confess their errors and show new enthusiasm by professing support. Through one means or another, the parent has suddenly come to realize that identification with the policy of the Party is the correct path of revolutionary happiness. Young people, who often have the benefit of more education than their parents, are also supposed to set an example for parents by following the correct revolutionary line in thought and action.

Another important agent of political socialization is the education system. Most people in China are able to get an elementary school education, fewer receive a middle school education, and only a select few reach the university level. In all levels of the education system, political study is emphasized in the curriculum. Teachers must demonstrate a high degree of affinity with correct ideological precepts. Advancement in education and especially promotion into the higher education system are partly determined by the political attitude of the student.

Still another agent of political socialization is the peer group. Nearly all Chinese (the exception being some of the isolated minorities) live in close proximity to other people. They associate with others in school, at work, and in the activities of daily life. Out of these associations, political ideas are indirectly established. The Party, recognizing the importance of peer group socialization, has led in the formation of mass organizations designed to act as agents of socialization.

Some of the mass organizations include students' organizations, women's organizations, trade unions, professional associations, cultural associations, and friendship organizations. For a time, some "democratic parties" that had cooperated with the CCP prior to 1949 were permitted to function, but they disappeared during the Cultural Revolution. In fact, most of the mass organizations came under criticism during the Cultural Revolution and subsequently disappeared or were reorganized. Some have reemerged, like the Women's Association, which has held national and provincial congresses regularly since the mid-1970s. The Communist Youth League (CYL) and the Students' Federation were replaced by the Red Guard movement during the Cultural Revolution. The CYL has been reorganized and is now functioning, but nothing has been said about a restoration of the Students' Federation.

The lapse of some of the mass organizations does not mean that the effort to socialize people on the basis of peer group has lessened. In fact, a requirement for political study has been maintained in every work unit, both urban and rural. Although the requirement for political study bears most heavily on CCP members, meetings are regularly convened for factory workers, students, production teams, PLA units, and other groups so that few are not involved in some group political study. Usually, the party members lead the study meetings, which emphasize correct thought and action.

A large propaganda apparatus is maintained in China to carry out this far-reaching socialization effort. With its headquarters in the Central Committee, the apparatus extends throughout China, even into the remotest areas. All the media are utilized to present a political theme. Besides Radio Peking in the capital, every province and major city has a powerful transmitter that carries regional news and political propaganda. Most urban homes have radio sets; some now even have television. In rural areas, wired broadcast stations have been established so that the peasants can listen even while working in the fields. Visitors to China note that in trains, airports, hotels, and other facilities one can listen to the message of the regime. In addition to the radio, there are inexpensive newspapers in every province and city and even in many rural areas. All films, plays, and artistic and literary works are closely supervised to insure correct political content. Shows and performances are circulated widely, often by semiprofessional dramatic teams that travel the country. Mao's dictum that politics should take command has been made reality by using the mass media to convey the regime's political message.

One of the most fascinating, and most open, forms of communication is the *tatzepao*, or wall poster. Mao encouraged a wall poster campaign during the Cultural Revolution; since that time, wall posters have been frequently used in campaigns to express diverse

Chinese students prepare wall posters (*tatzupao*) in the campaign to criticize Lin Piao and Confucius.

points of view. The *tatzepao* often take strong, flamboyant stands on current issues. They also frequently signal policy debates or decisions, even before official announcements. Foreign diplomats and correspondents often look at wall posters to see what kinds of issues are developing. Determining which posters are officially sanctioned and which are not sometimes provides the key to understanding power relationships in China.

The most authoritative printed media are *People's Daily*, a national paper that is the organ of the CCP Central Committee; *Red Flag*, the theoretical journal of the Party; and the *Liberation Army Daily*, the official organ of the PLA. To signal a major Party policy, these three publications will often produce a joint editorial. The Party journals in particular contain a specialized language for communicating with CCP members. In broadcasting, Radio Peking enjoys a primary role; many regional radio stations relay broadcasts from Radio Peking. These media direct a central propaganda theme for cadres, but the most important contact with individual citizens is probably through the group discussion mentioned above. Martin K. Whyte has observed that nearly everyone in China belongs to some small group that conducts political discussions.[23] All citizens are expected to participate in political study, the subject of which is often a theme from Mao's works, which are circulated throughout China, a recent editorial, or some other Party pronouncement. Usually the cadres lead the discussions.

What is the result of this emphasis on politics? Several conclusions can be drawn. Whyte's research demonstrates that much political study has become ritualized in China, suggesting that the average person is apathetic about politics. His conclusions are supported by my own experience. In 1973 I was visiting an elementary school teacher from Canton who had just arrived in Hong Kong with his family on an exit visa. He seemed very blasé about things political and appeared much more concerned about the price of shoes and medicine. Others who have interviewed persons leaving China report similar responses. On the other hand, some do become enthusiastic about the regime and its policies—they are likely to become activists and eventually be recruited for Youth League or CCP membership. There are also those who, for one reason or another, oppose the regime. It would probably not be incorrect to describe political attitudes in China as resembling a bell-shaped curve—that is, on one end a comparatively small number of people demonstrate a high degree of affinity with the ideology and policy being articulated in the media, a small number on the other end are disillusioned and would like to flee to Hong Kong, and the very large number in-between are largely apathetic.

The preceding may appear to contradict the "new socialist man" image of the Chinese people many visitors have who have looked at communes and factories first hand. In fact, although it is true that many aspects of Chinese society have been transformed by the Communists, the changes probably have to do more with the latent socialization performed by economic modernization than with political indoctrination. There can be no question that the Communists have been successful in developing the transportation and communications networks and in improving the standard of living. There have been great advances in public health and education; a barefoot doctor curing a peasant's illness likely has a greater socializing influence than a year's worth of political study meetings. The results of mass socialization efforts are mixed; there have been definite changes in political attitudes among the Chinese people, but most probably remain apathetic to political life, becoming involved only out of necessity.

SOCIETY

One of the primary values of Maoist ideology is egalitarianism. In building a socialist society, the Chinese Communists hope to erase the "contradictions" between social classes, between urban and rural elements, between Han and minority groups, and other contrasting distinctions that exist in Chinese society. As noted in the previous section, these contradictions are to be eliminated or resolved through the mobilization of society. How much has been accomplished? This section briefly examines various groups in Chinese society, focusing on peasants, urban workers, young people, women, and minorities.

Peasants

About 85 percent of China's 900 million persons—about 765 million people—are peasants. The peasantry, having gone through land reform and the socialist transformation of agriculture, are organized into people's communes, that is, production teams and production brigades. William Parish observes that the typical production team consists of about thirty households farming about fifty acres of land. In many areas the team is no more than a small village or part of a large one.[24] There have been efforts to promote the brigade of the commune as the basic unit of production, during the Great Leap, but in general the production team continues to be the basic unit. Parish also notes that many teams are composed of relatives through lineage or marriage.

The income of the peasants is based upon work points, a system for measuring the amount of work performed by a production team. An adult male putting in a full day's work can earn ten points, women and children can generally earn less. Work point allocations are determined by meetings of the team, and a cadre keeps a record of points earned by a household. When team income is received, it is divided according to the total number of work points earned by the household.

Although this point system would seem to guarantee equal wages for equal work, such is not the case. Because of geographic differences that influence production—the quality of land and availability of water, for example—income varies greatly from team to team. Moreover, the compensation of peasants for work performed is greater in areas where more is produced. Consequently, it is possible for a small adult household in a rich area to be comparatively prosperous, while a large family in a poor area could earn less than it consumes and be constantly in debt.[25] Also, prosperous communes are much more able to afford construction of hospitals, dental clinics, and other services so that, depending on location, some peasants are better off than others.

Income is also derived from private plots of land and private livestock. In some areas, the income in cash from the sale of one pig can amount to more than is earned by team labor for an entire year. Consequently, private income is important for savings, and for occasions like births, deaths, weddings, and festivals. One of the ongoing debates in China has been about how much private property should be allowed, and if it should be allowed at all. For the peasant, it now constitutes a very important source of income and in the opinion of many observers, makes collective life palatable.

The economic system of the peasants greatly influences village sociology. Parish observes that some features of traditional life have endured, including family responsibility to the aged and infirm, and the infrequency of female inheritance. Although the political power of the extended clan was finished by land reform, family ties remain strong in rural China. There is a continuing desire to have male progeny, and children are sometimes kept out of school so they can take care of private plots while parents work for the team.[26] There is still a tendency in rural areas for families to have four or five children (to insure one or two sons) before considering birth control. In the mid-1970s the government introduced economic penalties for those

A commune's granaries. Mao Tse-tung exhorted the Chinese people to "store grain everywhere," and each commune is expected to have a grain reserve.

families who had more than two children, however it has generally favored education rather than coercion to limit population growth.

Most estimates of population growth in China average around 2 percent annually, not extremely high when compared with other developing countries, but a considerable challenge considering the already large number of people and the limited amount of arable land. Many analysts believe that China's agriculture has barely kept pace with population growth; China's strategy for economic development under the concept of self-sufficiency has been to accumulate agricultural surplus to aid in financing capital construction in heavy and light industry. Consequently, success in agriculture is vital to China's economic development. China has had to import grain from abroad to feed its population, but has been able to produce enough rice for export to keep a balance. Taken together, these circumstances show that China's villages and the peasantry are the key to China's future.

The peasants' standard of living is much higher now than it was in 1949. In fact, economic improvement, combined with other factors previously noted, has helped preserve some of the traditional aspects of Chinese families (e.g., care for the elderly, large families). Also, public health has been greatly improved. Disease is still an ever-present threat to the villager, but life expectancy has increased. The barefoot doctors—a system of traveling paramedics—have reached most of China's rural areas, and many commune headquarters have clinics or hospitals to treat serious illnesses. The life of the Chinese peasant today is an interesting mix of traditional and modern features.

One further comment should be made about China's peasants. During land reform, they were classified as being rich, middle, or poor according to the amount of land they possessed or worked. In spite of economic changes in rural areas, this classification has remained, and few persons have been reclassified. Consequently, a peasant classified as "rich" may be relatively poor, and a "poor" peasant relatively well-off. The thrust of Party policy has been for cadres to concentrate on working with poor and lower-middle peasants. Because these groups have benefited most from the CCP's policies in rural China, they are more likely to be active supporters of additional changes. The majority of the mobilization campaigns are thus specifically directed at these groups.

Urban Workers

About 15 percent of China's total population can be considered urban. China has some of the world's largest cities, three of which—Peking, Shanghai, and Tientsin—have administrative rank equivalent to province. During the first five-year plan, the government invested heavily in existing urban industrial centers, which lead to rapid population growth prior to 1957. Since that time, however, China's urban population has remained relatively stable. More efforts have been made to develop industry in outlying areas, and urban population growth has been controlled by requiring urban youths to emigrate to rural areas and by preventing rural migration to the cities.

The urban family is likely to be employed in industrial enterprise with both parents working. Children are placed in schools and day care centers or sometimes remain with a grandparent at home. City housing is poor by American standards but is usually better than in rural China. City dwellers are on the average more prosperous than rural peasants. Prices for food and rent are higher in the cities, but higher incomes more than make up for the difference. Many urban families have bicycles, radios, sewing machines, and other goods that a rural peasant family may only dream of owning.

Workers are salaried, with incomes dictated by an eight-grade wage system based on seniority and skill. Technically, women receive equal pay for equal work, but in most areas they do not perform equal work. They are usually employed in industries that pay less, so they usually earn less. Nonetheless, the joint income of a family is normally sufficient to meet family needs with about 10 percent left over for savings.[27]

The trade union movement in China has been relatively moribund since the Cultural Revolution. Workers belong to small groups associated with the enterprise in which they are employed and are expected to engage regularly in political studies. The right to strike has been guaranteed by China's new constitution promulgated during the meetings of the Fourth National People's Congress in January 1975. However, work slowdowns or stoppages are considered to be counterrevolutionary. On occasion workers have effectively gone on strike by failing to meet production goals. During a number of recent mass campaigns, the Chinese press has reported that counterrevolutionaries have been actively disrupting factory production. Also, during the movement to repudiate the "Gang of Four," it was reported that some cities experienced an increase in criminal activity such as bank robbery, rape, black-marketeering, and prostitution.

The urban resident is more susceptible to the mechanisms of

political socialization than his rural counterpart. Not only does he have more access to newspapers and broadcasts, but he is also much more likely to attend a play, a film, or some other cultural event. The mass campaigns, with the exception of those specifically designed for rural areas, usually begin in urban areas and later filter out to rural areas. By being in close proximity with others, the urban resident is more easily influenced by the police, the public security apparatus, and other agencies of government.

China's cities are not plagued by the poverty and slums characteristic of cities in other developing countries. Visitors report clean streets, orderliness, no beggars, little motorized traffic, almost no crime—almost a sense of dullness. Some of China's large cities do have slum-type housing, but the government has taken steps to improve the quality of housing. China has also become more aware of the problems of industrial pollution in urban areas. So long as the government exercises strict control over the population growth rate in the cities, the comparatively good quality of life is likely to be maintained.

Whyte discovered that it is easier to have class status readjusted in a city than in a rural area.[28] The bourgeois classes were largely reformed during the early 1950s, but they still retain that identification. Like the poor and lower-middle peasants, the workers are included in the favored group according to CCP theory and practice, but they are likely to have a higher income and better access to education and other social amenities than the peasants.

Young People

About 60 percent of China's population is under the age of 25. The young-old dichotomy has been particularly troublesome for the Chinese Communists. In 1973 about 127,000,000 students were enrolled in primary school, about 35,000,000 in middle school and about 200,000 in higher education.[29] Although enrollment in higher education has rapidly expanded since that time, the competition to get into college or university remains extremely keen.

During the Cultural Revolution, the education system was attacked for fostering elitism through an admissions system favoring sons or daughters of cadres, urban residents, and those from undesirable class backgrounds who had a good educational background. The schools were closed for about three years and then reopened with a radically altered system. Gradually, however, aspects of the former system have been restored, including examinations, grades, and a renewed emphasis on technical subjects. Some of the Cultural Revolution reforms have been continued. Before admission to a university or higher technical school, a middle school graduate must spend a period of time, usually about two years, working on a commune or in a factory. Besides taking a competitive examination, the student must be recommended for advanced study by the unit to which he or she was assigned. The student's application must be approved by higher levels in turn, where political requirements are weighed heavily in admissions policy.[30]

Many urban middle school graduates are expected to volunteer to go to a rural area and permanently integrate with the peasants. This massive *hsia fang* has exceeded 10 million youths since the Cultural Revolution.[31] Not volunteering to go either to the countryside or to one of the border areas to engage in physical labor is taken as an indication of political unreliability. Most young people who go to the rural areas appear to make the adjustment. However, there are those who try to get back to the urban areas, and some of these illegal returnees engage in criminal activity since they cannot get ration cards or work permits. Still others try to escape to Macao or Hong Kong, embittered by the prospect of remaining the rest of their lives in a rural area.

China has been faced with the problem of educated unemployed— that is, there have not been enough jobs in technical fields to support those who have adequate training. The *hsia fang* of young people is one way of addressing this problem. At the same time it is hoped that sending young people with a middle school education to the countryside will help to facilitate technical development in rural areas and help to eliminate the distinctions between urban and rural people. By sending the urban youth to a rural area, perhaps education can be promoted. Of course, inexperienced as the urban youths are in agricultural production, they are not always welcomed by rural dwellers. In any event, in spite of the problems, the process of sending young people to rural areas has enabled China to cope with problems of urban overcrowding and the educated unemployed. At the same time, the program of integration will probably help transform the political attitudes of urban youths.

A principal aim of the Cultural Revolution was the creation of "revolutionary successors" to the passing generation. How have China's youth measured up? On occasion Mao Tse-tung expressed dissatisfaction with China's young people, but most of them are loyal productive citizens, even though they may not have achieved the high ideological standards Mao had in mind.

There is discontent, some of it open,[32] but China can probably rely on the generation raised since 1949 to carry on the effort to modernize and to achieve other major goals of the revolution.

Women

Some of the most significant reforms made by the Chinese Communists have involved the status of women in society. In traditional China women were regarded as inferior to men. Male children were preferred, and girls were often considered a liability; in some instances female infants were even drowned by poor families. Girls were generally married at an early age, and the bride entered the home of the husband's family, where she was often regarded as little more than a servant. Suicide was not an uncommon reaction to the restricted female role.

At the turn of the century, Chinese governments began to adopt a more progressive attitude toward women. Footbinding and some of the oppressive marriage customs were made unlawful, although few of these measures were rigorously enforced. With the passage of the marriage law in 1950, the "liberation" of women became a greater reality. The law was somewhat relaxed in 1953, but its provisions did require willingness on the part of both parties before a marriage could be contracted. It prohibited polygamy, concubinage, child marriages, and greatly restricted the lavish gifts associated with contracts of marriage. It also made divorces easier to obtain and granted women equal property rights with men.[33]

Concomitant to the marriage law was the desire of the authorities that women be engaged outside the home in productive activities, be educated, and be politically mobilized. Peasant women had traditionally worked the soil with their husbands, and the development of industry gave urban women a way to join the work force as well. The contributions of women to household income and the increased use of birth control have done much to establish greater equality for women.

Discrimination does still exist, however. As noted earlier, though technically they receive equal pay for equal work, their work is not usually considered to be equal to that of men, so they get paid less. Only a few have been able to rise to positions of high responsibility in political affairs. For example, it is generally believed that the power of Mao's wife derived from Mao and her other male associates prior to her purge. The highest-ranking Chinese woman is Chen Mu-hua, who is an alternate member of the Politburo and serves as minister of economic relations with foreign countries. Other prominent Chinese

Women are expected to play an important role in the Chinese economy. This Tibetan woman operates a tractor on a state farm.

women include Teng Ying-ch'ao (Madame Chou En-lai) and Soong Ch'ing-ling (Madame Sun Yat-sen). The Chinese Communists frequently point to women as exemplary peasants and workers, but they admit that women have not yet achieved full equality and that much remains to be accomplished. Chinese Communist ideology regards the equality of women as a class problem that will be resolved as the class struggle is continued.[34]

Minorities

The national minorities of China comprise only about 6 percent of the total population, but they tend to live in the strategically important border areas like Inner Mongolia, Sinkiang, Tibet, and Southwest China.[35] The minorities come from as many as 200 different groups. A central problem for the Chinese Communist authorities has been how to integrate these peoples and their respective territories into the national framework.

The Communists have essentially adopted a carrot-and-stick approach to the minorities. Originally CCP policy reflected the Soviet federal plan. However, once power was achieved in 1949, the idea of federalism was abandoned. Minorities were to have "autonomous regions" governed much like the provinces of China. Under the principle of regional autonomy, they were to receive special consideration in the development of language, culture, and religion, and in implementing socialist reforms. There are now five Autonomous Regions in China—Inner Mongolia, Sinkiang Uighur, Ning-hsia Hui, Tibet, and Kwangsi Chuang—and a larger number of autonomous administrate subprovincial units.

Prior to 1957, the CCP made good on its promise of special consideration for minorities. In 1958 a policy of more direct assimilation was adopted. The change in policy caused some resentment and contributed to the Tibetan revolt in 1959 and the Kazakh exodus in the early 1960s. Policy was once again modified to pay more attention to minority problems, but the hard line was reinstated with the Cultural Revolution. In response to Mao's statement in 1964 in which he supported the struggle of black people in the United States by asserting that the class question "must be resolved through class struggle," the Party proceeded to emphasize once again a more assimilationist approach. At the end of the Cultural Revolution, policy shifted back to more favoritism and less force in dealing with minorities.

In dealing with the minorities, the Chinese Communists have encouraged the migration of Han Chinese colonists to minority regions and have stationed the PLA in the border regions for both national defense and internal security purposes. The local economy, transportation services, and communications systems within the minority areas have been improved, and minorities have been given favorable treatment in recruitment as cadres, CCP members, and PLA soldiers. For this reason, minority separatism does not seem to be a serious threat at present, but the Chinese Communists have not achieved full integration or assimilation of minority peoples. This contradiction will likely continue in the foreseeable future.

CONCLUSIONS

China is a revolutionary society. The Chinese Communists are committed to changing the values, beliefs, and attitudes of the people and to achieving greater egalitarianism in the social structure. They are also committed to such goals as modernizing China's economy and achieving equality with other powerful nations like the United States and Russia. Their blueprint is to be found in the Thought of Mao Tse-tung, which emphasize will and struggle, self-reliance, the mass line, and contradiction. Although Mao's ideological prescriptions are often modified to suit the times by his successors, the basic desire to mobilize and transform society continues.

The goals of the Chinese Communists are to be met through socialization of the Chinese people, through mass campaigns, through propaganda, and through economic development. In comparing the China of today with the China of 1949, it is evident that considerable progress has already been achieved. Today there is greater interaction between the rulers and the masses of China than at any point in previous history.

We have made some generalizations about types of people in China, peasants, workers, young people, women, and minorities. Each of these groups has unique problems that the authorities are grappling with. Overall, what can be said about Chinese society? Perhaps the best statement can be made through a comparison. India is another country with a large population. With difficulty India has been able to maintain an essentially democratic political system with a good deal of political freedom. Yet, India also has great disparity between wealth and poverty. Many of India's millions are undernourished; there is famine and starvation. In China, people do not go hungry, but the do not enjoy much political freedom either.[36] Political participation is expected, but it is not usually spontaneous or without restraint. An evaluation of this entire situation is likely to be influenced by the observer's own sense of values. If the observer prefers political freedom, he will probably prefer India and be suspicious of the overwhelming Chinese effort to achieve social mobilization. If he prefers a full stomach, reasonably good health care, and a better standard of living for the masses, he will probably look with favor on the Chinese experiment and see beauty in "the picture being painted" upon the Chinese masses.

CHAPTER THREE

Political Institutions
and Processes

The force at the core leading our cause forward is the Chinese Communist Party. We must rally most closely round the Party Central Committee headed by Comrade Hua Kuo-feng, uphold the unity and unification of the Party, strengthen the sense of organization and discipline, obey the Party Central Committee in all our actions, persist in taking class struggle as the key link, adhere to the Party's basic line, persevere in continuing the revolution under the dictatorship of the proletariat, consolidate and develop the achievements of the Great Proletarian Cultural Revolution, grasp revolution, promote production and other work and preparedness against war, strive to win still greater victories in the socialist revolution and socialist construction, and further consolidate the dictatorship of the proletariat in our country.

—Editorial in *People's Daily, Red Flag,* and *Liberation Army Daily*[1]

In the previous chapters we have considered the political environment of China. Now we will look at the political process itself, examining both institutions and policy making. The Chinese Communist Party is at the head of China's political institutions, but the government bureaucracy and the People's Liberation Army also have important roles. We will see how these institutions work together to make authoritative decisions for the Chinese people.

THE CHINESE COMMUNIST PARTY

Formal Organization

The Chinese Communist Party had over 35 million members in 1978. It is the world's largest Communist party, yet it is small in comparison with China's total population. As indicated by the chapter epigraph, it is intended to be the leader of China's revolutionary cause. There have been several governing constitutions for the CCP, the most recent one having been established by the Eleventh CCP Congress in August of 1977. This constitution establishes the formal organization of the Party.

The new Party constitution reflects the struggle against the "Gang of Four." In his report on the constitution to the Eleventh CCP

Congress, CCP Vice-Chairman Yeh Chien-ying indicated that a number of changes had been made to correct deficiencies in the former constitution, which had been exploited by the "gang." The constitution is divided into a general program and five chapters. The general program outlines the nature and goals of the Chinese revolution, pays tribute to the role of Mao Tse-tung, and exhorts Party members to advance along the Marxist-Leninist line.

Chapter One of the new CCP constitution outlines the requirements and duties of the members. Members must be "revolutionary" persons who have reached the age of eighteen. They must be recommended by two party members, examined by a Party branch, and approved for probationary membership by higher Party committees. The probationary period is a new feature added to prevent groups like the "Gang of Four" from rapidly packing the membership with their supporters. In his report, Yeh noted that over half of the thirty-five million CCP members had entered since the Cultural Revolution, and, of these, seven million had attained membership since the Tenth Congress in 1973. Some of them were "bad elements" and others were duped by the "gang." Probationary membership will permit the weeding out of unqualified persons and will strengthen the ideological qualifications needed for attaining full membership. Chapter One also specifies the obligations of members and stipulates procedures for removing them from the Party.

Chapter Two specifies the Party's organizational system, which is democratic centralism. Democracy is to be utilized in the selection of members, the discussion of policy, and the transmission of information from lower echelons to higher echelons. The centralized principle means that once decisions have been made at higher levels they will be correctly implemented by lower levels. "The individual is subordinate to the organization, the minority is subordinate to the majority, the lower level is subordinate to the higher level, and the entire Party is subordinate to the Central Committee." Party congresses from the highest level on down are to be the leading bodies, but the Central Committee and respective Party committees at various levels can perform the leading function when the congresses are not in session. Decisions are to be transmitted collectively, though Party committees, and under the concept of mass line, should encourage individual initiative. Structures should be kept simple and reports on work made regularly. All Party committees are to establish commissions for inspecting discipline, a new feature of the constitution. Party organs may be established in state agencies and units of the PLA, and all other organizations in China must accept CCP leadership.

Chapter Three states that the National Party Congress will be held every five years unless special circumstances dictate otherwise. The Central Committee is elected by the Party Congress and it in turn elects the Politburo and the Standing Committee. The Politburo exercises the powers of the Central Committee when the latter is not in plenary session. Chapter Four states that local Party congresses should be convened every three years unless special circumstances dictate otherwise. These congresses also elect various secretaries and party committees.

Chapter Five discusses the basic units of the Party, and decrees that branches, general branches, or primary committees are to be set up in factories, mines, communes, offices, schools, shops, neighborhoods, companies of the PLA, and other primary units in accordance with size and circumstance. This chapter also outlines the functions of the local units, which are assigned the major role in achieving correct political socialization of members and seeing to it that Party policies are properly implemented.

Political Dynamics of the CCP

Prior to the Cultural Revolution in 1966, it was believed that the CCP was a relatively stable institution. Since the Cultural Revolution, most analysts point to instability at the highest levels. The Cultural Revolution resulted in organizational changes like the abolition of the Secretariat, and each Party congress has made changes in the constitution. The Tenth CCP Congress held in the fall of 1973 was concerned with rebuilding and consolidating the Party apparatus. The Eleventh CCP Congress held just four years later reflected the transition to post-Mao leadership.

A brief review of events since the Ninth CCP Congress in 1969 will demonstrate what has been happening. In 1969 the Standing Committee of the Politburo consisted of Mao, Lin Piao, Chou En-lai, Ch'en Po-ta, and K'ang Sheng. Ch'en, who had once served as Mao's personal secretary, was purged sometime in 1970. Lin Piao was said to have been killed in an airplane crash in Mongolia after failing to bring about a coup and attempting to flee to the USSR in 1971. In 1973, at the Tenth CCP Congress, the Standing Committee consisted of Mao, Chou, K'ang, and Wang Hung'wen, Yeh Chien-ying, Li Te-sheng, Chu Teh, Chang Ch'un-ch'iao, and Tung P'i-wu.[2] By 1976 Mao, Chou, K'ang, Chu, and Tung had died. Li was dropped from the Standing Committee (though he remained a member of the Politburo). Wang and Chang were purged as part of the "Gang of Four," leaving only Yeh as part of the original Standing Committee. Teng Hsiao-p'ing became a member of the Standing Committee in

FIGURE 3.1

CHINA'S LEADERSHIP

CCP Position	Name	Other Positions in Party and State Organizations
Chairman, CCP Central Committee	Hua Kuo-feng	Premier, State Council; Commander-in-Chief, PLA
Vice-Chairmen, CCP Central Committee	Yeh Chien-ying	Chairman, Standing Committee of National People's Congress
	Teng Hsiao-p'ing	Vice-Premier, State Council; Chief of Staff, PLA
	Li Hsien-hien	Vice-Premier, State Council
	Wang Tung-hsing	Head, General Office of the Central Committee; Commander 8341 Security Unit
Full Members, CCP Politburo	Wei Kuo-ch'ing	First Secretary, Kwangtung CCP Committee; Political Commissar, Canton MR
	Ulanfu	Chairman, United Front Work Department; Vice-Chairman, National People's Congress
	Fang I	Vice-Premier, State Council; Chairman, Academy of Sciences
	Liu Po-ch'eng	PLA Marshall
	Hsu Hsih-yu	Commander, Canton Military Region
	Chi Teng-kuei	Vice-Premier, State Council; Political Commissar, Peking Military Region
	Su Chen-hua	First Secretary, Shanghai CCP Committee; Political Commissar, PLA Navy
	Li Teh-sheng	Commander, Shenyang Military Region
	Wu Teh	First Secretary, Peking CCP Committee
	Yu Chiu-li	Vice-Premier, State Council; Minister, State Planning Commission
	Chang Ting-fa	Commander, PLA Air Force
	Chen Yung-Kuei	Vice-Premier, State Council
	Chen Hsi-lien	Vice-Premier, State Council; Commander, Peking Military Region
	Keng Piao	Vice-Premier, State Council; Chairman CC International Liason Department
	Nieh Jung-chen	Vice-Chairman, CC Military Affairs Commission
	Ni Chih-fu	Secretary, Shanghai CCP Committee
	Hsu Hsiang-chien	Vice-Premier, State Council; Minister of National Defense
	Peng Chung	Secretary, Shanghai CCP Committee
Alternate Members, CCP Politburo	Chen Mu-hua	Vice-Premier, State Council; Minister, Economic Relations with Foreign Countries (female)
	Chao Tzu-yang	First Secretary, Szechuan CCP Committee
	Saifudin	Former First Secretary, Sinkiang CCP Committee; Vice Chairman, National People's Congress

1974, was removed in 1976, and was reinstated in 1977. Hua Kuo-feng was added to the Standing Committee when he became Party vice-chairman in 1976. The Standing Committee elected at the Eleventh CCP Congress includes Hua Kuo-feng (CCP chairman, premier of the State Council, commander in chief of the PLA), Yeh Chien-ying (CCP vice-chairman, defense minister), Teng Hsiao-p'ing (CCP vice-chairman, deputy premier, chief of staff of the PLA), Li Hsien-nien (CCP vice-chairman, deputy premier), and Wang Tung-hsing (CCP vice-chairman, possibly serving as minister of Public Security). Other members of the Politburo are shown in Figure 3.1.

The composition of the Politburo and the Standing Committee demonstrates a balance between military experts, government bureaucrats, and economic specialists. There are no career military officers on the Soviet Politburo, yet eight of China's top twenty-five leaders have had military careers. Compared with the Tenth Politburo, the Eleventh also has a greater number of state economic planners. It would seem that a kind of "military-industrial complex" may dominate China's future politics. It is also interesting that no women have full membership status on the Politburo. Chen Mu-hua, an alternate member, is the only female in China's top leadership. Wu Kuei-hsin, a woman alternate member of the Tenth Politburo, was dropped but retains Central Committee status. The Eleventh CCP Congress reaffirmed the Hua-Yeh-Teng leadership and demonstrated the transition of leadership. The transition goes beyond a succession of names to an entirely new leadership style. China's "old guard" leaders who have been with the revolution since the Long March are gradually giving way to a new generation, and there has been a shift from the charismatic to the organizational type of authority. The charismatic Mao has been replaced by the Party bureaucrat. Prior to his meteoric rise between 1973 and 1976, Hua slowly worked his way up through the ranks in Hunan, Mao's home province.[3] His authority is based not on ideological contributions or a dynamic personality, but rather on political skills gained through experience at various levels of the CCP hierarchy.

It is necessary to look at the top leaders of the CCP, since they are the ones who make the major decision affecting the people of China, but it would be incorrect to focus solely on these individuals. The CCP is a large bureaucracy, and like all large organizations, power is effectively wielded at lower levels as well. Immediately below the Politburo and its Standing Committee is the Central Committee. The Tenth Central Committee of the CCP (Central Committees are named after the Congress at which they are elected) consisted of 319

Chairman Hua Kuo-feng and Vice-chairman Yeh Chien-ying, Teng Hsiao-p'ing, Li Hsien-nien, and Wang Tung-shing (from left to right) meet with delegates for the National Science Conference.

members, 195 regular members, and 124 alternates (alternates do not have the right to vote, although they do attend the meetings). Of these, roughly 100 were representatives of the bureaucracy, about 80 were military officers, and about 100 were worker-peasant representatives. In comparison with the Ninth Central Committee, the number of military representatives declined and the number of civil bureaucrats increased. The shift from military to civilian membership was indicative of the effort to strengthen and rebuild Party organization after the throes of the Cultural Revolution.[4] The political turmoil that resulted in changes in the Politburo also affected the Central Committee.

The Eleventh Central Committee consists of 201 full members and 132 alternates. Of these, 110 were full members of the Tenth Central Committee and 20 were alternates. This means that 71 new members of the Central Committee, or just over one third, were promoted from the ranks, while a number of former members were dropped. Part of this reflects the purges associated with the struggle against the "Gang of Four." There are presently 14 full and 24 alternate women members of the Central Committee, a very low number considering the emphasis that Chinese Communist propaganda has placed on achieving equality for women. All provincial first secretaries are full members of the Central Committee.

Meetings of the Central Committee are irregular and infrequent. Meetings of the entire committee are called "plenary sessions." The Eighth Central Committee (1956-69) held only twelve plenary sessions. The Ninth Central Committee (1969-73) held two, and the Tenth Central Committee (1973-77) held three. Meetings of the Central Committee are called to ratify major decisions. For example, the third plenum of the Tenth Central Committee passed resolutions restoring Teng Hsiao-p'ing to positions of responsibility and purging the "Gang of Four." From time to time, however, the Central Committee has been the scene of political struggles as Mao and his opponents tried to mobilize committee members in support of their respective policies.

Connected to the Central Committee are a number of working committees responsible for policy implementation. Committees like the Military Affairs Committee, the Control Commission (responsible for Party discipline), the propaganda organs, and other working groups function as adjuncts to the Central Committee. In the past, the Party secretariat was responsible for day-to-day policy implementation, but after its abolition during the Cultural Revolution other unspecified organs became responsible for this function. The committees functioning as adjuncts to the Central Committee are particularly important in developing national policy.

During 1950-54 and 1961-67 the Party maintained six regional bureaus as administrative divisions. In 1976 there was discussion as to whether these regional organizations might be revived. There are no Party congresses at these levels that appear to be primarily concerned with policy transmission. Immediately prior to the Cultural Revolution the regional bureaus often imparted policy guidance to the provinces under their jurisdiction. If the bureaus are reintroduced, they will likely serve a similar function.

Below the national level, each province and the three special municipalities (Peking, Shanghai, and Tientsin) have a Party congress and a Party committee headed by a first secretary. These provincial congresses serve about the same function as the national congress, that is, they lend legitimacy to decisions already made and signify important changes in leadership. Leadership changes in the provinces have reflected the dynamics of national politics. For example, after the purge of the "Gang of Four," sixteen of twenty-nine provincial and municipal leadership positions changed. Some were the result of new appointments of first secretaries, others were the outgrowth of purges and replacements, and one consisted of transferring the first secretary of one province to another.

In a recent article, Robert A. Scalapino analyzed the functions of 168 full secretaries at the provincial and municipal level and compared the individuals serving in that position in 1975 with those who had served in 1971.[5] His article concluded that the number of career military officers holding provincial secretariats was declining, and the number of representatives of mass organizations from Cultural Revolution days was increasing. He also observed that China's heartland, had more secretaries with close connections to the Party center, whereas secretaries in frontier areas were more likely to be military officers. This analysis demonstrated that younger cadres have been able to move up, even though some older cadres have been rehabilitated since the Cultural Revolution. Scalapino predicted that the continually changing pattern of career backgrounds in the provinces would contribute to future political instability. The provincial situation since 1976 seems to bear out Scalapino's predictions. Whether the new Hua leadership will bring more stability remains to be seen.

Below the provincial level on the *hsien,* or county level, are the

Members of the Standing Committee of a county CCP committee hold a meeting to discuss theory.

rural Party congresses and Party committees and the urban municipal congresses and committees. Below the *hsien* are the basic level units, which include the commune, street (in rural areas), and groups such as the school, factory, mine, or PLA unit. The size of the Party branch usually reflects the size of the unit in which it operates. Each Party organization from bottom to top is responsible for selecting its own leadership. However, these appointments must be confirmed by higher levels. Thus, a Party branch secretary in a commune must be approved by the county Party committee. This method insures that higher echelons will have control over selections at lower levels. For this reason, the "election" of Party representatives is largely a ratification of decisions made at higher levels.

The officers of the Party are called *kan-pu*, or cadres. There is some confusion over the term cadre since not all members of the Party are cadres and not all cadres are members of the Party. As used here, the term "cadre" refers to a person who holds an official position in the Party or state bureaucracies, is salaried by the state or the Party, and is engaged in political-administrative work. Other types of officials are sometimes called cadres (e.g., road construction engineers and technical specialists in factories) but we will use the term for political officers only. There are as many as 4 million Party cadres doing the administrative work of the Party. A cadre's salary and rank depends upon his level (i.e., local, provincial, or national) and position.

Party cadres are particularly concerned with administering the affairs of the Party. They are responsible for dues collection, political study, and the unending stream of reporting associated with Party activity. Although cadres (both Party and government) have an enviable position in terms of status and income, they are also the first to be criticized when a policy change is in the offing. This is particularly true of the basic level cadres who are responsible for transmitting Party directives to the masses. At one time a cadre might be criticized for commandism—for trying to force the people without adhering to the mass line—and at another time be accused of tailism—not being forceful in his leadership of the masses. The Party constitution clearly states that criticism and self-criticism will be an intimate part of a Party member's life; this is particularly true of the cadres at the lower levels.

Another characteristic of the political dynamics of the Party has to do with secrecy. Party meetings, particularly at the national level, are rarely announced in advance or publicized until after they are concluded. Meetings are not open to the public, though official reports about decisions are well-publicized through the media. Much of our information about the inner workings of the Party comes from analyzing formal pronouncements and statements from refugees, or from unauthorized leaks like wall posters, captured documents (the Nationalist government on Taiwan has occasionally obtained official CCP documents), or the Red Guard tabloids. Because of the high level of secrecy surrounding the decision process, information about the workings of the Party is sketchy. Little is really known about the formal organization of the Party (e.g., the composition of the various committees and commissions adjunct to the Central Committee).

In 1977 it appeared that the organization of the Party was going to undergo a major overhaul. Shortly before his disgrace Teng Hsiao-p'ing authored a document entitled "On the General Program for All Work of the Party and the Country," which called for a major reorganization of the Party. It was condemned as a "poisonous weed" during his disgrace, but since his rehabilitation it has been praised as a "fragrant flower."[6] Hua Kuo-feng, in a number of major speeches, has emphasized the work of what he calls "party-building," a theme also developed in *Red Flag*. It seems reasonable that the Eleventh

Congress will lead to some organizational changes in the CCP, but how much of this will be made public is uncertain.

Recruitment and Composition

Although any revolutionary who has attained the age of eighteen is eligible for CCP membership, membership is actually very selective. The last information about Party composition, made available in 1957, stated that about 67 percent of the Party were peasants and about 14 percent workers. At that time 25 percent were under the age of twenty-five, 67 percent between the ages of twenty-five and forty-five, and 8 percent were older than forty-five. About 10 percent were women.[7] Because of the rapid expansion of Party membership since that time, it is likely that these figures are no longer representative. We would expect to find more young people and probably more women in the Party now.

The primary source of recruitment prior to the Cultural Revolution was the Communist Youth League. By 1959 this organization numbered around 25 million. During the Cultural Revolution, the League came under attack and was not mentioned publicly for several years. In the 1970s the League began holding congresses again and received public attention. No figures about its membership have been given.[8] As the work of Party building continues, it is probable that the Youth League will once more become a primary recruiting source.

Another source of Party members is the army. PLA volunteers go through a highly competitive selection process, and it is not surprising that many are also qualified for CCP membership. Well over 50 percent of the PLA soldiers are members of the CCP or of the Youth League, and all officers are members. There have been numerous accounts in the media about how PLA soldiers are recruited for CCP membership after demonstrating courage and determination in facing some difficult problem or challenge.

During the Cultural Revolution, recruitment for Party membership was often associated with political activism. Some Red Guards were admitted to the Party, as were other workers, students, and peasants who became involved in various campaigns. Indeed, political activism still remains an important criterion for selection as a member of the CCP. Reports in the press indicate that some of the middle school graduates who are sent to rural areas are admitted to the CCP after demonstrating their enthusiasm by hard work and perseverance. Those actively seeking CCP membership must volunteer to work on whatever campaign is being developed at the time. Those who are actively involved will quickly come to the attention of Party leaders.

Motivations for joining the Party are varied. Some want to join because the Party is a prestigious elite and they see Party membership as an avenue to status, and perhaps a better material life. The less opportunistic are inclined to identify with the ideological values articulated by the Party. They see CCP membership as a way to serve—to build the new China. Whatever the motives, CCP membership is in great demand, but few are able to get in. Published accounts suggest that Party membership is earned by those who have distinguished themselves through some special service, through constant political study, and through connections with other CCP members. Many people spend two years or more proving themselves, and when they do become members, they are expected to continue their activity even more rigorously. If the rewards of CCP membership are great, the hard work associated with membership is also likely to be great.[9]

It would seem then that there will be a tendency for the Chinese Communist Party to become more organized and routinized—in essence, more bureaucratic. It will continue to grow, but the growth will be controlled and supervised. At the same time, the Party will strengthen its control over other institutions, state organs, the military, and mass organizations. Perhaps the evolution of a "new class" of Party careerists is inevitable in a large country with serious developmental problems, but in a time of leadership transition, it is unlikely that there will be a massive capitulation to bureaucratism. The struggle between ideology and organization will continue.

GOVERNMENT

Formal Organization

According to Marxist-Leninist theory, the political institutions of the state are the instruments of class rule. The role of the Party is to give leadership to the revolution; the state is to serve as the "dictatorship of the proletariat." This concept has been modified somewhat in most Communist countries, but particularly in China, where the national constitution specifies that state organs are to be led by the CCP. Generally speaking, the role of the Party is seen to be that of making policy, while the work of state is to implement policy. It will be useful in comparing Party and government organization to refer to Figure 3.2.

The most recent Chinese national constitution was promulgated

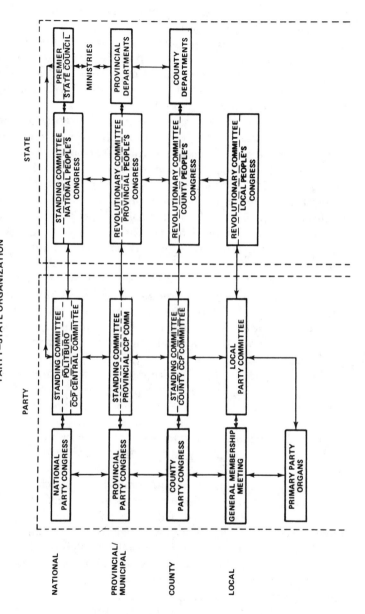

FIGURE 3.2

PEOPLE'S REPUBLIC OF CHINA
PARTY–STATE ORGANIZATION

on March 5, 1978, by the Fifth National People's Congress. Prior to that time the governing state documents were the 1954 and 1975 constitutions. The 1978 constitution is divided into a preamble and four chapters. Chapter One outlines the general principles of the PRC. Chapter Two discusses the structure of the state, Chapter Three outlines the rights and duties of citizens, and Four has brief articles dealing with the flag, the national emblem, and the capital.

Among the significant general principles are these: The Communist Party leads all the people and will exercise control over the state. All elected people's congresses at the various levels will practice democratic centralism. The Autonomous Regions, where national minorities reside, are inalienable parts of the PRC. There are two types of ownership of the means of production: socialist ownership by the whole people, and socialist collective ownership by working people. The state sector of the economy is the leading force in the national economy, and the state may nationalize natural resources and property when necessary. Peasants on communes are guaranteed the right to private plots of land and private livestock. All matters are to be conducted under the ideological precepts of Marxism-Lenism and the Thought of Mao Tse-tung; counterrevolutionaries will be suppressed. The chairman of the CCP is commander-in-chief of the PLA, which at all times is a fighting force, a working force, and a production force.

The principle of state structure is that the National People's Congress is to be the highest organ of state power under the leadership of the CCP. The Fifth National People's Congress consisted of 3,497 deputies elected from the provinces, Autonomous Regions, municipalities, and the PLA. It was elected for a term of five years, though the term may be extended or shortened, and is to meet annually. When the Congress is not in session, its formal business is to be conducted by its Standing Committee. The chairman of the Standing Committee, presently Yeh Chien-ying, acts as China's ceremonial head of state assisted by several vice-chairmen. Governmental powers are to be supervised by the State Council, which legally operates under the jurisdiction of the People's Congress and its Standing Committee. The State Council consists of the premier, now Hua Kuo-feng, the vice-premier, and some ministers; it supervises the work of the various ministries, directs the national economy, plans the state budget, and directs state administrative affairs.[10]

People's congresses are to be elected at the provincial and lower levels. The revolutionary committees, which served as the permanent organs of these congresses on the provincial and lower levels, are being abolished and replaced by other organs according to Hua Kuo-feng's report on the work of the government issued to the Fifth National People's Congress. Though the exact nature of the new organs has not yet been specified, they will probably be similar to the people's committees that existed prior to the Cultural Revolution. Autonomous Regions are to be governed in the same manner as provinces. A people's judiciary is to be established, including a Supreme Court and a Supreme People's Procuracy, with courts and procuracies also at lower levels. The Procuracy remained dormant in China for many years; its resurrection in the new constitution is taken by some observers to reflect more procedural emphasis in Chinese law. The constitution also provides that the masses will be involved in public trials.

Among the rights and duties of citizens are the duties to support the Party and the state, and to defend the country. Citizens eighteen and over have the right to vote, the right to receive an education, and the right to work. Old people have the right to material assistance in illness and disability. Citizens can complain if they feel their rights are being abused. They enjoy freedom of speech and assembly, the right to strike, and the right to believe or not believe in religion. Women are to have equal rights with men; the state protects marriage, the family, and the mother and child, but it also officially encourages birth control. The rights of overseas Chinese are protected, as are those of revolutionaries who seek political asylum in China.

In his speech on the work of the government, Hua Kuo-feng endorsed Chou En-lai's 1975 proposal to achieve comprehensive modernization for China by the year 2000. He disclosed a ten-year (1976-85) economic plan that proposes increasing agricultural production by 4 to 5 percent annually and industrial production by 10 percent. Steel production is to nearly triple to 60 million tons, and grain output should increase from the present 275 million tons to 440 million tons. Hua also said that China would construct 120 large industrial complexes, including 10 iron and steel plants, 9 nonferrous metals centers, 8 coal mines, 10 oil and gas fields, 30 power stations, 6 mainline railroads, and 5 ports. These would create 14 strong industrial areas. Population growth is to be reduced to less than 1 percent annually over the next three years. His speech affirmed the point that the primary work of the government will be comprehensive development.[11]

Political Dynamics

The term "parallel hierarchies" has been used to explain the relationship between party and government in some Communist countries. In China the hierarchies are not always specific since there is express Party supervision of all aspects of government work. During the Cultural Revolution disruptions often made Party and state relationships unclear; the revolutionary committees at the various levels were originally hybrids of CCP and government administration. The Tenth CCP Congress in 1973 symbolized the reconstruction of Party organs, and the Fourth National People's Congress in 1975 symbolized the reconstruction of state organs. The Eleventh CCP Congress in 1977 and the Fifth National People's Congress in 1978 have made it clear that the formal distinctions between Party and state will be maintained. It appears that a new system of parallel hierarchies is being established.

There are a number of techniques used by the Party to control the government. First, the national constitution specifies that all state organs must accept Party leadership. Second, Party leaders are also assigned top government positions (note Figure 3.1). For example, Hua Kuo-feng, besides being chairman of the CCP Central Committee, serves as premier of the State Council and commander-in-chief of the PLA. Teng Hsiao-p'ing serves as a vice-premier and PLA chief of staff, and Yeh Chien-ying is chairman of the National People's Congress Standing Committee. Other Politburo members hold vice-premierships and ministerial posts. All government ministers are members of the CCP Central Committee. All government cadres, whether Party members or not, are recruited through Party-directed staffing and personnel procedures. All civil servants are expected to participate in political study, usually led by Party cadres.[12]

The National People's Congress serves a largely ceremonial function. It meets only sporadically, and when it does, it ritually ratifies previous decisions and receives reports from various ministers on government work. Members of the Standing Committee are usually involved in meeting foreign delegations and performing other ceremonial functions of state. These activities receive a good deal of attention in the Chinese press but have little to do with the exercise of power.

More significant is the work of the government ministries. The ministries are important in implementing policy decisions. In the past there has been constant tension between the demands for professionalism in ministerial affairs and the demand for ideological correctness. This tension between "red and expert" was a primary factor in the Cultural Revolution, which resulted in the disruption of many ministries. The current government under Hua, Yeh, and Teng, is committed to a policy of modernization by the year 2000, so it seems likely that professionalism will be emphasized, perhaps at the expense of a purely Maoist ideology.

Like Party affairs, the work of most government ministries is highly secretive. Glimpses of governmental operations have been obtained from former cadres who have left China, from formal reports and speeches reported in the media, from leaked documents, and in some cases from official dealings. For example, recent exchanges between China and the United States have permitted greater insights into the workings of some government commissions. Businessmen who have had dealings with the Ministry of Foreign Trade understand something of the Chinese decision process from negotiating contracts. Perhaps future exchanges will shed even more light on government operations.

It was previously stated that governmental operations are to be supervised by the Party. Not all state cadres are CCP members, yet the nature of their responsibilities allows them to exercise power. As always, large bureaucratic organizations have a tendency to develop organizational values and norms independent of those dictated by any ideology. Similarly, officials often have individual goals that are not congruent with either organizational or ideological goals. In China this problem came to the surface during the Cultural Revolution when the Red Guards accused many Party and government cadres of bureaucratism, careerism, and other deviations. The purges that resulted may have temporarily checked some of the tensions, but as former cadres were rehabilitated during the post–Cultural Revolution period, the issue began to resurface.

One answer to the problem is the *hsia fang*. During the Cultural Revolution many cadres were sent to "May 7 Cadre Schools," so named because of Mao's directive on May 7, 1967, that cadres should experience the revolution by engaging in physical labor, political study, and by actually integrating with the masses.[13] In the past, cadres had been sent down to lower levels to "purify" themselves, so the Cultural Revolution's *hsia fang* was not altogether new. Thousands of cadres spent one or two years in the schools. At first being sent to a May 7 Cadre School appeared to be punishment; subsequently it became a token of one's revolutionary credentials, and cadres eagerly volunteered to attend the schools. After participating in the schools, most cadres could expect to be restored to their original positions or to positions of similar rank.

In addition to *hsia fang*, the requirement for political study and criticism help curb bureaucratic tendencies. Nearly all officials have been criticized at one time or another; some have been sharply criticized and humiliated. Those who have been rehabilitated after having undergone severe criticism, state publicly that while it was not always a pleasant experience, it was one that opened their eyes to the needs and demands of the masses and made them more sensitive to their obligations.[14]

At the provincial level and below, the organs of government are called revolutionary committees. With few exceptions, the chairman of the Party committee in a given area is also the chairman of the revolutionary committee. The revolutionary committees, created during the Cultural Revolution, as noted above, were hybrid organizations that combined Party and state committees. As the Party was rebuilt, the revolutionary committees gradually became the leading government organs, replacing the people's committees that had performed this function prior to the Cultural Revolution. The constitution now gives legal sanction to this status of revolutionary committees.

In rural areas, the revolutionary committees extend to the commune level. Those who visit China, and tour the communes are often met by revolutionary committees that represent each commune's political activists. Below the commune level, the brigades and teams have organizations, but they do not have revolutionary committees. Also, in many parts of rural China there are state farms operated by farmers salaried by the government. These farms are often used for mechanization, experimentation, reclamation, and other tasks.

This system of dual administration by Party and government officials seems to have worked quite well in rural areas. Mark Gayn argues that the Chinese Communists have succeeded in establishing an honest and capable rural administration that has, over the past years (1) achieved a more equitable pattern of social justice than existed before the revolution, (2) made a more effective use of rural manpower, and (3) achieved self-sufficiency in food production.[15] Gayn attributes these successes primarily to the efforts of young, energetic Party cadres who give good leadership. Although some of his conclusions might be disputed, most visitors and analysts would agree that the accomplishments of state and Party management in rural areas surpasses anything achieved before the revolution.

In urban areas the municipal organs are also headed by a revolutionary committee. Below them are the street offices (consisting of about 5,000 households), the residents' committees (500 households), and the residents' small groups (20 households). Each of these levels have cadres who work closely with Party cadres to insure that order is maintained and other municipal affairs properly conducted.

The government is also responsible for public security, which is managed by the Public Security Ministry. Although visitors to China frequently comment on the low visibility of uniformed policemen, a large secret police apparatus does exist. Dossiers are kept on all citizens, and troublemakers are speedily dealt with. Recently there have been reports of criminal activity, including murder and robbery, in some of China's large cities. There were reports of looting during the massive earthquake that destroyed Tangshan and also reports of sabotage attempts at key railway junctures.

Criminal prosecutions are conducted by the public security apparatus through "popular courts," which are often nothing more than an assembly of the masses pronouncing cumulative judgment on undesirables. It is uncertain how large or extensive the prison system of China is,[16] but there are probably two types of offenders. One class of criminal lawbreakers are simply sentenced to jail as punishment. Another class of "criminals," however, are the political offenders, who may be sent to labor camps until they are deemed worthy of rehabilitation. The public security system supports political socialization to maintain the control of the regime.

This complex system of Party and government administration is authoritarian. In spite of constitutional guarantees, most unorthodox expression in China is likely to be anomic, that is, in mass demonstrations, wall posters, or in some form of underground or criminal activity. This is not to say that the people of China have no freedom. Under the principle of the mass line there are opportunities for the people to express opinions or to make demands. Although the opportunities are carefully controlled and channeled, they do exist. The Chinese people are not just a nation of blue ants or "new socialists."

The point of this discussion is that any administration is constrained by the society in which it operates. Just as the society is mobilized and changed through political controls, so must the administration adjust to meet the disparate needs of society. The cadre is sometimes placed in the unenviable position of meeting state production goals on the one hand, and meeting the peasants' or workers' needs for resources on the other. The cadre's burden is heavier still in the knowledge that any mistake may result in criticism or even dismissal. Under these circumstances, achieving competent government administration is a challenging task. The Chinese

Communists are constantly experimenting—sometimes encouraging
a decentralization of power and local initiative, sometimes encouraging a greater centralization of power with less local initiative—but
the system seems to be achieving some success. The precise
relationship of Party and government organs will also continue to
change, and it is this willingness to adapt that has enabled the
Chinese Communists to maintain power.

THE PEOPLE'S LIBERATION ARMY

Formal Organization

Mao's dictum that "political power grows out of a barrel of a gun"
has not been forgotten. The military has frequently been called upon
to participate directly in Chinese politics. During the Cultural
Revolution the PLA established martial law in some areas and
participated heavily in civil administration in others. Though it has
somewhat reduced its participation since 1973, as an institution it
still figures prominently in political affairs.

The state constitution specifies that the PLA is a fighting force, a
working force, and a production force. Its task is defined as serving
"to safeguard the achievements of the socialist revolution and
socialist construction, to defend the sovereignty, territorial integrity
and security of the state, and to guard against subversion and
aggression by imperialism, social-imperialism and their lackeys."[17]
The constitution also specifies that the chairman of the CCP is the
commander in chief of the armed forces.

The military command structure includes the Military Affairs
Committee within the CCP Central Committee and the Ministry of
National Defense under the State Council. Immediately under these
comes the chief of staff, who is responsible for the military chain of
command, and the director of the General Political Department, who
is responsible for the system of political commissars within the
military. Presently, Hua Kuo-feng as Party chairman is commander
in chief of the armed forces, Hsu Hsiang-chien is minister of national
defense, and Teng Hsiao-p'ing is chief of staff. Chang Ch'un-ch'iao,
prior to his purge served as director of the General Political
Department.

The PLA is composed of about 3,600,000 people;[18] some 3,000,000
are in the army, 300,000 are in the navy, and about 300,000 are in the
air force. China is divided into eleven military regions; each is named
after the city where the headquarters is located, with the exception of
the Sinkiang Military Region. Each region is headed by a military

commander. Three of the key regional military commanders are members of the Politburo—Ch'en Hsi-lien (Peking), Li Teh-sheng (Shenyang), and Hsu Hsih-yu (Canton). They control about one third to one half of China's total armed forces. The military regions are further subdivided into military districts, with each province constituting a military district.

The PLA is divided into main force units and local force units. Main force units are administered regionally, but they are under central command. Main forces include 121 infantry divisions, 10 armored divisions, 3 cavalry divisions, 4 airborne divisions, 40 artillery divisions, and 41 railway and construction engineer divisions. Local forces include some 40 armies made up of infantry divisions and 110 independent regiments. Each army generally includes 3 infantry divisions, and 3 artillery regiments; in some cases there are also 3 armored regiments.

The Chinese Navy has about 60 submarines, 8 destroyers, and a host of smaller support craft. It also has a naval air force and about 28,000 marines. Most of the navy is employed for coastal defense. The regular air force has over 4,000 combat aircraft, most of which are aged MiG 15s, 17s, and 19s. Duration of service in the army is from 2 to 4 years, in the air force from 3 to 5 years, and in the navy from 4 to 6 years. Officers are recruited from the ranks. In 1965 rank insignia were abolished, so officers are presently distinguished by position title rather than by insignia.

China's strategic capabilities include about twenty to thirty intermediate range ballistic missiles, and about thirty to fifty medium range ballistic missiles. The missiles are liquid fueled and have nuclear warheads. China has launched earth satellites, but has not actually tested an intercontinental ballistic missile (ICBM). China also has sixty-five Tu-16 medium bombers capable of delivering nuclear weapons to strategic targets. It should be noted that China's military posture is primarily defensive; China is capable of striking the USSR and other targets on its periphery with nuclear weapons but most effort has gone into defenses against any attack. China has emphasized the acquisition of antiaircraft and antitank weapons, and conducts special training of soldiers for operations in case of invasion. Recently, China has sought to purchase foreign technology in order to upgrade defense capabilities. These purchases include aircraft and communications equipment from the United States, a jet engine factory from Britain, and various items from other countries.[19]

The small size of China's total armed forces compared to the whole population enables the PLA to demand the highest quality in its

PLA soldiers receive instructions on antitank warfare.

volunteers. In prerevolutionary China, service in the armed forces did not bring status or prestige; in fact, soldiers were generally despised. The situation has been reversed, and today military service is eagerly sought after by young people. Service in the military brings automatic status and prestige, and may lead to Party membership or some other career avenue as well. Those wishing to join the PLA must pass rigid physical examinations and must demonstrate correct political attitudes. They must also be recommended by their production teams or factory units; only the very best applicants are selected for service. An adjunct to the PLA is the armed militia of about 5 million people, which is organized into 75 divisions and an unknown number of regiments. Other militia, like the urban militia and the ordinary and basic militia, numbering several more millions receive some training but are unarmed.

Political Dynamics

The PLA has often been at the center of political activity in China. After liberation in 1949, the country was divided into regions supervised by Military Control Commissions. As Party and government authority was established, the military tended to withdraw from active involvement. The Soviet model was used for the professionalization of the PLA. However, the process was never fully completed. The history of the PLA, that is, of an armed force based on the masses and supported by them, conflicted with the professionalization model. This issue figured in the dismissal of P'eng Teh-huai from the position of defense minister in 1959.

During the early 1960s the PLA became a vehicle for the study and propagation of Mao's thought. This movement was apparently orchestrated by the new defense minister, Lin Piao. During the Socialist Education Campaign ranks were abolished, and the people of China were exhorted to learn from the PLA as the most correct exponent of Maoist ideology. During the Cultural Revolution the PLA supported Mao, albeit with some reluctance. A number of Mao's opponents in the PLA were purged, and Lin Piao's supporters won some commanding positions. Lin himself was named Mao's successor. After the purge of Lin there was another overhaul in the command structure. The position of chief of staff has been particularly vulnerable over the past few years, and the job has changed hands several times because of political turmoil.

Perhaps the best observer of this process in the Chinese military is William Whitson, who has provided considerable insights into the high command of the PLA.[20] Whitson observes that political involvement in military affairs is related to an ongoing system of personal ties and career patterns carried forward from preliberation times. Particularly important is the field army system. China is geographically divided among five field armies, each army having jurisdiction over certain regions, which are not necessarily contiguous. Politics at the center of the system reflected a balance of influence among the various field armies until Lin Piao sought to "stack" the center with representatives from the Fourth Field Army. After Lin's purge, an effort was made to reestablish an equal balance. Whitson has also made a detailed study of provincial level leaders and their affiliation with the field armies. There is a remarkable correlation between the field army/system career patterns of most provincial governors and the field army location of their assignment. Thus, the field army system has bearing on civilian as well as military leadership.[21]

Whitson's conclusions have been hotly debated by other scholars. Modifications have been necessary to accommodate events like the shift of key regional military commanders after the Tenth Party Congress in 1973, the first time such a shift had occurred in China. Nevertheless, his demonstration of the influence of the military in political affairs is an important contribution to our understanding of Chinese politics.

The military has been at the center of some of China's most important political debates over the years. One major issue concerns the question of professionalism versus politicization. Debate has continued since the PLA first tried to experiment with the Soviet model. Those who favored professionalization also apparently favored greater military expenditures for modern arms, the maintenance of a separate professional officer corps, and more emphasis on military training than on political indoctrination. Those who opposed this view, including Mao, argued that men are more important than weapons, that the past success of the PLA was based on its intimate relationship with the people, and that ideological indoctrination was necessary to maintain this relationship. A compromise that favored Mao's position prevailed through the Cultural Revolution. Mao and his supporters got military help in maintaining their power, but steps were also taken to improve the quality of weapons. Now that Mao is gone more emphasis will probably be placed on modernization of weapons and military training. It should be noted, however, that this is only a question of emphasis and not a zero sum game in which military professionalization implies a total lack of political indoctrination or ideological commitment.

A related issue is the question of how intimately involved the PLA should be in civil administration. During the 1949-54 and 1967-71 periods, the PLA was directly concerned with civil administration in many parts of China. The time spent in these functions necessarily detracted from the ability of the PLA to prepare for war. After the Sino-Soviet border incidents of 1969, the PLA began to withdraw from civil administration and concentrate more on defense preparation. The relationship of the military commander and the political commissar is not very clear; if the military withdraws from civil administration and spends more time on strictly military functions, how will the role of the commissar be affected?

Another issue—one the Chinese cannot escape—has to do with the allocation of scarce resources. China's annual gross national product (GNP) is just over $300 billion, of which perhaps $20 billion goes for national defense. With all the emphasis on modernization and the other routine demands, there are bound to be conflicts over the budget. Choices must be made for allocating funds to heavy industry, light industry, agriculture, and other priority items as well as defense needs. Even in the defense budget there have been disagreements as to whether China should seek rapid advance in high technology (missiles, electronics, and nuclear warheads) or try to modernize conventional capabilities. Also, different geographic regions have different defense priorities; it would not be surprising if military commanders in North China preferred an improvement in air defense capabilities and Southern commanders preferred developing naval strength.

Still another issue has been the relationship between the PLA and the militia. The PLA has not always been anxious to take on the responsibility of training and maintaining the militia. At the same time, recent charges against the "Gang of Four" claim that they sought political of the militia and that they planned to use the militia to assassinate key military commanders, seize control of the armed forces, and stage a counterrevolutionary coup.[22] This charge is probably an exaggeration, but it does illustrate the problem of relations between the PLA and the militia.

These are only a few of the issues related to the role of the PLA in political decision making.[23] We will now turn our attention to some of the PLA contributions to various aspects of political life, especially in the areas of political control, production, political socialization, and national defense.

Control. The PLA is responsible not only for defending China against foreign enemies but also for insuring central authority in

PLA soldier gives political instruction to members of a county militia.

times of crisis. It already been noted that from 1949 to 1954, and
again from 1967 to 1971, the PLA was an important agent for stability
when other political institutions were weak. During the Cultural
Revolution, the PLA established martial law in many provinces. It
crushed a rebellion in Tibet in 1959, and has established order during
various provincial disturbances like the ones connected to the purge
of the "Gang of Four." It also maintained order after the massive
Tangshan earthquake of 1976. In national minority regions, the PLA
has neutralized attempts toward greater autonomy and has helped to
insure that these border regions will remain an integral part of the
nation.[24]

Production. The PLA is to be a productive force as well as a fighting
force. In areas where PLA bases are established, soldiers frequently
assist the people in planting, harvesting, and other work. Annually
several million man-days are allocated by the PLA to assisting the
masses. At the same time, the PLA tries to be self-sufficient,
producing its own food, medicines, and other essentials. PLA bases
usually have farmed land, small factories, and other productive
facilities designed to reduce the demand on central finances for
supporting the PLA. These activities also ensure that PLA soldiers
have plenty of work to do in addition to their military training. The
PLA has formed a Production and Construction Corps, which
operates in some of the border regions. This corps is staffed with
civilians who immigrate to the frontier regions as PLA representa-

tives. The corps opens lands for colonization and operates state farms, mines, mills, factories, and other facilities. There are probably about 4 million people involved in corps projects.

Socialization. The PLA performs a number of activities related to political socialization. PLA doctors often treat civilians when other medical care is not available. The PLA also sponsors traveling teams that entertain in rural areas. During the Socialist Education Campaign and the Cultural Revolution, the Chinese people were urged to learn from the PLA. Revolutionary heros and martyrs like Lei Feng are presented as examples of exemplary personages who should be emulated.[25] The PLA participates with the people in political study sessions and other activities. All of these activities help indoctrinate the troops, and provide a means of integrating the soldiers with the workers and peasants while indoctrinating the people as well.

Defense Policy

The major function of the PLA, like all military organizations, is to provide national defense. Since 1949, the PLA has been involved in several major conflicts and lesser actions. The first major conflict, and the largest, was the Korean War. In the Chinese view, the United States threatened the sovereignty and territorial integrity of China with the United Nations invasion of North Korea. Chinese forces intervened in October 1950 and fought the United States for three years. The Korean War was extremely costly for the Chinese but helped the nation regain some pride after more than a century of humiliation.

The next major combat engagement was against India in 1962. The territorial dispute with India was unresolved in spite of the generally friendly relations between the two countries in the 1950s. After the Indian government adopted a "forward policy" in the disputed territories and refused to heed Chinese warnings, the Chinese attacked and pushed the Indians back. The campaign ended after a brief period; the Chinese partially withdrew and called for negotiations. There have been no negotiations, but the convincing display of Chinese power discouraged the Indians from making further moves.[26]

The 1969 clashes with the USSR were similar to the clash with India, in that territorial sovereignty was a major issue. Though not all of the facts are certain, it appears that the Chinese initiated the first incidents and the Soviets initiated the later clashes. The fighting was brief and resolved no issues, but it involved division-sized units and resulted in substantial casualties. For a time it appeared that China and the USSR might go to war; tensions remained high, but neither side engaged in serious military provocations.[27]

Another effective use of Chinese military power occurred in the Paracel Islands dispute of 1974. A well prepared and well trained Chinese force drove South Vietnamese forces from several islands in January, capturing forty-eight Vietnamese soldiers and an American advisor. This use of power backed up China's legal claims to these territories.[28]

All of these major combat involvements were associated with the Chinese goal of maintaining territorial integrity and national sovereignty. All of them occurred near Chinese territory or in disputed areas where Chinese military power was effective. Both legal and historical justifications were presented by the Chinese to support their use of force. Thus, in those instances the use of force by China can be considered cautious.

There have been other kinds of involvement. In 1959 the PLA skirmished with Nationalist forces over the two small islands of Quemoy and Matsu. (Located just off Fukien province, they are presently held by Nationalist forces.) During the early 1960s the PLA provided construction support to North Vietnam for repairing damage caused by U.S. bombing and to Laos for building a road to Northeast Thailand. The PLA has also provided advisors to insurgent movements in various parts of Asia and Africa; involvement in Latin America is more obscure. In addition the PLA contributed advisors during the construction of the Tanzan railroad, constructed with Chinese aid.

Beyond combat involvement to defend territorial integrity and national sovereignty and limited advisor support to liberation movements, Chinese forces have been employed in a defensive manner in accordance with Chinese defense policy. After the outbreak of the 1969 clashes, China began a movement to prepare for war with the USSR as the major threat. Prior to that time China considered the United States to be the biggest threat. After the United States withdrew from Vietnam and other parts of Southeast Asia, and the Sino-Soviet dispute escalated, China's strategy reflected the changes. Most Chinese forces are now positioned to counter any Soviet attack along the northern border. China has embarked on a massive civil defense program in the event of a conventional or nuclear attack. This program includes storing food and provisions, digging underground tunnels, and encouraging the development of inland industry, thereby dispersing China's hitherto concentrated industrial targets.

Meanwhile, official Chinese statements reflect the belief that there will be a major war between the superpowers, the USSR and the United States. China supports the system of defensive alliances in Western Europe, and the U.S.-Japan Mutual Security Treaty. China refused to participate in SALT (Strategic Arms Limitations Treaty) or other disarmament negotiations, saying that these are just part of the collusion and competition tactics of the superpowers to insure their own nuclear supremacy. In essence, China's strategy has been to modernize its armed forces and to prepare for war, while acting cautiously in the international arena. The USSR is viewed as the greatest threat; consequently, China encourages forces that will discourage the ambitions of the USSR.[29]

Many demands are made on the PLA. It is expected to provide China's national defense as well as contribute to internal security, production, and political socialization. With this variety of tasks and challenges, it is not surprising that the PLA, as an institution, constitutes an important element of Chinese politics.

THE POLICY PROCESS

Now that we have examined China's three major political institutions, we will look into the policy process itself. Several phases of the policy process can be identified: the manner in which conditions that necessitate a policy decision arise, the manner in which policy is derived, and the manner in which policy is implemented. By no means are all the facts pertaining to these phases available but some generalizations can be made. First let us examine an important feature of policymaking in China—the existence of informal groups or factions.

Factions in Chinese Policymaking

Nearly all analysts of the Chinese policy process agree that there are informal groups or factions among Chinese leaders that sometimes cooperate and sometimes contend with each other. There is no agreement whatsoever on what constitutes the basis of the factions, how the coalitions are formed, or even exactly how the policy process is affected by these informal groups.[30]

The Chinese themselves use a model that may be called the "struggle between two lines." As the Chinese see it, there are two kinds of leaders, those who take the socialist line and those who take the revisionist or capitalist line. Throughout CCP history there have been secret capitalist roaders and splittists who have been able to reach the highest echelons of political power, including Kao Kang, P'eng Teh-huai, Liu Shao-ch'i, Lin Piao, and most recently, the "Gang of Four." The struggle between the faction that supports the revolution and the one that is composed of counterrevolutionaries, traitors, and revisionists is part of the class struggle that must continue until communism is achieved.

The two-faction analysis is repeated in the Western press, albeit with modifications. Newspaper accounts frequently speak of the dichotomy between "radicals" and "moderates." The "radicals" are represented by Mao and the Shanghai group. They are radical because they prefer revolution to modernization, and ideology to pragmatism. The "moderates" prefer modernization to ideology. They are people like Chou En-lai and Teng Hsiao-p'ing, who are pragmatists concerned with building China into a modern country even if it means sacrificing excess ideological baggage.[31] A more sophisticated two-faction analysis has been presented by Doak Barnett.[32] Barnett uses the terms "Maoist" and "non-Maoist" in his two-type approach to Chinese issues, though he also recognizes shades of difference within the types. Barnett believes that struggle between these two factions will continue, even now that Mao has died, but he ultimately forecasts victory for the "non-Maoist" line.

A somewhat more complex model of factionalism was introduced by Michael Oksenberg and Steven Goldstein.[33] They came up with a four-way model based on two assumptions: (1) there is genuine political struggle over issues and (2) the key question underlying most issues is how China is to modernize. The four groups include (1) "militant fundamentalists," who stress ideological mobilization of the people, espouse an almost fanatic antibureaucratism, and desire to minimize contacts with the outside world; (2) the "radical conservatives," who want to preserve the essence of the revolution with selective borrowing of technology from the West; (3) the "eclectic modernizers," who are willing to sacrifice some revolutionary goals in order to achieve modernization and are eager to establish good relations with the West; and (4) the "Westernized Chinese," who prefer a Western or Soviet developmental model to the one China presently pursues. Some of the very radical elements that appeared during the Cultural Revolution are examples of militant fundamentalists, Mao is an example of a radical conservative, and Chou En-lai is an example of an eclectic modernizer. Westernized Chinese are hard to identify because their line is unpopular; if they were to espouse it publicly they would probably be purged.

The Oksenberg-Goldstein model has been roundly criticized. Michael Pillsbury argues that the work of Nathan, Whitson, Solomon, and others demonstrates that organizational ties, shared experiences, and other factors must be examined as well.[34] Kenneth Lieberthal proposed a three-way model based on the two issue orientations, ideological persuasions, and organizational backgrounds.[35] Lieberthal's groups include (1) the "Peking group" composed of high ranking cadres, primarily from the central bureaucracy, who favor modernization and connections with the West, (2) the "Shanghai group," composed of what is now known as the "Gang of Four," which is less inclined toward ideological compromise, and (3) the "military group," composed of the key regional military commanders and central military leaders primarily concerned with national security. Andrew Nathan, Tang Tso, and other scholars are continuing to investigate the nature of factions in China, and more models will probably be forthcoming.[36]

The various models all assume that the policy process is characterized by the formation of coalitions on various issues. The struggle for political office is also an aspect of the competition. The purge of the Shanghai-based "Gang of Four" does lend some credence to the idea of informal groups or factions. However, the composition of coalitions can be confusing. Chiang Ch'ing (Mao's wife) is characterized as having been an enemy of Chou En-lai, and the factional models above would seem to place her in that role. Yet, Chiang Ch'ing claimed the premier as an ally in her discussions with Roxanne Witke.[37] The models do suggest some of the variables entering into the composition of informal groups that must be considered as part of the policy process. Some of them are discussed below.

Personality. In leadership situations, human relations are clearly a significant factor. In fact, the personality variable is most often used when analysts and commentators from Taiwan view the political situation in China, which demonstrates that the Chinese themselves believe personality to be the most important factor. Personality influences who gets along with whom, what kinds of alliances are formed, and whether temper or patience will prevail in a given situation. For example, Chou En-lai was able to succeed in many instances by sheer force of personality. Chou had an ability to make alliances with other key individuals at crucial times. Another example can be seen in the struggle to succeed Mao. It has been widely reported that Chiang Ch'ing tried to get the support of Ch'en Hsi-lien, but that, partly because of his personal dislike for her, he decided to back Hua Kuo-feng instead. Indeed, Chiang Ch'ing was reported by Roxanne Witke to have borne large grudges against a number of other leaders. When her position was exposed, her enemies were only too happy to take advantage of it.

Ideology. Clearly, there are differences over ideological interpretations. This is demonstrated in the conflict between Teng Hsiao-p'ing and the "Gang of Four." Originally, Teng was condemned as a capitalist roader within the Party because the proposals he made for modernization and Party reorganization were said to negate the class struggle. Teng's contributions were condemned as "poisonous weeds." After his rehabilitation, it was said that his contributions were in fact "fragrant flowers," that he had taken the correct position all along, and the "Gang" had tried to distort what he was actually saying.

Policy. Closely related to the issue of ideology is that of policy. If a certain ideological point of view is to be taken, how is this to be reflected in policy? An individual who favors rapid modernization may see private plots of land for peasants as a means of accumulating agricultural surplus. Another individual may believe that maintaining private plots of land impedes the transition to socialism and communism. One military leader believes that China must not form alliances, and should rely strictly on its own resources to develop military power. Another may believe that rapid modernization of the armed forces requires increased contacts with advanced foreign countries. Perhaps each individual in the upper Party echelons has a unique view on how ideology and policy must interact; this can make consensus difficult to achieve.

Career Pattern. Ideas on both ideology and policy are likely to be influenced by the career pattern of the individual. An army man like Yeh Chien-ying, who was with Mao from the early days of the revolution, has had very different experiences from a person like Hua Kuo-feng, who rose through the Party ranks. Career patterns help determine personal alliances through the protégé system that so often characterizes authoritarian countries. Chiang Ch'ing owed influence to her position as Mao's wife. Teng Hsiao-p'ing was a protégé of Chou En-lai, and on and on. Furthermore, a person in a particular career pattern is likely to have a different outlook from someone in another career pattern. For example, a person who has had a career in agricultural development may have different budget priorities than a PLA regional commander. There can be generational differences, influences in the protégé system, and differences in bureaucratic experiences—all of which influence the system of alliances that form as part of the decision process.

Phases in Policymaking

In recent years, social science analysts have categorized certain phases of the policymaking process. The first is interest articulation wherein various demands are made on the decision makers. The second is interest aggregation, in which the interests are combined into policy alternatives. The third consists of decision making, in which a selection is made from several alternatives. The fourth phase is policy implementation, in which the alternative selected is put back to the society. The final phase, feedback, arises when consequences of the decision invoke new demands.[38] Whatever the terminology, there do seem to be identifiable phases in the decision process.

In China, it is the responsibility of the Party to supervise the entire process. There is no neat dividing line to separate one phase from the next; all aspects of decision making occur simultaneously. For example, the decision to rehabilitate Teng Hsiao-p'ing was predicated on conditions that resulted in the purge of the "Gang of Four." Nevertheless, for purposes of clarity we shall isolate and examine some phases in the policymaking process.

Interest Articulation. In the first phase, interest articulation, the necessity of a decision is presented to the policy makers. Interest articulation is one element of the mass line coming from the masses. That is, cadres at all levels must be open to inputs from the people. Obviously, some of the issues that arise in society can be handled at the local level. A cadre assigned to the production team can get advice on what work ought to be done in the fields the next day and take it from there. Many of these decisions are routine and are affected largely by circumstances. Some issues get pushed to higher levels. General issues concerning matters of national policy like economic management, agricultural policy, and foreign affairs are brought to the attention of the Politburo and perhaps even the Central Committee.

Demands or interests arise from several sources. Probably the major source is feedback from the consequences of earlier policy decisions.

Wall posters at Tachai criticize Chiang Ch'ing's plot to seize top Party leadership. The posters are an example of government-controlled interest articulation.

For example, in 1975 Chou En-lai announced a decision that the country would seek comprehensive modernization by the year 2000. A campaign to build Tachai-type brigades throughout the country was launched as part of this program. Provincial leaders were expected to set goals and to mobilize human and natural resources to meet them. Their decisions in turn created new demands for resources like mechanized farm equipment and fertilizers to help achieve the goals.

Another source of demands comes from organized groups like the Party, the government, and the PLA. These organs, as we have noted above, each have their own particular perspectives on issues. Groups like the youth, women, and minorities also make demands. All of these groups are represented to some degree in the upper echelons of power and can influence decisions. An examination of a recent debate over cadre promotion shows how decision making is affected. Immediately after the Tenth CCP Congress, a large number of the cadres who were purged and humiliated during the Cultural Revolution began to be restored to positions of authority. There was also a large number of new cadres and Party members recruited on the basis of their activisim during the Cultural Revolution. The newer cadres were often opponents of those who were being rehabilitated. Some officials felt that the new cadres should be promoted more rapidly; other powerful leaders objected, and some urged that the newcomers be put through a period of experience and "rectification" before they were promoted. These differing demands were not only the results of differing points of view; they were attempts to adjust power within Chinese institutions. A major reason for Teng Hsiao-p'ing's purge was that he favored the older rehabilitated cadres, thereby subordinating the interests of the Shanghai group, which based its support on the younger cadres. When Teng was rehabilitated and the "gang" was purged, there continued to be trouble from supporters of the "Shanghai group."[39]

Besides the demands that flow from the environment and from organizations, there are demands that come in a sort of diffuse manner. Peasants still fail to meet production goals or tacitly resist a campaign to improve production, as they did during the Great Leap. They may hoard grain instead of giving it to the state during a period of administrative disruption, as they did during the Cultural Revolution. Workers may resist Red Guards entering the factories. Young people sometimes refuse to stay in rural areas and try to get back to urban areas. These types of demands may not be articulated openly, but they do constitute a position on a particular issue to which the leaders must sooner or later respond. Most interest articulation in China occurs through organized channels, that is, the Party controls the types of demands that will be expressed. Other groups and organs have little or no autonomy with which to express themselves. The speaker at a women's congress, for example, is likely to "demand" that the Party's policy toward women be implemented. Also, the Party must view demands within the ideological context. A demand for "greater personal liberty" would probably be viewed as counterrevolutionary. "Legitimate" demands are those which conform to current ideological tenets—if the tenets change, the demands must change. Interest articulation that occurs outside proper channels, or goes against ideological principles, is usually suppressed (this is not always the case, as illustrated by Mao urging the Red Guards to challenge the Party apparatus, or by the nationwide broadcast of a wall poster denouncing the Education Ministry for restoring examinations).

Interest Aggregation. The demands that arise from a country as large, geographically diverse, and politically organized as China are, of necessity, complex. As we have pointed out, many issues are routine and can be handled at the local level. Nevertheless, as conditions change, new policies must be formulated at the national level. These policies must take into account the various demands arising from the countryside, the cities, peasants, workers, young people, minorities, Party members, non-Party members, and other segments of the populace. If the Party channels and controls interest articulation, it also largely determines aggregation. (Aggregation means that various demands must be combined into policy alternatives.)

An illustration of what is involved in aggregations is provided by the massive earthquake that struck Tangshan in Hopei Province in July 1976. A city of one million was almost completely destroyed, and the surrounding areas were heavily damaged. In this case, the demand for action arose from the environment, and the demands were numerous and complex. People had to be provided with emergency relief, factories had to be rebuilt, and production had to be restored. What priorities would be established?

A central delegation headed by Hua Kuo-feng was dispatched to the stricken area. Hua met with Liu Tzu-hou, first secretary of Hopei Province, and other local officials. Reports were made and views were exchanged. Before final decisions could be reached, the officials had to investigate the seriousness of the damage and make recommendations as to the solution. Meanwhile, the PLA was called upon to provide emergency relief, and supplies were rushed in from the Shenyang, Peking, and other military regions. Local Party committees took charge of emergency operations, searching for buried victims and providing medical care, food, disease control, and public security against looters and vandals. As the emergency efforts continued, the leaders considered programs for reconstruction.

After considerable discussion, some alternatives were prepared. Not all of the alternatives were made public, but according to subsequent published reports, one alternative was to move at a slow pace and concentrate on rebuilding less severely damaged industries before acting on the more seriously damaged facilities. Another alternative was to concentrate efforts on the most damaged sectors, while encouraging workers in less damaged areas to repair things as best they could until greater assistance was available.[40] Alternatives for rebuilding housing also had to be considered.

In all of this activity, the Party organs took primary responsibility, and utilized other organs in an assisting capacity. Because the Party leaders were also leaders in government and military affairs, coordination of effort was made easy. After the alternatives were assessed, it was decided to stress production in the Kailuan coal mine and to form shock troops of workers to rebuild the other industries. (Porcelain workers, for instance, were mobilized to rebuild the porcelain factories.) Experts from several mining institutes in other provinces were called in to see how the Kailuan mine could best be restored to production. Attention was also directed to reconstruction of the railroad facilities adjacent to the mines. Thus, there is clearly a close relationship between interest aggregation and policymaking.

Effective interest aggregation—that is, interest aggregation that enables decision makers to concentrate on viable alternatives—depends on accurate communication. One of the problems that has plagued China in the past is the lack of accurate information. For example, the decision to embark on the Great Leap was in part based on faulty information about the situation in rural areas. Cadres, pressured to produce results, sometimes inflated production figures to create the impression of success. This problem has also been associated with more recent political problems. The "Gang of Four" and their supporters are said to have given faulty statistics about the situation in some provinces in order to make themselves look good. Tan Chen-lin, vice-chairman of the Standing Committee of the National People's Congress, informed several foreign delegations that China had no accurate population figures because the provinces tended to report births accurately but deaths inaccurately, in order to put themselves in a more favorable position for resource allocation. Clearly, good communication and effective information are important to all phases of the policy process. Given the weaknesses in this area, China's leaders have a serious problem when it comes to making workable decisions.

Decision Making. It is the Chinese Communist Party that is responsible for making decisions. More precisely, it is the Party leadership on all levels, that is responsible for policy decisions. We have already noted that informal groups operate in the decision-making process not only at the national but at the local levels as well. Although Mao's injunction to avoid splittism is consistently repeated at Party and public gatherings, unity has not always been easily achieved.

Mao was often able to maintain control of the Party through his charismatic leadership. Chang points out that Mao often had to mobilize support in certain quarters to get what he wanted.[41] However at times, as during the period of 1958 to 1966, Mao was not able to get his way, and other Party leaders were able to withstand some of his initiatives. After Mao's death and the purge of the "Gang of Four," it appeared that a coalition of military, Party, and government bureaucrats was forming; this broadbased coalition met an initial test in the decision to rehabilitate Teng Hsiao-p'ing, and to hold the Fifth National People's Congress in the spring of 1978.

At the national level, most decisions are made by Party leaders within the Politburo. On key decisions, when consensus cannot be easily arrived at, the Central Committee will sometimes get involved, as during the Cultural Revolution. Little is actually known about meetings of the Politburo, but some of the documents leaked during the Cultural Revolution indicate that discussions are often lively and pointed. [42] An example is the decision to purge Teng Hsiao-p'ing. Teng's opponents wanted to get rid of him once and for all but his supporters refused. They finally compromised on a resolution dismissing him from his positions but allowing him to retain his Party membership to see if he would repent. The escape clause eased his later rehabilitation.

Meetings of Party leaders are frequent. Thus the members of the Politburo do not just meet with each other, but are likely to consult with ministry officials when matters affecting that ministry are involved. Some members of the Politburo give more attention to foreign policy questions; others give more attention to domestic policy. Members of the Politburo who do not have a strong power position in their own right (e.g., Ch'en Yung-kuei) do not have much impact on decision making.

The role of each leader is likely to be determined by the relative amount of power each wields. The three regional military commanders are crucial to important decisions because of their military support. Teng Hsiao-p'ing and Li Hsien-nien have strong support from the government bureaucracy. Hua Kuo-feng's power is based on his experience, on his supposed endorsement by Mao, and, most importantly, on his ability to command the respect and support of other powerful individuals. Thus far, Hua has apparently been successful. If he is able to continue to consolidate his position as Party chairman and to boost his personal legitimacy through propaganda he will lead the Party and govern China.

The effort to achieve consensus helps to legitimize policy once it is decided. On important matters the Central Committee will be convened to issue a resolution concerning the particular policy question involved. These resolutions are quickly transmitted and hailed throughout the nation. Often a rally or celebration is called to accompany the resolution. Hundreds of thousands of people gather in Peking and other cities to join in these mass rallies. Provincial and local Party committees meet within one or two days to "hail" the decision that has just been made. It is interesting to note that, whatever the decision, the process is almost identical. When Teng Hsiao-p'ing was purged, millions demonstrated to express support. All the provincial party committees hailed the decision. When he was reinstated just over a year later, the people once again demonstrated support as the party committees hailed the decision. Although the quick change may be disheartening to some and confusing to others, the hoped-for effect is to create legitimacy for policy decisions.

As might be expected, there is a good deal of debate among scholars as to the exact nature of decision making in China. Exactly who is involved? What factors are paramount in a given decision? We can only hint at the answers to these questions. What we have tried to point out is that China's leaders are confronted with a variety of complex demands from which they must arrive at alternatives and decisions. Decisions cannot be separated from one another because most issues are linked to each other: a decision concerning agricultural policy influences industrial and military policy as well. All issues must be examined on the basis of ideological factors or constraints. This process is not unique to China by any means, but the nature of ideology and society in China is such that the decisions themselves are unique.

Policy Implementation. The primary role for implementing policy is assigned to the government bureaucracy, carefully supervised by the Party. Central decisions are quickly communicated through the media and through official documents to the lower levels. Meetings are held within various organs and units to discuss how policy is to be implemented. As might be expected, there is considerable political maneuvering during this process.[43] Oksenberg observes that there is great diversity in bureaucratic communication according to the function of the ministry; there is also diversity between geographic regions. Organizational procedures that have origins in the prerevolutionary period are only gradually adjusting to technological changes.[44]

The issue of centralization versus decentralization has characterized the implementation process. The basic question is to what extent lower-level officials should seek guidance from above in adjusting policy to fit particular circumstances and how much they should use their own judgment. This is, of course, risky for the cadre. If he relies too heavily on guidance from above, he may be criticized as having a slave mentality or as being inflexible. On the other hand, if he goes too far on his own, he may be accused of trying to establish an "independent kingdom"—seeking to serve his own political advantage by manipulating policy. According to Mao's criteria, a good cadre is one who is both flexible and responsive to leadership, but attaining the correct balance is often difficult.

Policy implementation is also influenced by the forces that affect other aspects of policy making. An individual's personal ties, his bureaucratic perspective, his personality, and other factors will necessarily influence the manner in which he implements policy. When a campaign is in progress, there is usually a work slowdown while cadres try to assess the situation before acting. They often wait to see "which way the wind is blowing" before taking initiatives.

The risks involved can be demonstrated by the fall of Ch'iao Kuanhua, who was appointed foreign minister at the Fourth National People's Congress. Ch'iao was primarily a professional diplomat but he had been elected to the Central Committee at the Tenth CCP Congress. He was an effective spokesman for China's foreign policy interests but became too closely associated with the Shanghai group. After the purge of the Shanghai group, Ch'iao also lost his position and was replaced as foreign minister by Huang Hua. Ch'iao's dismissal was not a failure of policy but a result of his failure to disassociate himself from the "Gang of Four."

In spite of such difficulties, the Chinese bureaucracy seems to work quite well. Businessmen who deal with officials from the Ministry of Foreign Trade generally acknowledge that the Chinese are very professional. The low degree of crime and corruption points to effective administration. The Tangshun earthquake crisis can once again serve as a good example of effective policy implementation. In spite of the severe damage, the difficulty of rebuilding, and the public disturbances associated with the earthquake, within a year officials could point to considerable progress in reconstruction.[45]

That policy implementation is effective does not necessarily mean that the policies themselves are effective. We have already noted that sometimes tacit resistance to policy occurs, as during the Great Leap and the Cultural Revolution. Furthermore, because of unanticipated consequences or mistaken judgments, not all policies achieve their original objectives. In the event of a policy failure, however, there is a tendency to blame officials rather than policies. When something goes wrong, it is deemed to be the fault of counterrevolutionary elements, misguided cadres, or both. It is these individuals who become responsible for erroneous "lines," and not the organs themselves. For example, when the Chengchow Railroad Bureau, a key railroad juncture failed to meet car-loading quotas for nineteen months in succession and coal loading expectations for fifty-three months in a row, it was blamed on the "Gang of Four" and their "hatchetmen" in the division. Only after the workers were mobilized to repudiate this influence was the plan properly implemented.[46]

Feedback. In his essay "On Practice," Mao indicated that experience contributes to the correct view just as ideology helps to interpret experience. As experience is gained, policy must go forward in a dialectical process. Mao, himself, had apparently learned from past policy failures.[47] This approach enables the Chinese Communists to adjust policies when they fail or are only partially successful.

A number of scholars of Chinese politics believe that the history of the CCP is characterized by several policy oscillations. At the beginning of this section, we noted several periods in Chinese politics that seemed to be characterized by major policy shifts. There can be no question, for example, that the policies followed in 1962 were considerably different from those attempted in 1958-59. There is no agreement among scholars, however, as to precisely how policy change should be viewed. Andrew Nathan has criticized a number of models of Chinese politics for showing policy oscillations when in fact there were none.[48] Edwin Winkler responded to Nathan with the assertion that policy issues are interconnected, and that there are major shifts that are historically significant.[49]

There have unquestionably been changes in both foreign and domestic policies from time to time, reflecting both the individuals in power and the changing ideological perspectives of Mao and other leaders. The principal reason for these changes has been an evaluation of the success, partial success, or failure of past policies. The evaluation process is colored by the same factors that influence other aspects of Chinese policymaking.

SUMMARY

Policymaking in China, as in other societies, is complex. The process of making policy is continuous, with leaders engaged in nearly all phases at all times. Given the nature of large organizations like the ones that exist in China, policy is made as it is implemented. What the policymakers decide in Peking may not be the same thing that the cadre in the production team implements, despite careful Party supervision and unified leadership.

We observed previously that Mao's dictum that politics should take command is a reality in Chinese society. In order to socially mobilize and transform China's masses, it has been necessary to construct large bureaucratic organizations, such as the Party, the state, and the PLA, not to mention a host of suborganizations responsive to CCP leadership. The Thought of Mao Tse-tung is not sympathetic to large bureaucratic organizations. The tensions between ideology and organization were patently manifest during the Cultural Revolution. It is within this background that efforts to make policy in China must be understood. In the following chapter, we will consider what some of these policies have been, and what factors are likely to influence policy in the future.

CHAPTER FOUR

Issues and Problems

In times of difficulty we must see the bright future and not bend or swerve; in times of victory we must not lose sight of the difficulties ahead and must guard against conceit and impetuosity. We are fully confident that under the leadership of the Central Committee, the Chinese people will surmount all conceivable difficulties and work miracles . . .

—Hua Kuo-feng[1]

The past chapters have provided insights into the ideological and environmental framework in which politics are decided and the structures and processes by which policy is made. This chapter examines the primary issues and problems facing China. To facilitate our discussion, we distinguish between domestic policy issues and foreign policy issues, although this is an arbitrary separation— domestic and foreign policies are invariably linked.

DOMESTIC ISSUES

Major domestic issues can be divided into three subcategories. The first is that of political stability. In his speech before the Eleventh Party Congress, Hua Kuo-feng said that China was entering a period of consolidating the gains made during the Cultural Revolution in the past eleven years (1966 to 1977). Those eleven years were characterized by political instability, but Chinese leaders now apparently hope to solve the continuing problems of factionalism. The second category is that of economic development. China must feed a growing population and yet mobilize sufficient resources to meet the developmental goals outlined by the leadership. The third and related category is that of social development. What impact will economic modernization and political institutionalization have on social change?

Political Stability

We have already pointed out that Mao's concepts of revolution are not necessarily conducive to political institutionalization. That is, his ideas are opposed to the process of bureaucratization that invariably occurs in large organizations like the Party, the state bureaucracy, and the PLA. However, it appears that China has made the greatest economic progress when political institutions have been more stable, as in the period after the Great Leap Forward, and prior to the Cultural Revolution.

The tension between the desire for revolutionary change and the desire for economic modernization and national power has been manifest in political instability. P'eng Teh-huai was purged in 1959 partly because he opposed Mao's ideas on social mobilization of the peasantry as well as other aspects of the Great Leap. Similarly, Liu Shao-ch'i was accused of advocating and implementing "revisionist" policies that heightened bureaucratism at the expense of social change.

Other issues have also divided the Chinese leadership. Matters of foreign policy and national defense, military professionalization, wage scales and ownership of private plots, and the issue of who is to exercise power have all figured largely in the long period of political instability. We noted the purges of Liu Shao-ch'i, Ch'en Po-ta, Lin Piao, and the "Gang of Four" in the past ten years, not to mention the ups and downs of Teng Hsiao-p'ing. It seems obvious that there has been a constant struggle for power among China's leaders for at least the past decade.

What is uncertain is how the death of Mao and the gradual departure of others of the old guard will affect Chinese politics. Since the purge of the "Gang of Four" and the Eleventh CCP Congress of August 1977, there has been a definite effort to establish a stable leadership capable of achieving consensus on the issues. The present coalition seems disposed to emphasizing economic modernization, perhaps at the expense of some of the revolutionary goals Mao strove for.

Nevertheless, many of the issues remain the same, and there are likely to be differences of opinion. There are different organizational perspectives, and if political stability is maintained, these differences are likely to become stronger and possibly encourage continued political conflict among China's leaders. Should Hua and his supporters in the present ruling coalition fail, there will undoubtedly be some who will challenge their leadership. It is interesting to note

Scene from a revolutionary opera. "Azalea Mountain." Cultural expression in China often reveals ideological shifts. Some operas that were once popular are now heavily criticized, while those once denounced are now praised and performed.

that in the USSR after the death of Stalin, it was difficult for would-be successors to maintain control, although the rulers of North Vietnam have been able to achieve and maintain consensus after the death of Ho Chi-minh (admittedly, there was a war on, which did heighten the need for consensus). Succession to the charismatic Mao Tse-tung will be no easy task. Political stability in China will depend greatly on the nature of the issues and how the sides line up on them.

A related issue is that of ideological continuity. The "gang" and other Chinese leaders differed over the interpretation of Mao's legacy as embodied in his Thought. The Shanghai group insisted that the revolutionary aspects of his Thought should be emphasized in policy. As noted earlier, the "gang" believed that political mobilization should take precedence over economic incentives in achieving development. They also believed it was necessary to promote younger cadres recruited for their activities in the Cultural Revolution rather than to restore those cadres who had already fallen into patterns of bureaucratic behavior. These and other policy preferences of the so-called radicals stemmed from Mao's idea that the achievement of socialism can only come through a continuing struggle.

This fundamentalist interpretation of Mao's Thought has now apparently been modified or discarded by his successors. They have reinterpreted Mao to give new emphasis to the goals of building a powerful country through economic development. If economic development requires political stability and that sacrifices some of the antibureaucratic aspects of ideology, then so be it. Mao himself will continue to enjoy status and prestige as his successors appeal to his legacy to enhance their own legitimacy. Nevertheless, his ideas will become modified as the new leadership seeks to develop the nation. This does not necessarily mean that there will be no future shifts toward a more radical ideological stance. Observers of Chinese politics were unable to predict the Cultural Revolution and its accompanying ideological thrust. It is possible that another such movement could emerge, but with Mao gone and no charismatic leader evident, it seems less likely that such a movement will occur.

Economic Development

A primary goal of the Chinese revolution has been the achievement of economic modernization. As has been noted previously, during the Fourth National People's Congress Chou En-lai called for comprehensive modernization by the year 2000. Hua Kuo-feng has reiterated this goal, which will be a major undertaking, since China, by nearly every indicator, is far behind the industrialized world. China's gross national product is about $310 billion (roughly equal to that of France). China is severely lacking in some of the elements required to support a modern industrial economy.[2]

The organization of the Chinese economy has permitted central state control while also permitting flexibility at the local level. The state owns and operates key industries and controls communications and transportation. Provincial and municipal governments operate other large enterprises, and local county governments operate small-scale industries. All of these operate under a state plan, but consultation among the various levels allows for the integration of local plans and goals with the state plan. In agriculture the state has a unified plan, but provinces, counties, communes, and brigades also develop plans that are taken into account in formulating the state plan. The movements to learn from Tachai and Taching specify production goals and organizational techniques other enterprises are to learn from.[3]

According to most analysts, the key to China's economic future lies in its ability to improve agricultural production. If China is to achieve rapid economic development, it must increase agricultural production by about 2 percent annually, enough to feed the population and still provide capital for the materials necessary to supply growing urban industries. Only 15 percent of China's total land area is conducive to growing crops, and most of it is already under cultivation. Production increases will probably have to come through increased use of chemical fertilizers and irrigation in areas north of the Yangtze River.[4]

In the past China's industrial growth has generally been rapid and uneven, with disruptions occurring during the Great Leap and the Cultural Revolution. Industrial growth has occurred partly at the expense of mass consumption. During the early period of Communist rule, wealth was redistributed so that there was greater equality, but the standard of living has not improved rapidly since 1949. Many goods, like cloth and cooking oil are rationed. This permits a more even distribution of goods and thus greater equality among the population, and it also enables the government to accumulate profits for reinvestment in industrial development. The Chinese people are encouraged to save any excess. The profits can also be used by the state for economic development.

One analyst of the Chinese economy believes that China can achieve a 7 percent annual industrial growth rate over the next few years by the use of effective investment techniques, the continued control of mass consumption, and technology obtained through foreign trade.[5] In order to achieve this kind of growth, China's leadership will have to make some ideological concessions (that is, be willing to sacrifice mass campaigns that create turmoil in the economy) and further develop trade relations with technologically advanced Western countries.

The same analyst recognizes that increased economic development could lead to ideological tensions between leaders. After all, the fairly rapid economic achievement that helped convince Mao to embark on

Bustling Shanghai dock reflects the desire of current Chinese leadership to expand foreign trade.

the Great Leap Forward later turned into an economic disaster. Rapid growth in both agricultural and industrial development requires political stability, but may itself contribute to political instability.

There are other variables that will affect China's economic development. Most analysts believe that China's economic infrastructure must be improved, including its transportation and communications systems. China will also have to increase its energy production and foreign trade. In the past, China's growth has been predicated on investment in areas that could produce quick returns. In the future more investment will have to be made in areas that do not yield quick returns, but are essential to modernization. For example, China may develop its oil refining capabilities to produce more petroleum for domestic consumption and export, but this will require the importation of oil drilling and refining equipment from abroad, at considerable expense, several years before returns are received. In the machine tool industry there is now a demand for high precision equipment instead of the less costly equipment produced in the past. These contingencies must be met if rapid development is to occur.[6]

Although China's total foreign trade amounted to $13 billion in 1976, several problems remain. A major requirement for China has been chemical fertilizers. China imports both fertilizer and the facilities for manufacturing chemical fertilizer. China is also purchasing plants in the iron, steel, petrochemical, synthetic fibre, petroleum, and power generation industries. These purchases have been expensive, yet China has thus far rejected long-term financing or loans. Plants are purchased on either a cash-and-carry basis or a deferred payment basis over a five year period.[7] In the past, China has financed these purchases from abroad through exports of silk, textiles, and other raw materials. Until 1976 China had massive trade deficits—as high as $1 billion in 1974—but by 1976 China began to offset deficits by increasing its petroleum export capability. A number of sources estimate that China could be a major oil exporter by the mid-1980s.[8]

A continuing problem will be feeding China's ever growing population. China has had to import grain from abroad, even during years when weather and conditions have been favorable. In the event that prolonged drought or other severe weather conditions hit China, it would be difficult to achieve the 2 percent agricultural production increase needed for rapid economic development. Failures in agriculture would have severe implications for other sectors of the economy. Consequently, the task of building China into a major economic power by 2000 will require not only good management by skilled leadership, but also good fortune.

Social Change

The goal of building China economically has sometimes been subservient to the goal of mobilizing China's masses in pursuit of a socialist society. The major campaigns of the 1950s, such as Land Reform and the socialist transformation of agriculture, were the most far reaching efforts to transform the country. More recent campaigns have sought social change but not on such a large scale. The Cultural Revolution sought a more effective integration between urban and rural areas through the exchange of people and technology, but the results were limited. In some respects the reforms of the Cultural Revolution have been rescinded by the adoption of new admissions requirements and examinations in the education system, the rehabilitation of formerly purged cadres, and alterations in the system of sending young people from urban areas to the countryside.

Mao believed that social change could be induced through correct education, indoctrination, and, most importantly, through experience. He also believed that social change could precede economic advances in the society. By transforming social consciousness, the conditions for building a strong socialist China could be accomplished. Mao's successors seem to have a view somewhat closer to classical Marxism, that is, through economic transformation social change will come. China's leaders believe that economic development and social change must be encouraged jointly. The speeches of Chinese officials in recent years have consistently stressed the relationship between production and correct political ideas. Improvements in consciousness will permit greater production; greater production evidences correct political attitudes.

It is likely that efforts to transform society will be based on continued campaigns with limited political goals. As noted in the preceding section, in order to advance China's economy rapidly, it will be necessary to limit growth of mass consumption. The Chinese people will be continually called upon to make sacrifices in order to meet economic goals. An editorial in the *People's Daily* just after the Eleventh Party Congress, for example, stated that from the sacrifice of the masses would come the profits required for capital investment.[9]

The major direction of campaigns will be to explain the sacrifices that must be made and to check the tendencies toward individualism or selfishness that might obstruct the nation's economic goals. Undoubtedly, the masses will be called upon to continue to emulate those who have made personal sacrifices to improve production. Art, music, literature, and drama will continue to emphasize the themes of self-reliance, hard work, and dedication to the cause of socialism.

In Chapter Two, we raised the issue of personal freedom; we noted that perspectives on human rights in China are determined by the values of the observers. Although achieving economic goals will necessarily limit mass consumption, the regime will continue to seek ways to adequately feed and clothe the Chinese people. It will also seek to improve health care and education. There is no tendency to lessen controls on expression. Speeches, the print media, and the arts will continue to reflect the correct "line" implemented by the propaganda organs of the Central Committee. There may, however, be some broadening of expression. Since the purge of the "Gang of Four," some previously banned types of music and films have been made available. Whether this is a genuine broadening of standards or merely a shift in ideological interpretation brought about by the "gang's" downfall is not yet clear.

As we have said before, no government functions independently of the society it governs. Just as the policies of the Chinese Communists are designed to change society, changes in society will affect and shape the nature and policies of the government. Consequently, the efforts of the regime to foster social change will ultimately affect the government itself. It is widely anticipated that sometime in the 1980s the population of China will approach one billion people. Given these large numbers of people, the ambitious goals and objectives of the Chinese Communists, and the ongoing process of interaction between political structures, ideology, and the society, the politics of China should be both dynamic and interesting.

FOREIGN POLICY ISSUES

Among the goals of the Chinese revolution have been the achievement of territorial integrity, the development of national power, economic modernization, and the achievement of socialism. These goals are related to both domestic and foreign policy. While a full analysis of the nuances of Chinese foreign policy is not possible here, we can give an overview of China's policies in light of the goals mentioned above.

Relations with the United States

Beginning with World War II, the United States cast itself in opposition to Chinese Communist goals. Although the United States had contacts with Mao and the Communists in Yenan, for various reasons it was decided to support Chiang Kai-shek. This support continued through the Chinese civil war and became firm after the conclusion of a Sino-Soviet Treaty in 1950 and the ensuing Korean War. In 1954 the United States signed a Mutual Defense Treaty with the Nationalist Chinese government on Taiwan. This treaty continues to remain in force, and the United States is the only major country to maintain formal diplomatic ties with the government in Taiwan.

To the Chinese Communists, this constituted intervention in the Chinese civil war and it prevented Peking from achieving territorial unification. The Chinese regarded the United States policy of military containment (forming alliances with countries on China's periphery) and economic embargo as hostile acts. As a result, relations between the United States and China were bad for two decades. There were sporadic meetings between representatives of the two countries in places like Warsaw, but little was accomplished. Relations appeared to be at an all-time low during the height of the Vietnam war. Some people in the United States wanted to bomb North Vietnamese sanctuaries in China, and some Chinese leaders advocated an escalation of Chinese support to North Vietnam, including armed intervention if necessary.[10]

The deterioration of relations between China and the USSR (discussed in the following section) escalated through the Cultural Revolution, bringing them to the verge of armed conflict in 1969. Thus, the Soviet Union became China's antagonistic contradiction. At the same time, United States policy toward China began to change. The Nixon Administration announced its intention to withdraw U.S. forces from Vietnam and eased travel restrictions, trade restrictions, and other restrictions involving China. In 1971 Secretary of State Kissinger visited China and arranged for a visit by President Nixon. The 1972 visit and the issuing of the Shanghai Communique ushered in a new era of better relations between the United States and China.

With the Shanghai Communique, the United States symbolically withdrew from the Chinese civil war, acknowledging the position of the Peking and the Taipei governments that there is but one China. Subsequently, the United States and China established liaison offices in Washington and Peking that now serve as embassies in all respects except name. Although objecting to Taiwan's denial of membership in the United Nations, the United States permitted the Peking government to assume China's seat in the UN Security Council and the General Assembly. Trade between the two countries also began to

U.S. President Richard Nixon visited China and concluded the Shanghai Communique in February 1972.

develop and by 1974 the United States had become China's second largest trading partner.

Nevertheless, full normalization of relations between the U.S. and China has not yet occurred. Secretary of State Vance made the Carter Administration's first official high-level visit to China in August 1977 to explore future possibilities, but apparently no firm commitments were made by either side. The outstanding issue continues to be Taiwan. China's public position is that the United States must sever its diplomatic relations with Taipei, abrogate the Mutual Defense Treaty, and withdraw all U.S. military forces and installations from Taiwan before full normalization can occur.[11] Thus far the United States has been unwilling to accept these conditions, and Peking has been unwilling to give full assurances that the Taiwan question would not be resolved through force.

According to public statements, China regards the United States as a superpower in competition with the USSR for world domination. The Chinese also claim that competition between the USSR and the U.S. will ultimately result in world war. Although the Chinese government hopes to have good relations with the U.S. government and the American people, U.S. "imperialism" is to be opposed under all circumstances.[12] The Chinese also oppose a precipitous U.S. withdrawal from the Pacific area, fearing that it would invite increased Soviet intervention. The Chinese have expressed support for the U.S.-Japan Security Treaty, and generally endorse the North Korean position, although they have advised against North Korean military action in South Korea. In essence, China hopes that U.S. power and influence will balance Soviet power and influence in the Pacific area.

Relations with the USSR

As far as the goals of the Chinese revolution are concerned, the United States and the USSR have reversed roles. The United States now recognizes China's territorial integrity and has created conditions favorable to China's foreign trade; the Soviet Union has territorial, ideological, and political disputes with China, and has proposed an Asian Collective Security System, which the Chinese regard as an effort to encircle China and contain its influence.

The territorial dispute stems from the unequal treaties concluded between China and the tsarist government of Russia. The USSR once renounced these treaties, but the territories were never returned to China. The Soviet Union now insists that these treaties be used as the basis for any territorial negotiations. The Chinese have outlined a five-point position calling for the USSR to disavow the unequal treaties so that a new treaty can be concluded on the basis of mutual sovereignty and equality.[13] The Russians are afraid that once they renounce the unequal treaties the Chinese will demand that much of the territory be returned to China. Several years of intermittent negotiations have not resolved the territorial issue, and both sides have staged a military buildup. The USSR has nearly 50 divisions— approximately one million troops—with tanks, airplanes, nuclear weapons, and other modern weapons assigned to areas in Central Asia, Mongolia, and Siberia for border defense. The Chinese have a similar quantity of manpower, though their forces are not as well equipped. In 1969 territorial tensions erupted into violent confrontations in which more than 800 Chinese and over 30 Russians were killed. The situation has eased somewhat, but it remains volatile.

Another issue dividing the USSR and China is ideology. Since the denunciations of Stalin in 1956, the Chinese have questioned the leadership of the USSR in interpreting the Marxist-Leninist heritage. The Chinese accuse the Khrushchev and Brezhnev regimes of being "revisionist," and encouraging a restoration of capitalism in the USSR. The Chinese point to the growth of bureaucratism, favoritism, and privilege in the Soviet Communist Party to substantiate their claim. Meanwhile, the Russians believe that since the Eighth CCP Congress the Chinese have gone astray. Both sides have engaged in a series of bitter polemics. The Chinese Communists charge that the USSR has become a social imperialist country since its intervention in Czechoslovakia in 1968. The USSR accuse the Chinese of being fascists rather than Marxist-Leninists. These charges are rooted in differing interpretations of Marxist-Leninist doctrine pertaining to the class struggle, the dictatorship of the proletariat, and so on.[14]

The third area of dispute is political and stems from the other two. The Chinese Communists historically did not enjoy a comfortable relationship with the Soviet Communist Party, particularly after Mao came to power in the mid-1930s. The Chinese Communist revolution did receive some Soviet support, but when Mao met with Stalin in Moscow in 1950 to conclude an alliance, a number of issues were left unresolved. The territorial question was left open, and the Chinese rejected a proposal for Soviet naval facilities or other bases on Chinese territory. Soviet aid during the First Five-Year Plan was crucial, but limited, and it came with strings. When the Chinese became dissatisfied with the Soviet model of industrialization in the 1950s, it hastened the withdrawal of Soviet advisors, technicians, and assistance between 1958 and 1960. Perhaps the crowning blow in the political dispute came in 1962 when the USSR essentially endorsed India's position in the border conflict between China and India. The result of the growing political dispute was a split in the world's communist movement, with some parties favoring the USSR and others China. The Chinese and Russians now vie with each other for leadership of the international communist movement.

During the Cultural Revolution the Soviet Embassy was attacked by Red Guards, and Soviet diplomats were humiliated. Relations were strained nearly to the breaking point. Then the 1969 border dispute erupted, and it appeared that the two countries might go to war. Since that time, relations between them have remained hostile. Inasmuch as China now regards the USSR as the primary contradiction in foreign policy, it has generally sought to limit Soviet influence in Asia and in other parts of the world. The Chinese have endorsed a strong NATO alliance, maintaining that the principal Soviet threat is in Europe, rather than in Asia. China has pursued good relations with nations that have had a falling out with the USSR, like Egypt and Chile. Chinese policy in Southeast Asia is motivated by concern about the prospect of Soviet encirclement. There is perhaps greater concern that the USSR will attempt political intervention than military intervention. Liu Shao-ch'i was declared to have been "China's Khrushchev" during the Cultural Revolution.

Lin Piao was ostensibly killed in an airplane crash while trying to escape to the USSR. These charges, whether true or not, reflect Chinese concern with the possibility of Soviet support to a political faction or group within the Chinese leadership.

There can be no quick solution to the long-standing territorial, ideological, and political disputes that divide China and the USSR. Most of the differences are bound to continue, and the prospects for improved Sino-Soviet relations are not good. There could be some improvement if some of the political issues are resolved, but a return to the Sino-Soviet alliance of the early 1950s seems unthinkable. Competition with the USSR, an expansionist global hegemony as far as the Chinese are concerned, is likely to continue into the forseeable future.

Relations with Japan

Perhaps even more than the West, Japan symbolized China's hundred years of humiliation. Japan's full-scale invasion of China during World War II set the stage for eventual Communist victory. At the end of the war, China was able to reclaim territories taken by Japan, and there are presently no major outstanding territorial issues save for the Senkaku Islands, which have a way of becoming important at unpredictable intervals.

The postwar alliance between Japan and the United States precluded full normal relations between Japan and China; trade between the two countries fluctuated. After the Nixon visit to China, the Japanese moved quickly to normalize relations with the People's Republic. The Sato government, which the Chinese claimed was planning a revival of Japanese militarism and expansionism, gave way to the Tanaka government, thus allowing a change in the Chinese position. Japan granted full diplomatic recognition to China and severed formal diplomatic relations with Taiwan. However, Japanese investment in Taiwan has continued unabated, and the former Japanese embassy continues to perform diplomatic functions in everything but name. Japan and Taiwan have worked out a number of agreements, like the now-famous air accords, by which non-flag-carrying agents of the national airlines of each country fly to the other; Peking looks the other way as far as these continuing economic ties are concerned.[15]

The conclusion of a full peace treaty between China and Japan has presented many difficulties. Japan has balked at Chinese insistence that a clause committing both sides to opposing any third country that seeks hegemony be inserted in the treaty. The Japanese correctly believe that this is an anti-Soviet gesture on the part of the Chinese. Certainly, the USSR has made no secret of its belief that the "anti-hegemony clause" is intended to be anti-Soviet. The Japanese, still looking for prospects in the development of Siberia, are reluctant to conclude a treaty that is blatantly anti-Soviet in tone. Nevertheless, both sides have claimed that they seek a quick conclusion of the negotiation of a peace treaty.

In an effort to embarrass the USSR, the Chinese have endorsed Japan's claim to the Southern Kurile Islands, which the Soviets took at the end of World War II. The Kurile Island issue, together with problems over fishing rights and other political and economic differences, have precluded good relations between Japan and the USSR. Further, China has endorsed the U.S.-Japan Mutual Security Treaty as a barrier to Soviet hegemony. China has also used the prospect of trade to woo the Japanese. Japan has become China's number one trading partner, and the prospects of Chinese oil and future economic opportunities in China appeal to Japanese business.

Overall, China hopes to profit from Japan's economic strength, without fostering better relations between Japan and the USSR, or encouraging any policies that might lead to Japan's acquisition of nuclear weapons and a strong military capability. China has urged the North Koreans to be cautious, believing that an invasion of the South could quickly escalate to a major conflagration involving the United States and possibly Japan. Such an invasion would almost certainly bring about full-scale Japanese rearmament, which would not be in the present interests of China. It seems likely that economic ties between Japan and China will continue to develop since the two countries are natural trading partners. However, considering the fact that the two nations have differing economic and political systems, as well as divergent ideological views, it cannot be expected that all will be smooth between them.

Relations with Southeast Asia

Also of great importance for China is Southeast Asia, which was historically under China's suzerainty. Although China long ago gave up major territorial demands in this area, it is still believed that Southeast Asia has a special relationship with China because of the past historical ties.[16] China's policy toward these areas has been varied. Prior to the Cultural Revolution, China generally advocated good state-to-state relations based on the Five Principles of Peaceful Coexistence, which came out of the Bandung Conference in 1955. During the Cultural Revolution, China seemed to favor "people's war" in the Southeast Asian countries, and endorsed liberation movements in Thailand, the Philippines, Vietnam, Cambodia, Burma, Malaysia, and Indonesia. Many of these insurgencies received political and material support as well as verbal encouragement from China.[17] At the end of the Cultural Revolution China's policies again began to shift. China advocated normalized state-to-state relations, and after the Nixon visit many Southeast Asian countries moved rapidly to normalize relations with China.

At present, all of the Southeast Asian countries, with the exception of Indonesia, maintain diplomatic relations with Peking. However, China has found that its earlier endorsement of "people's war" was easier to make than to get out of. One of the Five Principles calls for nonintervention in the internal affairs of the respective countries, and China normalized relations with Southeast Asian nations on this basis. In spite of the legal pledge, China has continued to support some insurgencies, probably because of concern that the USSR might seize the upper hand if China were to withdraw support. Were China to completely abandon the insurgencies, it would be abandoning one of the government's ideological principles as well, and would risk increased Soviet involvement on China's periphery. Mostly, the Chinese have been trying to "have their cake and eat it too"; that is, Peking has tried to have good relations on a state-to-state basis, while maintaining some influence in certain insurgencies. How long this policy can endure remains to be seen.

One of the most serious challenges to Chinese policy stems from Indochina. During the war against the United States, North Vietnam was able to get aid from both China and the USSR. Since the end of the war and the reunification of Vietnam, the Vietnamese have played the USSR and China against each other. The Chinese are embarrassed by territorial disputes with Vietnam and by the possibility that Vietnam might grant a naval facility to the USSR. At the same time, China is concerned with Vietnamese intentions pertaining to Laos and Cambodia. China has had good relations with Cambodia, but the USSR appears to have the advantage in Vietnam and Laos. Historically, there has been animosity between the Chinese and the Vietnamese. Even though both are communist countries and the Vietnamese revolution owes much to the Chinese precedent, the Sino-Soviet dispute, territorial problems, and other political and economic issues have resulted in a competitive Chinese-Vietnamese relationship. The clashes between Cambodia and Vietnam demonstrated the awkwardness of China's position in Indochina. Peking generally sided with the Cambodians but tried not to alienate Hanoi.

Other Foreign Policy Issues

There are other complicated foreign policy issues facing China. Not the least of these has to do with border states like North Korea, Mongolia, India and Pakistan. China has given strong verbal support to the North Korean stand on the overall Korean problem, but has also tried to restrain Kim Il-sung for reasons noted previously. The North Koreans had a falling out with the Chinese during the Cultural Revolution, but relations have been patched up. North Korea steers a somewhat neutral course in the Sino-Soviet dispute but in recent years has tended to lean toward China.

Mongolia is firmly allied with the Soviet Union and has strongly denounced the Chinese Communist leadership. Mongol leaders are fearful that China might one day try to reclaim Mongolia. However, a border treaty was concluded between the two countries in 1962, and formal diplomatic relations and some minor trade are maintained. The Chinese have not publicly denounced Mongolia or the Mongolian leadership but China constantly propagandizes about the Soviet exploitation of Mongolia.

Since the border war with India in 1962, relations between China and India have been strained. India has received strong support from the USSR; consequently, China formed an alliance with Pakistan. China has good relations with Nepal and is wary of Indian actions in Sikhim and Bhutan. Generally, the relationship between China and India is competitive, as both countries offer other developing countries divergent models of development. In 1977-78 relations between China and India began to improve gradually but there was no indication that their border dispute would be quickly resolved.[18]

China's policy in Western Europe has been one of seeking to contain Soviet influence. China supports the NATO alliance and has extensive trade with Germany and other European countries. Only recently China has begun to woo Western European Communist parties that have become disaffected with the USSR. China also seeks good relations with Eastern European countries like Romania and Yugoslavia, while denouncing Soviet hegemony in Eastern Europe. China has had only minimal support from radical elements in European Communist parties. Albania, China's only ally in Eastern Europe, has recently shown signs of disaffection. Enver Hoxa apparently disapproves of China's ideological shift to the right and China's increased contacts with the West.

In Africa, China obtained some influence through the construction of the Tanzam railway, China's most significant foreign aid project.

China has competed with the USSR for influence in some liberation movements. For example, the Chinese supported the Union for Total Independence (UNITA) insurgents against the Soviet-supported Popular Movement (MPLA), which took power in Angola. China gives verbal support to the blacks' struggle against the ruling whites in Rhodesia and South Africa. During the Cultural Revolution, several African states suspected Chinese involvement in plots to overthrow their governments, but since that time China has been able to achieve correct if not good state-to-state relations with most African countries.[19]

Sino-Soviet competition is also reflected in China's policies in the Middle East. After Egypt's President Sadat cancelled agreements with the USSR and sent Soviet advisors packing, China agreed to supply spare parts for Egypt's Soviet-made aircraft. China has endorsed the Arab position vis-à-vis Israel but has avoided commitment to UN resolutions dealing with the Middle East. Chinese propaganda points to the Middle East as a primary example of competition among the superpowers.

During the 1960s a principal argument against the seating of the People's Republic in China's seat at the UN was that Peking would be "obstructionist." Now that the People's Republic has been a member for some time, the record indicates otherwise. China has used the UN as a forum to support the aspirations of Third World countries verbally but has not obstructed any major Security Council resolutions. Usually, on major UN resolutions such as the ones pertaining to the Middle East, China does not vote "yea" or "nay" or even abstain; rather, the Chinese delegate just reports that China is "present." China has increasingly gained acceptance in other international organizations, nearly always at the expense of Taiwan.[20]

China and the World

Former Secretary of State Kissinger envisioned a world in which five major actors—the U.S., USSR, Western Europe, Japan, and China—would balance in interests and power. Though China is a nuclear power, it is not yet a world power.[21] China does not have the ability to project its power outside Asia; thus Chinese influence on world politics is limited.

In the Chinese perception, the major problem in world affairs is competition among the superpowers that they believe will eventually lead to world war. The Chinese insist that China will never become a superpower that seeks hegemony over the world as do the other superpowers. Of course, the Chinese do not now have the capability of exercising the role of superpower; however, time could change this. If China achieves its goal of becoming an industrialized, economically modern state, its foreign policy is likely to change also. We are not saying that China will become a hegemonic beast, seeking once again to hold dominion over Asia; we are only saying that as China develops and the situation changes, so will China's interests. At a minimum, China will want to have predominant influence in East Asia's international relations.

China is now establishing the self-respect that comes from dealing with other countries as a sovereign equal. As Chinese power develops, maintaining this respect will require new commitments. At the same time the development of power has an incentive of its own. China, as the largest nation, with a strong economy and a strong military, as well as its past historical and cultural traditions, will certainly be looked to by other Asian countries.

Meanwhile, China is a regional, rather than world power. China will continue to make pronouncements about situations in Africa, Latin America, and the Middle East, but for the time being, China's immediate political problems are related to Asia. As already noted, the first priority issue is relations with the USSR. China sides with any nation and supports almost any cause that can help to counteract Soviet influence. China is secondarily concerned with the roles of the United States and Japan relative to East Asia.

It appears that China will continue to follow present policies with some gradual changes. Full normalization of relations with the United States is not likely in the immediate future, but the countries will continue to talk and trade. The development of a special relationship with Japan is also likely to continue. China will support a U.S. role in Asia so long as it counteracts Soviet influence.

Conclusions

The goals of the Chinese revolution have centered around achieving territorial unification and sovereignty, promoting the national economy, attaining power and status in the international community, and achieving socialism. Hua Kuo-feng and his associates among China's leaders have committed themselves to accomplishing many of these goals by the year 2000. As we have seen, this will require a prodigious effort on the part of the Chinese people and liberal doses of good fortune.

The Chinese leaders believe that these goals can be best accomplished by a continued emphasis on state planning and controls of political, economic, and social affairs. The agents of political socialization will continue to emphasize sacrifices that must be made by the people, but there will probably be no mass campaigns of the depth of the Great Leap Forward or the Cultural Revolution. Some of the elements of Maoist concepts pertaining to the struggle against political institutions in order to achieve permanent social revolution will probably be forsaken. The events of the Eleventh CCP Congress and the new Central Committee indicate that cadres once condemned for bureaucratism are making a comeback, while those who are identified with mass mobilization campaigns like the Cultural Revolution have suffered setbacks.

China's present situation is not unlike the early 1960s when the planners and technocrats were in command. Perhaps the Cultural Revolution, as some have asserted, was the last gasp of revolutionary ideology in China. The demands of modernization usually produce unprecedented institution building; the party, state, and other political structures must become increasingly routinized. China may be led to the year 2000 by a group similar to the Soviet leadership, except that there will probably be more professional military men in high political positions.

Whether the revolution gradually becomes institutionalized or not, there can be no doubt that the issues and problems facing China will not be conducive to harmony among China's leaders. The informal process of struggling for power will continue, though it is not likely to result in upheavals like the ones that shook China from 1966 to 1976. In his report on the Constitution before the Eleventh Congress Yeh Chien-ying stated:

> Our Party and our country are now at an important point in history when we are carrying forward our inherited revolutionary tradition and forging ahead into the future. The great victory we have won in smashing the "gang of four" marks the successful conclusion of the first Great Proletarian Cultural Revolution in our country and the start of a new period in China's socialist revolution and socialist construction.

China is entering a new era. How much of the "inherited revolutionary tradition" will be carried into the future remains to be seen. Perhaps the major political tests for the Chinese Communists are still to come.

PART TWO

JAPAN

CHAPTER FIVE

Historical Background

> Party government is run-of-the-mill government; we cannot wish it to be the very best, yet it cannot be the very worst either.[1]

These words, written in 1928 by a Japanese observer of the political scene, proved to be extremely perceptive. Writing several years prior to the end of party government, he did not know how much foresight he had. It was left to military officers and bureaucrats to demonstrate to Japan and the world the kind of depths to which "the very worst" government could lead a country.

This review of Japanese political development prior to World War II will stress the role of political parties, focusing on the thirteen-year period of 1918 to 1931. It would be a disservice to the reader if we did not make it clear that other actors competed with political parties for power in Japan and, in fact, from the time of the enactment of the Meiji constitution in 1890, these other actors held center stage. Nevertheless, understanding the development of parties is crucial to our comprehension of the contemporary system.

In theory the Meiji constitution was unique in modern experience, vesting all executive, legislative, administrative, and judicial authority in the emperor. In practice, the actual involvement of the emperor in more than a ceremonial capacity became rare indeed after the death of the Meiji Emperor in 1912.

The authority to use power in the emperor's name was delegated to

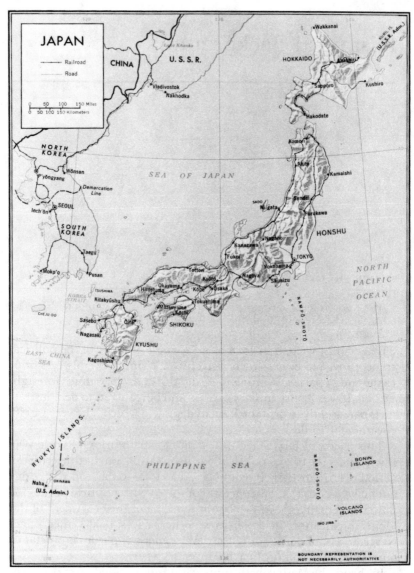

Note: Okinawa is no longer under U.S. administration; it was returned to Japanese jurisdiction in 1972.

various agents. Of special significance was the fact that operational authority over the navy and military was placed in the hands of general staffs and nonmilitary power was given to a prime minister and cabinet. Civil control of the military did not exist. Legislative power was divided between the cabinet, which had certain rule by decree prerogatives, and a bicameral legislature consisting of a House of Peers and a House of Representatives. Both Houses shared powers to initiate laws, question members of the cabinet, assign taxes, and approve budgets. Judicial authority was, in the tradition of the European code, divided into judicial and administrative courts. Local government was responsible to the central government and had little power to initiate. Civil servants and military officers served the Emperor—*not* the people.

In essence, the system was basically authoritarian in tone, with various elites competing for power. In practice a delicately balanced sharing of power evolved among the following actors: (1) the Meiji oligarchs as eventually institutionalized in the *Genro,* or Elder Statesmen; (2) military and naval elites; (3) higher civil bureaucrats; (4) leaders of the major political parties; (5) the zaibatsu, or large corporate interests; (6) the hereditary peerage in the Privy Council and House of Peers.

Any gain in one actor's power usually came as a result of some concomitant reduction in that of another group. This account deals with the early attempts of the political parties to gain a greater share in government. Advances were made in the years following World War I but they did not stem from changes in the Meiji constitution. When domestic and international circumstances altered in the late 1920s and early 1930s, the early parties could not demand the necessary support from the people—partially for reasons of their own making—nor could they cite legal authority. It was then that the parties became anachronistic to the system.

Political parties—actually political associations—first appeared in Japan in the 1870s. These early groupings, called *jiyu minken* (loosely, "free people power"), did not exhibit characteristics normally associated with the roles assumed by modern political parties. In general, they were negatively oriented protest movements interested primarily in ending the era of government by certain influential clan factions (*hambatsu*). Their membership consisted of former samurai displaced by the new political order of the Meiji government, young intellectuals, conservatives who resented the numerous reforms, and government officials who had resigned their posts with the infant Meiji government due to policy differences.[2]

Slowly these associations began to assume the characteristics of bona fide parties. Programs were formulated, leadership was acknowledged, and they began to seek political power rather than just an end to clan government. This, of course, did not happen overnight. In fact, it took several direct alliances with leaders of the oligarchy to give the parties the legitimacy they desired and arrangements with big business to provide the money they needed. Oligarchs such as Ito Hirobumi and Katsura Taro eventually realized that political movements could help them in their quest for power. At the same time, party association with the two prestigious oligarchs provided the fledgling groups with increased credibility.

The Era of Taisho Democracy

It was not until 1918 that party government came to Japan in a manner that approximated Western tradition. As a result of the victory of the democratic powers in World War I, articulate Japanese experienced a new respect for and desire to emulate democratic models. The prewar autocratic regimes used by Japanese leaders as patterns for the nation's modernization lay in ruins. Japan had found herself at war with her one-time mentor, Germany. The concepts of Wilsonian liberalism reached Japan, and there were many who felt the time had come for their implementation and incorporation. It was a period characterized by the temporary coalescence of embryonic labor groups, leftists, intellectuals, liberal politicians, and Christian social activists.[3] All these groups professed, if they did not fully understand, the tenets of liberal democracy.

Although altruistic motives played a role in establishing a certain intellectual mood in Japan in 1918, they were not the reason for the initiation of party government in Japan. In 1918 Prime Minister Terauchi Masatake was the head of a "transcendental cabinet" (so called because the premier had no connection with the parties in the lower house of the Diet). As a result of inflation, and dissatisfaction over the economic disruption of the war, rice riots broke out in the provinces and spread to the cities. Terauchi fell from office and a search for his replacement was begun by members of the Genro. After canvassing the likely candidates and finding none willing, the job fell to Hara Kei, leader of the *Seiyukai* (Political Friends Association) of the lower house.[4] This was the first time that a commoner had been chosen to head the government, and the first time that the prime minister and the majority of his ministers came from one party.

There were expectations that the selection of Hara would lead—as in the British case—to the establishment of responsible party government. Advocates optimistically pointed to the fact that the political elite had coalesced around several major parties as in Great Britain. Civil and military elements favored the *Doshikai Kenseikai* (Like-minded Persons Party and Constitutional Government Party) coalition led by Kato Komei, while those more "politically" motivated tended to associate with the Seiyukai led by Hara Kei.[5]

Although major parties did indeed exist, were elected to the Diet, and engaged in parliamentary debates, those who believed that Japan was about to embark into an era of responsible party government were a bit premature. They did not fully appreciate the power of the existing extraconstitutional Genro system or the force of the complete multiple elite structure. The Genro had the power to remove government leaders without recourse to elections,[6] which helped them assure the continuance of "benevolent bureaucratic authoritarianism."[7] However, as time passed, so did members of the Genro; in 1918 only three remained. It was hoped by some that once all members of the Genro had died or retired, true parliamentary government could be realized instead of the pseudo phenomenon that existed under oligarchic tutelage.[8] Even the decision to appoint Hara Kei prime minister was made by the Genro. Japan was on the road to responsible party government, but 1918 merely set an historical precedent; it remained for the future to honor that precedent.

Hara came to office, as mentioned previously, when the ideas of Western democracy were vibrantly challenging the domestic status quo. Demands for social, economic, and political reforms were increasing. Measures concerning "universal manhood suffrage," social welfare, trade unionism, and reforms of the educational system were called for.[9] Students and workers burst forth with radical demands for a reconstructed and modern Japan.

Hara did not see himself as a visionary reformist. He sought to reduce the power of the oligarchs, and he saw his selection as prime minister as a measure of his success. His programs hardly reflected the growing desire for national reform. Such policies as "the strengthening of national defenses, . . . the development of transportation and communication . . . and . . . the encouragement of trade and industry" did not evince any proselytizing spirit for him or his party.[10] In fact, in 1920 he dissolved Parliament to avoid a showdown on a suffrage bill that had the Kenseikai's backing.[11] When it came to labor reform, his government followed a pattern of suppressing strikes by force.[12] However, he did reduce the amount taxpayers had to pay in order to qualify to vote. Lowering the qualifying sum from ten to three yen produced an increase in the electorate of more than two million. Of course, it primarily benefited the small landowners, who just happened to be staunch supporters of his party, the Seiyukai.[13] Hara also began to open some bureaucratic posts to party appointees. His foreign policy was moderate and generally opposed to Japan's expansion.

Although Hara and the Seiyukai did not carry the reformist torch, the Kenseikai under Kato was much more receptive. In fact, its membership included a perhaps more "progressive" mix of individuals than did the Seiyukai. Not being in power has the tendency to raise the level of rhetoric. Kato's party's program consisted of: "the institutionalization of constitutional government, an extension of the suffrage and respect for civil rights, stabilization of the people's livelihood, a solution to the labor problem, and the improvement of education."[14]

The issue of universal male suffrage absorbed the attention of the Diet through the early 1920s. Hara, however, did not live to see the conclusion of this great debate, for on November 4, 1921, he was assassinated by a youth protesting corruption of the Seiyukai.[15] He was succeeded by his finance minister, Takahashi Korekiyo.

Takahashi was unable to command the party's loyalty as Hara had, and the Seiyukai broke into factions. The Kenseikai, the major party in opposition, obtained only 24 percent of the lower house seats as opposed to 60 percent for the Seiyukai.[16] But the once powerful Seiyukai was torn by differences over the way to approach universal suffrage and other matters. The Kenseikai remained cohesive only on the hope that their leader, Kato, would be asked to form a cabinet. Such was not the case. One of the Elder Statesmen, Saionji Kimmochi, surveying the political confusion rampant in the Diet, chose to bypass the parties once again in selecting a prime minister and decided in favor of a "transcendental cabinet" headed by Kato Tomasaburo.

Of special note at this time is the tactical maneuvering that occurred between the parties. Rather than see Kato Komei, president of the Kenseikai, become prime minister, the Seiyukai agreed to support the nonparty recommendation of the Genro, Kato Tomasaburo.[18] Had they insisted on a continuation of party cabinets—or at least made an issue of it—perhaps the total cause of party government would have been aided. Between 1922 and 1924 three successive cabinets were formed by nonparty men. They were headed by Kato Tamasaburo, Yamamoto Gombei, and Kiyoura Keigo.

The return to "transcendental government" was abided twice by the disparate parties in the Diet and even supported for tactical reasons, as mentioned, but the choice of Kiyoura in 1924 caused party leaders and Diet members to doubt if there would ever be a return to parliamentary government led by the parties. In the face of such dismal prospects, the Kenseikai, the Seiyukai, and a minor party, the Kakushin (Reform) Club, united in the Movement for Constitutional Government. All parties of the Diet—save the Seiyuhonto, which split off to support Kiyoura's government—called for a return to the party cabinet system.[18] They issued a proclamation demanding:

1. the establishment of a system of party cabinets;
2. the suspension of the arbitrary and monopolistic power and special privilege of the oligarchs;
3. joint action to achieve these purposes; and
4. repudiation of the Kiyoura government.[19]

This surprising show of unanimity brought about the dissolution of the Diet and the fifteenth general election. Held in May 1924, this election resulted in a significant strengthening of the Kenseikai to 33 percent of the House seats. The Seiyuhonto came in second with 25 percent of the seats; and Seiyukai won 22 percent and the Kakushin Club garnered 13 percent of the seats.[20] With Kato able to count on Seiyukai and Kakushin Club support in addition to his own party, the Kenseikai, it became clear that he possessed the support of as much as 68 percent of the membership of the Diet. It remained to be seen whether Saionji would recommend that another transcendental cabinet be formed or endorse Kato Komei; in tribute to the Movement for Constitutional Government, Kato was selected.

The Kato cabinet was formed in June 1924. This body was somewhat reform-minded, but erratic. Less than a year after the cabinet's attestation, the Universal Manhood Suffrage Law was passed, increasing the size of the electorate from three to fourteen million.[21] All men over the age of twenty-five who had lived in their electoral district for one year and who were not indigent were permitted to vote.[22]

The Kato cabinet was generally hailed for the suffrage law, but it was not acclaimed for a piece of legislation it endorsed and promulgated one week later called the Peace Preservation Law. This particular measure provided a sentence of up to ten years in prison for anyone found guilty of joining groups or societies desiring to change the constitution, the capitalist system, or the existing form of government.[23]

Kato also attempted reforms in other areas, more successfully in some than in others. In his attempt to modify the power of the House of Peers (the upper house) he had a measure of success. Although he could not reduce the power of the Peers, he was able to alter the body's composition. Rather than having so many members from the nobility, he increased the number appointed by the emperor—men chosen primarily for achievement. Kato also succeeded in reorganizing the imperial army and cutting military expenditures from 42 percent of the budget to 27 percent.[24] The price he paid was high. The elimination of four divisions was not accomplished by forcing the excess officers into retirement; they were attached to schools and universities to administer compulsory military training.[25] Some effort was also expended to revise the tax system and make it more equitable, as well as to support reform measures regarding education, local suffrage, and labor unions. He was successful in efforts to permit the existence of the labor movement and supported measures to improve the conditions of labor. However, these initiatives were not handled so as to capture the imagination and support of the people, and 1925 saw the end of the coalition upon which Kato depended.[26]

The parties lapsed again into interparty bickering and general immobility. Desire to implement programs was overpowered by an all-consuming desire for power. Public faith in the parties, never really impressive, began to erode even further. Thus, although a coalition with the Kenseikai might have been condoned for tactical reasons, the Seiyukai acted in its own interests after the first Kato cabinet and allied loosely again with the Seiyhonto. As a result, the Diet was fairly evenly split between the Kenseikai and the two opposition parties. Kato and the Kenseikai stayed in power because Saionji continued to place his faith in proven elements rather than risk giving the government to one of the leaders of the Seiyuhonto or Seiyukai, who still did not agree enough to form a united front.

Kato died on January 28, 1926, and so did the limited movement for reform. Kato was replaced by his lieutenant, Wakatsuki Reijiro, who lasted little more than a year. However, by the end of his tenure as prime minister, Wakatsuki was well on the way to establishing the base for a merger of the Kenseikai and the Seiyuhonto. The merger eventually took place in June 1927, with the formation of the Minseito. This new party offered a reform-oriented platform that incorporated many of the objectives needed to insure a reconstructed Japan:

1. Diet-centered politics under the emperor in which the demands of all the people are centralized . . . by means of

universal suffrage;
2. diplomacy based on international justice;
3. increased industrial efficiency to end the instability of popular livelihood;
4. equalized opportunities for education; and
5. public election of party officials.[27]

By the end of 1927 two major developments had occurred: there were now two principal parties in the Diet, and since the first Kato cabinet (1924) the prime minister had been chosen from a leading party of the lower house. These changes were not firmly established perhaps, but they indicated that the concept of party government was becoming more accepted and more difficult to overlook. The party system was to be sorely tested when the relatively tranquil period of the Taisho era came to an end with the death of the Taisho Emperor in December 1926, and the tumultuous Showa era of Emperor Hirohito began.

The March Toward Authoritarianism

When Wakatsuki Reijiro was forced to resign in April 1927, Saionji, the aged Genro, selected General Tanaka Giichi, president of the Seiyukai, as the new prime minister. He faced a serious economic crisis at home and imperialistic temptation abroad. Tanaka followed a somewhat more activist policy with respect to Japanese involvement in China than his predecessors, dispatching Japanese troops to Tsingtao in an attempt to thwart the new Chinese nationalism that was threatening the continuation of foreign interests in China.[28]

To avoid a vote of no confidence in January 1928, Tanaka forced an election, the first conducted under universal male suffrage. In this election the Seiyukai and the Minseito each won 46 percent of the House seats, and the proletarian parties won 2 percent (8 seats) in their first election. Certain irregularities that occurred during the election were attributed to Tanaka's Home Minister, Suzuki Seisaburo, who waged a war of intimidation against opposition hopefuls. Suzuki, using the Peace Preservation Law as his justification, arrested 1600 leftists for having dangerous thoughts.[29] This impropriety set off a Diet reaction that ultimately resulted in Suzuki's resignation.

The spirit of the nation was beginning to shift perceptibly. The parties, long interested in their tactical battle with the oligarchs, were seen by conservatives and traditionalists as spokesmen for selfish moneyed interests. Furthermore, "the halt these leaders had brought to the expansion of Japan's armed forces and empire appeared to be little more than treason."[30] During this era the parties did not help their own cause; the Minseito called the Seiyukai government (1927-29) a "Mitsui cabinet." When the Minseito returned to power in 1930, Prime Minister Hamaguchi was said to head the "Mitsubishi cabinet."[31]

By 1930 the population exceeded 60 million and was increasing at the rate of one million each year. Increased dependence on imports was noticeable and certain expansionist factions called for an increased empire in order to insulate Japan against international depression.[32] In addition to growing uneasiness and disaffection among the farmers, small businessmen, and others, military activists were increasingly restless at the progress of Chiang Kai-shek in China and sought action to prevent the loss of Japanese influence in Manchuria as a result of Chiang's consolidation of power.

The first indication of events to come occurred on June 4, 1928, when Chang Tso-lin, warlord of Manchuria, was killed when the train in which he was riding was blown up. Rightly or wrongly, Prime Minister Tanaka was blamed for this act and eventually forced from office. In essence he lost control of the army, and when Emperor Hirohito demanded that the officers be disciplined, Tanaka was rebuffed by the army, which claimed that it needed to accept no censure from civil government.[33]

The man picked to follow Tanaka was Hamaguchi Osachi, head of the Minseito, who formed his cabinet on July 2, 1929. He immediately set forth a policy of economic retrenchment, returning to the gold standard at home and adopting a policy of conciliation toward China. After six months he dissolved the Diet and called for elections to be held February 20, 1930. The Minseito won an impressive victory, gaining 59 percent of the seats. The Seiyukai, headed by Inukai Tsuyoshi, was able to obtain only 36 percent.[34]

Such sweet victory is often short. As the full impact of the economic disaster that had befallen the world reached Japan, the Hamaguchi cabinet became entangled in a test of will between itself and the Naval General Staff. The encounter occurred during the course of negotiations at the London Naval Conference of 1930. To avoid a breakdown in the talks, Hamaguchi accepted a compromise on the ratios for heavy cruisers that was slightly different from the desires of the Japanese Navy. He and his party were subject to scathing attacks from the press, the Seiyukai, the nationalists and the general public. The Seiyukai attacked Hamaguchi for "having neglected to follow the advice of the military experts."[35]

Through outright determination, Hamaguchi succeeded in having the treaty ratified by the Privy Council on October 1, 1930, but by the middle of November, he was the victim of an assassination attempt. Severely wounded, he died a year later and with him went the notion of civilian control over the military.[36]

Wakatsuki assumed the duties of prime minister from the ailing Hamaguchi, and his cabinet was witness to the beginning of almost unbridled military adventurism egged on by ultranationalist theorists who called for an expropriation of zaibatsu holdings, dissolution of the Diet, military rule, and return to the "grandeur" of imperial rule. In fact, in the spring of 1931, young officers imbued with such a spirit plotted a "Showa Restoration" but were discovered in time.[37] This ultranationalist drive was also reflected in the Mukden Incident of September 18, 1931, which heralded Japan's imperialistic conquests in Manchuria. Wakatsuki and his foreign minister, Shidehara Kijuro, repeatedly found themselves trying to explain army actions after the fact. Even at that, some army firebrands plotted to "exterminate the cabinet."[38]

Wakatsuki was unable to control the Kwantung Army in China or the Imperial Army, and after decisions were taken by the latter to reinforce the Kwantung Army, the beleaguered prime minister resigned on December 13, 1931. His most probable successor, and president of the Seiyukai, was Suzuki Kisaburo. Saionji, still influential as the last of the Genro, decided that Suzuki was too nationalistic and picked Inukai Tsuyoshi, unwittingly giving him his death warrant at the same time.[39]

The Inukai Cabinet

The nationalistic frenzy that had driven Wakatsuki to resign continued to intensify. By February 1932 the army expansionists had set up the "independent" state of Manchukuo in Manchuria, and members of the government and the zaibatsu were increasingly in danger of assassination from "patriots" belonging to the myriad of ultranationalist groups.

Amid this militaristic and expansionistic spirit, the eighteenth general election was held, and the Seiyukai won 68 percent of the seats at stake. The Minseito won only 31 percent. The candidates elected supported prevailing military policies; the brake on expansion was gradually being removed, and Japan was preparing to run headlong down the road of aggression.

With many ultrarightists believing that Japanese society had to be purged of party leaders, zaibatsu, and individuals representative of a liberal economic system, it was inevitable that party cabinets would be dissolved. On May 15, 1932, Prime Minister Inukai and others were assassinated. Saionji, the Elder Statesman and one-time president of the Seiyukai, chose not to select a party leader from the Seiyukai to replace Inukai because the party had become too outspokenly nationalistic. The era was over—and nonparty cabinets once again became the rule.

What had happened to cause this change? International depression brought unemployment in Japan to three million, a record unsurpassed even by the 1974-75 recession, which hit a much larger population. The political parties, due to their close identity with the zaibatsu and international trade, were blamed by the man in the street for the depression. Secondly, the advance of Chiang Kai-shek put great fear into army expansionists that even Manchuria might fall from their grasp if not quickly consolidated into the empire. Finally, liberal democracy seemed to fall from grace, in face of the new political approaches that were arising. Fascism and nazism offered a new hope for one-time adherents to authoritarianism.

The Advent of War

From 1932 onward, having lost the initiative of the twenties, the prewar parties became echo chambers for government policy. As Reischauer has stated: "What occurred was a small shift in the balance between the elites, the advantage passing from the parties to the services and the higher ranks of the bureaucracy. This small shift produced an enormous change in political climate and policy, setting Japan upon the course that led to disaster in World War II."[40]

In the lower house election of 1936, while the nation was experiencing the turmoil described, the more moderate and liberal Minseito still managed to outpoll the Seiyukai 44 percent to 37 percent. This election was followed only one week later by the last attempt by the ultranationalists to seize control of the government. The famous 2-2-6 Incident of 1936 (for February 26) was planned by young officers of the army's First Division to bring about the long-sought "Showa Restoration," but they were declared rebels and the attempt failed. In the wake of this increasingly serious threat from the lunatic fringes of the right, the army turned to setting its own house in order and greater attempts at public thought control were initiated.[41]

The last general election to take place before the war occurred in 1937. In this election the Minseito and the Seiyukai ended in a virtual tie, both winning 38 percent of the seats, although the Minseito received 90,000 votes more. Socialist gains continued but still did not bring them to major party status, as the socialist party Shakai Taishuto elected only 8 percent of the Diet members.

As Japan moved closer and closer to the chasm of World War II and found itself enmeshed in a full scale war in China, steps were taken to encourage political support. In 1937 a "movement for national spiritual mobilization" was created.[42] The overseer of this effort was the Central Alliance for the Mobilization of the National Spirit, which by 1938 encompassed some ninety-four organizations, including veterans groups, unions, and mayors' organizations. In October 1940, Prime Minister Konoe Fumimaro supported an extension of the concept and created the Imperial Rule Assistance Association (IRAA). This body replaced *all* political parties; they were dissolved and subsumed within the IRAA.

The IRAA never gained the status of a political movement. It was more like a bureaucratic conduit for the transfer of information from the top downward, and a means to mobilize the *tonarigumi*, or neighborhood teams, for firefighting, air raids, and other support activities. So prepared, Japan entered 1941 marching to an unopposed drummer called the IRAA.

THE MACARTHUR ERA:
THE YEARS OF THE U.S. OCCUPATION, 1945-1952

Although the U.S. occupation of Japan lasted one year longer than MacArthur lasted as Supreme Commander for the Allied Powers, it is fitting to name this particular period after the man who set the tone for what was one of the most successful programs of national rehabilitation in modern history. This terminology is even more appropriate when it is recalled that the years up to and including 1948 were years of significant reform. After that, external considerations began to weigh heavily as determinants of U.S. policy—two of the more important considerations being the development of the cold war and Chiang Kai-shek's increasing difficulties in China.

The occupation of Japan became, for all practical purposes, an American operation, due to MacArthur's determination not to abide interference from the Soviets. (At one point MacArthur is reported to have "threatened to lock up the whole Soviet delegation if they tried to resist him."[43]) The occupation went through two distinct phases. The first period was characterized by active pursuit of reform measures aimed at demilitarizing and democratizing Japan. The second phase, from 1948 onward, was a period of growing realization on the part of Occupation authorities that they have permitted the leftist genie to leave its bottle, and that perhaps something more than an economy capable of supporting Japan's peacetime needs was in order.

We shall examine this era of Japanese-American relations with an emphasis on the reforms that came in the early years when individual groups—youth, labor, farmers, women, and men between 20 and 25— were given new freedoms and new rights. The durability of these reforms was placed in the hands of the parochial interest groups themselves. An era of balancing elites was replaced by an era of countervailing influences and interests.

The mandate for the reform objectives of the Occupation was the Basic Initial Post-Surrender Directive, from which the U.S. forces in Japan operated. This document set the political and economic tone for the MacArthur interregnum. It had two ultimate goals: (1) that Japan would never again menace the world's peace and (2) that a government would be established embodying democratic principles. Methods to achieve these overall goals included: restricting Japan territorially to the islands of Honshu, Hokkaido, Kyushu, and Shikoku; the demilitarization of the state; encouragement of democratic and representative experiences for the Japanese people; and economic development to "strengthen the peaceful disposition of the Japanese people."

Based on these broad directives, the United States operated through the existing Japanese governmental bureaucracy to purge the government and schools of ultranationalist individuals, to circum- scribe zaibatsu power by dissolution, to increase the scope of the franchise, to institute collective bargaining, to initiate a comprehen- sive land reform, to introduce legal reforms for the nuclear family, to decentralize the national police, to give new autonomy to local government, and to oversee far-reaching educational reforms. All these measures have not remained intact. Over the years certain modifications have been effected, especially realigning the structure of big business and increasing the centralization of local government, education, and police.

One of the first items resolved by Occupation authorities—in retrospect, one of the most important decisions made by the Americans— was whether Emperor Hirohito was to be tried as a war criminal. MacArthur evidently had no preconceived course of action, but eighteen days after his arrival in Tokyo, he was visited by the emperor and decided that Hirohito would not be tried.[44] Several months after Hirohito's meeting with MacArthur, an Imperial Rescript was issued in which the emperor divested himself of any "divineness," and by February 1946 Hirohito was out meeting the people of Japan in his never-to-be-forgotten "crumpled gray hat."[45]

By early February 1946, MacArthur despaired of ever receiving from the Japanese government a "decent" or acceptable draft of a constitution to replace that of the Meiji Emperor. He ordered his own Government Section under General Courtnay Whitney to write a draft, insisting that three specific points be included:

1. Japan was to renounce war forever, abolish her armed forces, and pledge never to revive them;
2. Although sovereignty was to be vested in the people, the emperor was to be described as a symbol of the state;
3. The peerage was to be abolished, and the property of the Imperial household was to revert to the state.[46]

Within two weeks the draft was shown to the Japanese, who were still working on a draft of their own. They were completely shocked by the American document that so closely followed the American model. Under pressure from various Occupation authorities, the new constitution was concurrently announced to the Japanese people on March 6, 1946, by MacArthur and the emperor. It was adopted by the Diet on November 3, 1946, and took effect six months later. The constitution incorporated many important features into the Japanese political system; it:

1. derived the authority of government from the people;
2. made the emperor the titular head of state;
3. renounced war as a sovereign right of the nation;
4. gave extensive civil rights to all citizens;
5. abolished the peerage;
6. established equal rights for women;
7. adopted a parliamentary system of government based on a popularly elected bicameral Diet;
8. gave legislative and fiscal authority to the Diet;
9. put executive power in the hands of a cabinet responsible to the Diet;
10. created an independent court system with a Supreme Court that possessed the power of constitutional review over "any law, order, regulation, or official act"; and
11. decentralized local government.[47]

The Japanese were given one of the most progressive constitutions in the world, and it is a testimony to its concepts of building new interest groups and protecting their rights that it has remained unchanged for more than thirty years.

As the demilitarization of the nation progressed through the demobilization of the armed services and their return to the main islands, efforts were begun to rid the body politic of those individuals most closely connected with the goals and objectives of the old regime. Those to be purged fell into the following groups:

1. career military officers;
2. heads of secret or patriotic societies;
3. executives of financial groups that had exploited territories occupied by the Japanese;
4. former ambassadors to Germany and Italy between 1937 and 1945;
5. those who negotiated treaties with the Axis Powers;
6. officials of war production companies;
7. members of wartime cabinets and their special sections.[48]

The Occupation purge was conducted in a very uneven manner. Some individuals were protected by U.S. officials so their special skills could be utilized. In all, 220,000 were purged. The majority of those purged (180,000) were former military officers. Under provisions of this particular program, those purged could have been kept out of government or education and general positions of public trust until 1951.[49] However, due to the shift in Occupation policy in 1948, only 8,710 persons remained in a purged status when the system terminated in 1951.[50]

One of the inequities that both Japanese government and Occupation officials realized needed to be corrected was that of land ownership. In 1945 tenant land made up 53 percent of wet rice production, and the power of village landlords was based primarily on this situation. Hoping to preempt the Occupation on this matter, the Diet passed a land reform program in December 1945 allowing landowners to keep five hectares of property. The time-frame for implementation was seen as five years.

The reform did not go as far as desired, however, and the Occupation insisted that a more complete measure be drawn up. The second Land Reform Act of 1946 was considerably more severe, stripping absentee landlords of all property and allowing village resident landlords to keep only 2.5 acres of leased land. The maximum amount a farmer could own was set at 7.5 acres. The redistribution of land took approxmately two years to accomplish and tenancy dropped to below 10 percent. This far-reaching measure had the effect of destroying the economic and political base of local landowners and immediately gave a vested interest in the new government to the three million new landowners. Profits from the high price of rice at that time soon helped them reduce or eliminate their previous indebtedness.[51]

The zaibatsu, well aware that a similar reorganization was due to befall them, attempted to put their own house in order by a 1946 scheme called the Yasuda Plan. As a result of the plan—which was helped along by considerable Occupation prodding—zaibatsu family assets were frozen and taxed, and eighty-three holding companies were dissolved. The zaibatsu were broken into smaller components, and legislation was passed to prevent a rapid reconstitution. The effectiveness of these anti-monopoly measures was aided by the coincidental purge that removed top management figures from the immediate scene.[52]

Action against the zaibatsu was combined with legislation to encourage the role of labor unions. Three specific acts—the Trade Union Law, 1945; the Labor Relations Adjustment Law, 1946; and the Labor Standards Law, 1947—created a positive environment for unionism. By 1949 union membership had increased to an impressive 6.5 million.[53] Communists gained a disproportionate share of the initial leadership, but after the failure of a general strike in 1947 and through the combined efforts of SCAP (Supreme Command, Allied Powers) authorities and the Japanese government, their role was quickly reduced.[54]

Reforms in education and local government were also attempted. The years of compulsory education required were increased from six to nine. Control over schools was decentralized and given to locally elected school boards. Prefectures, cities, and towns were given extensive autonomous powers. Even the *tonarigumi* or neighborhood associations, which served as a control element during the war, were officially dissolved. This latter measure was not as successful as other reforms, and the local associations soon reappeared under different names.

By 1947, as mentioned previously, the pressures of international events forced a reevaluation of Occupation policies. The growing disagreement with Communist powers was one force pressuring for altered policies; the continuing cost of the occupation was another. This burden weighed heavily on SCAP officials, who wished to see Japan possess a healthy economy. Demilitarization had been the concern prior to 1947, but certain aspects of remilitarization became increasingly important after 1947. As a result, a significant turnaround in SCAP policy occurred. To bolster the economy the former zaibatsu were allowed to resume greater industrial activity, and economic recovery increased measurably. By 1950 and the Korean War, the rehabilitation of the industrial base had achieved "encouraging results."[56]

Efforts to end the Occupation through the enactment of a peace treaty were stepped up. In March of 1947, MacArthur made his first statement regarding a possible peace treaty. Other references followed, and a plan including a peace conference in Tokyo in July of 1947 was discussed. The plan came to naught due to "Allied" disagreements. In November 1948, the U.S. National Security Council took the position that the remaining period of U.S. occupation should be used to strengthen Japan economically and politically. A long-term relationship of friendship was becoming more likely.[57]

The June 25, 1950, invasion of South Korea by North Korea gave new impetus to the movement for a peace treaty. In September 1950, John Foster Dulles was appointed as special ambassador to negotiate the treaty. Continuing Soviet opposition led the American government to take the position that no "single nation had the perpetual power to veto the conclusion by others of a peace with Japan."[58]

Dulles, working with the other Allies, was able to resolve most noncommunist objections by July 1951, and a call for a September peace conference in San Francisco was issued. This conference, attended by representatives of the Allied Powers, produced a peace agreement that was signed by forty-nine nations, including Japan. The state of war was terminated, and Japan's sovereignty recognized. Japan, in turn, recognized her new boundaries and the fact that reparations, although modest, would be paid to the countries she occupied during the war. The Soviet Union and the People's Republic of China did not sign the treaty.

In addition to the peace treaty, a bilateral U.S.-Japan Security Treaty was signed. A special relationship between the United States and Japan was to continue based on the recognition of sovereignty and the needs of defense. The Occupation came to an end, but it left its mark on the institutions of Japan; it has continued to affect the political life of Japan to this day.

CHAPTER SIX

Political Culture and
Political Behavior

NIHONSHUGI AND THE JAPANESE POLITY

Japan have certain unique characteristics contributing to its overall makeup that all students of Japan, regardless of their specific interests, should know. These traits are the items that constitute the *Nihonshugi* of Japan—her "Japan-ness." Before discussing Japan's political culture, we will briefly look at these special characteristics.

Language

One of the more obvious items that sets the nation apart from the rest of the world is the Japanese language. It is composed of ideographic characters that individually and in combination impart ideas and concepts; thus, a background in any Western language will not provide much assistance in mastering Japanese. The language may be difficult for the average foreigner, but it also presents a formidable challenge to the Japanese themselves. In fact, the intense process of learning the 1800 or more characters by the end of the ninth grade requires a rigorous self-discipline on the part of the Japanese students. This language-induced discipline binds the Japanese closely to one another; they also share in the language's fine subtleties and humor. The language hurdle can keep all but the most resolute foreigners from intimate contact with the society.

Ultimately, Japan finds herself in a form of informational isolation. Data on foreign countries are readily available to the Japanese, but the reverse is not the case. Information received by

Japan as compared with data dispatched from Japan flows at an uneven ratio of twelve to one.[1] Any attempt to follow daily political events in Tokyo through accounts in leading U.S. newspapers or newsweeklies leads to significant informational gaps, not to mention frustration. This situation is not, per se, the fault of the Japanese; much of the blame rests on the great American infatuation with Europe. Yet, if informational exchange is to become equal, the Japanese themselves will probably have to foster any improvement.

Geographic Insularity and Resource Scarcity

A second important factor contributing to Japan's world view is its insularity and relative resource impoverishment. The Japanese archipelago stretches for over 2,300 miles along the eastern coast of the Asian continent; it has a total land area of approximately 146,000 square miles, but of this over 105,000 square miles are mountainous. The nature of the islands, the lack of retrievable raw materials, and the dynamic nature of the industrial sector produces a great dependence on external sources for goods to meet individual and industrial demands. For example, only 4 percent of the soy beans consumed by the Japanese are domestically produced. The same figure holds for wheat. All cotton, wool, bauxite, and rubber for industrial purposes are imported.

Other critical materials such as copper, coking coal, iron ore, and oil are imported, with percentages running from a low of 80.2 percent for copper to 99.7 percent for crude oil.[2] Such dependencies on foreign raw materials create significant vulnerabilities, as could be seen during the 1973 oil crisis. Japan is particularly dependent on energy imports. Only 11.5 percent of Japan's energy is obtained domestically; the rest, some 88.5 percent, is obtained from foreign sources. This dependence on foreign sources to sustain the Japanese way of life induces a paranoia that affects the highest policy maker as well as the average citizen.

Homogeneity

Another contributing factor of Japanese life and self-image is the ethnic unity or ethnic purity of the nation. Save for some 650,000 Koreans and a smaller number of Ainu, the nation is basically a homogeneous society. The Korean population is primarily a result of Japan's imperial period (1905-45), when Korean labor was encouraged to relocate in Japan. The Ainu are the remnants of a Caucasoid civilization that at one time inhabited the principal part of the islands of Japan. Like the American Indians they were unable to resist the tide of a more advanced civilization and were gradually forced northward, and today they are concentrated in the northern-most islands, especially Hokkaido.

There is another group, the *Eta*, that is racially Japanese, but it is the target of some discrimination. This group grew up around the ancient religious proscriptions against the consumption of meat, the slaughtering of animals, and the processing of leather. At one time they were required to live in segregated sections of Japanese villages with their station recorded on family records; today they exist as an officially liberated group. The term currently used to identify them is *Burakumin* (literally "village people"). Due to the dynamic nature of Japanese society, the *Burakumin* are being assimilated gradually, but some problems of discrimination remain and occasionally come to the fore as political issues.

Outside of these minor groups, the 113 million Japanese are ethnically similar. The resulting unity of purpose, common identity, and strong cultural heritage are important assets to the Japanese nation.

Goal Orientation

Another characteristic that has been part of Japan since the period of feudalism and the rivalry of neighboring *han* (feudal domain) is goal orientation (rather than ideological orientation). Most Japanese are relatively neutral about religion and ideological politics. Achievement orientation and competition were hallmarks of the *han* organization in early Japan. Each group competed with neighboring groups to excel in the production of some good or product. When the target—sometimes political, sometimes not—was articulated by the leadership, all members of the group strove for achievement. If the goal was changed by the leader, the group worked for success on the new goal. This particular characteristic served Japan well when challenged by the West in the mid-nineteenth century and it continues to be valuable today.

Vertical Organization

Another characteristic of Japanese society was the development of vertical organization rather than horizontal ones. In the period before the Meiji Restoration, society was organized very clearly. In Japanese it is characterized by the expression *shi-no-ko-sho*, which stands for nobility/samurai, farmers, artisans, and merchants. These groups represented a definite hierarchy. Loyalties were also very clear; unlike the Chinese, loyalty to the *daimyo*, or local lord, came before loyalty to the family. As might be expected, this resulted in personal dilemmas that have been recorded for posterity in the No and Kabuki art forms. In the prerestoration era (before 1850), the daimyo had ample authority to alter the goals of the group within certain limits. This feature has given the Japanese more societal resilience than societies where social organization is based on horizontal relationships or ideological norms. One of the more recent examples of this phenomenon was the rapid readjustment that occurred after World War II. The new leader, General MacArthur, set new goals and objectives for Japan and, generally speaking, the Japanese responded with a new sense of direction.

Vertical organization is critical to practically every group in Japanese society and plays a key role in interpersonal relations as well. Knowledge of the strength of vertical ties in Japan makes some political events far more understandable. The term most frequently used to explain vertical relationships is *oyabun-kobun. Oyabun* is thought of as the "parent" and *kobun* as the "child."

Reciprocal Relationships

Within the goal-oriented vertical organization of Japanese society, the workings of reciprocal relationship are exceedingly important. The terms used to capture this concept are *on* and *giri.* Within the vertical organizations stressing a senior-junior relationship, often another more subtle situation exists. In this relationship, *on* is the benevolent responsibility of the senior rank to provide some measure of security and reward to the junior member. In return, the subordinate has an obligation, *giri* ("duty"), to follow the desires of the more senior member. We in the West have several variants of this concept; often the notion of loyalty to a boss or superior is voiced.

The concept of *on* and *giri* comes from feudal times when the landlord had a benevolent relationship with his retainers (*on*). In return for the security and opportunity the landlord provided, the retainer had a strong sense of obligation or duty (*giri*) to the lord. A similar relationship can be found in many aspects of Japanese society today—particularly within the political system.

A striking example of *on* occurred during the recession that beset Japan as a result of the worldwide reaction to the 1974 oil crisis. A personnel manager of a medium-sized firm was forced to "pink slip," or terminate, some of the firm's long-term employees. After having notified the affected individuals, he committed suicide to atone for his inability to carry out his *on.*

The Decision-Making Process

The decision-making process is another unique aspect of Japanese society. It is closely tied to the *ringi* system. This system, frequently seen in Japanese bureaucracy and business, is one in which middle-ranking personnel create policy by initiating studies and papers at their level. Through a series of consensus-building exercises the ideas move ever upward in the chain of command until they are adopted by the organization as a whole. The *ringi* system represents a kind of decision making found in Japanese commercial or government organization, but it does not explain the decision-making system used by the ruling party to make national policy acceptable to the opposition and the national constituency.

In general, consensus must be obtained before a decision is made. The charge that a party, faction, or leader is "going it alone" is one of the most serious charges that can be made within the framework of the Japanese polity. Rule by majority—the norm in Western democracies—is not greeted in a favorable light in Japan. Edwin Reischauer points out in *The Japanese* that almost two-thirds of Diet legislation is passed by unanimous consent.[3] This reflects the remarkable effort by the ruling party to placate, as far as practicable, the opposition parties, paying close attention to criticisms they might have on particular bills. On selected major issues, the LDP must resort to forcing votes without waiting for consensus among the parties.

In the political world, decisions are first worked out within the LDP. Then bills are submitted to the Diet, thus forcing other parties to come to grips with the issues. Often, modifications recommended by the opposition parties can be accommodated in the proposed legislation, resulting in unanimity or consensus. On issues of an ideological nature, such as the various party positions toward the security treaty, multi-party consensus usually cannot be reached. In those instances the LDP often resorts to using a "ram-rod" to get legislation or treaties passed. The opposition may then take to the streets or, more likely, to the media. Great party opposition to LDP Diet tactics may result in a boycott of Diet proceedings. In such cases, after having passed the measure, the LDP, hat in hand calls for a meeting of the various secretaries general to apologize for acting tempestuously and to request a return to normal procedures.

It is easy to talk in general terms about the nature of decision making in Japan, but it may be more informative to follow one decision in detail to observe how the LDP reaches consensus on some contentious question. For a step-by-step description of the process, see the March 1977 issue of *Asian Survey*, which covers the eight years of maneuvering that went into Japan's ratification of the nuclear Non-Proliferation Treaty.

The Cyclic Nature of Japanese Society

Japan has another interesting historic feature which may have long-term consequences. The Japanese, by virtue of their relative isolation and inherent uniqueness, have been able to indulge in national introspection at times. At other times Japan has been the recipient of foreign religion, philosophy, techniques, and material goods.

Japan has turned inward against things foreign when faced with threats to its perceived security needs. During the Tokugawa era (1600-1868) the nation shut itself away. With the Meiji Restoration the self-imposed isolation was cast aside, but Japan withdrew again during the dark days of the economic depression of the 1930s which loosed forces that would be abated only with war, devastation, and defeat. After the war a new era of receptivity toward foreign ideas evolved. Whether Japan will repeat this cycle of history has yet to be determined. Much depends on the ability of the current political system to respond to foreign and domestic challenges.

JAPAN'S POLITICAL CULTURE SINCE INDEPENDENCE

We will now examine the major trends that have typified individual Japanese political experience since 1952, when the nation once again gained control over its own destiny. It is necessary to understand how voters changed after 1952 if we are to fully comprehend modern party development.

The typical voter in Japan is basically conservative. The political spectrum is generally divided between the conservative and the "progressive" or revisionist elements. Ever since the war, the vote for conservative candidates in national elections for the lower house has been greater than 45 percent of the total vote cast. Although conservatism has become characteristic of the Japanese body politic, a new general trend has set in, and each election finds the conservatives gathering a slightly smaller percentage of the vote. In the last election prior to World War II the conservatives—excluding the ultra-nationalists—obtained 76 percent of the vote;[4] in the 1976 election for the House of Representatives, the conservative vote was only 45.7

TABLE 6.1
Percentage of Votes for Japanese House of
Representatives

Dates	Conservative (LDP, NLC)	Socialist (JSP, DSP)
1946	46.3	17.1
1947	58.9	26.2
1949	63.0	15.5
1952	66.1	21.9
1953	65.7	27.6
1955	63.2	30.2
1958	57.8	32.9
1960	57.6	36.3
1963	54.9	36.2
1967	48.8	35.2
1969	47.6	29.1
1972	46.8	28.9
1976	45.7	26.9

percent. The general trend is shown in Table 6.1.

While the conservatives have been losing ground, the socialist ranks have also declined since 1960. One explanation is the increasing attractiveness of parties outside the conservative or socialist parties, like the Komeito and the Japan Communist Party (JCP). Another may be the general urbanization of the electorate and the resultant change in issue orientation of the voters. We will examine the specific characteristics of parties later, but at this time we have no reason to believe that either the Komeito or JCP will radically alter their vote-gathering capabilities. Continuing cooperation between the conservative Liberal Democratic Party (LDP), the New Liberal Club (NLC), and the conservative Democratic Socialist Party (DSP), will probably assure conservative rule for some time to come.

At the national level, the Japanese voter has tended to favor conservative candidates over the range of alternatives. This orientation is not likely to change significantly in the 70s. For example, a poll taken on December 7, 1975, by the *Tokyo Shimbun* in the Tokyo metropolitan area revealed that 59.7 percent of the respondents felt that a conservative government or a conservative-renovationist coalition government would be desirable in the future. Other polls by the *Mainichi* and *Asahi* indicated that more than 50 percent of respondents in the entire nation viewed themselves as either completely in favor of conservatives or inclined toward conservatives.[5]

The average voter in Japan has a very high level of participation in elections. The turnout for the first election after World War II was 72.1 percent; in 1967 it was 74.0 percent. The Japanese voter is obviously more inclined to exercise his right to vote than his counterpart in the United States.[6] A question often asked is whether the Japanese vote out of a feeling of duty—that it is the correct thing to do—or because of social pressure. This question was dealt with by Bradley Richardson in his book *The Political Culture of Japan*. His research inquired into the voters' attitudes about the relevance of politics in everyday lives, their ability to understand politics, and their feelings as to the instrumental nature of political involvement.

Richardson's research demonstrated that between one-half and three-fourths of the respondents were convinced of the meaningfulness of politics—both at a national and local level.[7] These figures compared favorably with similar surveys in West Germany and Great Britain. The figures were higher than in Italy, but lower than in the United States. However, the Japanese also demonstrated characteristics of *formalism;* that is, although they were greatly interested in politics—or indicated such—they did not participate individually to any great extent.

Efforts to determine how well the Japanese believe they understand politics at a national level were most revealing. It was found that only one-fourth of the respondents felt that they understood national affairs. Italy showed a similar low level of confidence, but voters in the United States and Great Britain were much more confident.[8]

On issues that directly affected their interests, Japanese voters were far more knowledgable; this was seen as evidence of an *instrumentalist* approach—a motivation based on the utilitarian value of voting. Some voters were found to have loyalties to certain groups or individuals and participated in politics because of those loyalties.[9]

Richardson compared levels of interest in politics in Japan and other industrialized states. The Japanese compared favorably in most cases, but when "strong interest" was tested, it was discovered that Japan lagged somewhat behind voters of other developed states. More Americans, for example, indicated a "strong interest" than did Japanese.[10]

Another aspect of Japanese political development since World War II is the manner in which citizens appraise governmental performance. According to the empirical research done by Richardson *ambivalence* is a central theme.[11] In general respondents were not strongly supportive of the output from the public process at the national level; they were somewhat more satisfied with local political efforts. Most Japanese endorsed the electoral process, but their responses were more critical when more substantive or issue-oriented matters were dealt with. When it came to Japanese attitudes toward the effectiveness of elections, more skepticism appeared. It was apparent that respondents considered the act of voting important, but they questioned the responsiveness of the men they elected. This kind of ambivalence is not confined to Japan. Richardson pointed out that the electorate in Great Britain, Germany, Italy, and the United States responded quite similarly. Negative orientations were found to be greater in urban areas than in rural districts.

The average Japanese's role in the political process was found to be quite passive. Some have suggested that most Japanese may not see a need to participate actively in politics because they are basically satisfied. This does not seem likely, for most Japanese do not voice satisfaction when asked about political matters. A public opinion poll published by the *Sankei* newspaper on February 24, 1975, showed that 80 percent of the respondents believed that politics did not reflect the wishes and views of the people. Only 1 percent of the respondents said that the wishes and views of the people were fully reflected in current political activity. The percentage of dissatisfaction was exactly the same in a poll taken a year earlier.[12] Another poll on political consensus published by *Mainichi* on March 23, 1975, showed that 78 percent of the respondents were dissatisfied with current politics. A *Yomiuri* poll in 1977 indicated that 72.7 percent were dissatisfied.[13]

The political passivity of most Japanese could be due to the fact that the average person is ill-at-ease in the political environment. Richardson's study found that many Japanese feel personally inadequate and hesitate to get involved for this reason. A more accurate explanation may be that norms regulating personal behavior in Japan do not stress self-assertiveness,[14] and active involvement in political affairs is somewhat denigrated.

In a perceptive study written in 1976, Tsurutani suggests that the disaffection of the Japanese voter is a symptom of the development of post-industrial politics. The politics of the industrial society, which is largely distributive in nature, is being replaced with more issue-oriented politics that is basically cross-stratal in nature. The problems of pollution, welfare, aging, and the like are not dealt with by the traditional political parties and therefore, according to Tsurutani, political activism by citizen movements instead of parties is becoming the norm. The average Japanese may feel insecure about traditional parties, but certain issues are attracting fuller participation in alternative forms of interest articulation.[15]

How do the Japanese vote, or why do certain voters vote repeatedly for certain candidates? Richardson has identified three categories of voting attitudes: "candidate perceptions, instrumental expectations, and party orientation." He found that Japanese voting is highly personal and that voting for a candidate was very important at local levels—less so at the national level. At the national level, "party" becomes an important determinant. There appear to be instrumental reasons behind the candidate or party choice, but Richardson found that "the main emphasis in voting attitudes in Japan is the candidate."[16] More recent data indicate that a large segment of the Japanese voting public refuses to be associated with any party, preferring to join the "floating vote," or independent vote as it is often referred to in the United States. A poll taken in November 1975, centering on Tokyo and Osaka, indicated that 48 percent of the respondents were not supporting any particular political party.[17] Thus, it is reasonable to assume that voters focus on individual candidates rather than parties.

Another aspect of Japanese political culture since World War II has been that voters in rural areas see a larger degree of instrumentalism in politics than do voters in the cities. However, rural voters are much more interested in their own politics than in politics on the national level. This "localism" can be explained by the social climate of the village, where greater frequency of contact and closer intimacy occur than in urban interactions. Rural voters also exhibit greater expectations from their vote than do urban dwellers. This is not surprising, if rural voters indeed see a greater degree of instrumentalism in politics; it seems natural that they would expect the elected representatives to follow through.[18]

The entire tendency of the rural voter in Japan to depend on elected officials may reflect the traditional norms of paternalism, or *on* and *giri*, the traditional Japanese concepts of reciprocity, more than is generally thought. In this case we might say the elected official receives the vote from the rural electorate and in return has an obligation of supporting or following through on election promises. If this is the explanation for higher rural satisfaction with the political system, it would demonstrate that there are still many traditional influences in Japanese political behavior.

This particular interpretation is strengthened by the fact that Richardson did find "duty" being cited frequently by rural voters as their reason for voting. He found that urban voters were more likely to cast their votes in response to party labels or the reputation of the candidate. Rural voters cast their votes on more pragmatic and personally immediate grounds.[19] With the growth of the nonparty or independent segment in the urban areas, urban voters may be more issue-oriented than in the past, which supports Tsurutani's theory of a Japan moving toward greater political involvement through groups other than parties. Richardson found that education played a most important role in influencing rural and urban political attitudes.[20] The more educated voters in urban areas were more likely to be attracted to issues and parties than the country voters, but the individual played the most important role.

Standard differences caused by age were also evident in Richardson's research. Generally, middle-aged voters were found to be more involved in politics than the very young or the very old. Young and middle-aged voters were drawn to the relevance of national politics; older voters were more involved in matters of local concern. Age also plays a very interesting role in the measure of positive acceptance of political acts. Richardson found that older voters who grew up during the prewar era remained socialized to an unquestioning acceptance of the decisions of political leaders.[21]

Because of the greater interest in national politics, both young and middle-aged individuals place comparatively greater emphasis on parties than on candidates—but this was only a comparative aspect, for generally, all Japanese voters place greater stress on candidates than on parties.[22]

The differences Richardson discovered are supported by recent data. For example, when asked "Do you support a specific political party?" 27 percent of the respondents in their twenties replied "yes," as compared to 31 percent of those in their thirties, 36 percent of those in their forties, 40 percent of those in their fifties, and 48 percent of those in their sixties.[23] Greater support for leaders according to age was also confirmed by polls taken in June and September of 1975. The questions asked concerned support for the Miki cabinet; the results are shown in Table 6.2.

In summary, Japanese political culture contains significant elements of *conservatism,* as well as a high degree of *formalism*—that is, a sizable majority of the electorate considers politics to be relevant, but only a small portion of these citizens would become actively engaged in the political process beyond participation in elections. Further, Japanese voters are *ambivalent* about the effectiveness of their vote. The feel that their vote can restrain politicians, but they are not sure how much of a positive force it can be. *Localism* has been

TABLE 6.2
Percentage Popular Support for Miki and Fukuda
Cabinets

Cabinet	Teens	20s	30s	40s	50s	60s
Miki						
June '75						
Support		22	27.6	39.3	47.5	50.5
Sept '75						
Support	31	35	38	49	62	63
Fukuda						
June '77						
Support		20	21	30	40	47

Source: Data reflected in the Tokyo Shimbun,
June 3, 1975, Sankei, September 2, 1975, and the
Asahi, June 5, 1977.

identified as a fourth major aspect of political life in Japan today.
The average voter is more interested in local politics than in national
issues. A fifth trait, *personalism*—a greater concern for the candidate
than for the party—rounds out the major characteristics of the
Japanese voter.[24]

Differences exist between urban and rural voters and voters of
different ages; there are also differences in aspects of instrumentalism
and levels of political involvement. In essence, Japan is similar to
other industrialized states. Trends toward dissatisfaction and
cynicism with politics are cause for concern; Tsurutani sees in these
trends developments that will be shared by all industrialized
democracies. As states change from industrial to postindustrial states,
political parties—the handmaidens of industrial-based clients—will
be slow or unable to meet the needs of the citizenry. In such cases
citizen movements will fill the void, manned principally by middle-
class and middle-aged enthusiasts. Such movements are too attractive
not to be co-opted by the existing political parties. It will be the
challenge of the conservatives to react and attract these groups. Since
Japan is basically conservative in orientation, the conservative party
must make efforts to regain public confidence if faith in the political
system is to be genuinely restored.

THE ELECTION PROCESS

How does a person gain the blessing of a party as a candidate in an election in Japan? Each party has a slightly different process; our discussion will concentrate on the system that has evolved in the LDP.

Technically, anyone who is a Japanese citizen can run for the lower house. All he or she need do is register a letter of intent and post a one-million-yen government bond at least four days before the election. However, there is quite a difference between what is technically possible and what is really possible, if the candidate wishes to be elected and sponsored by the Liberal Democratic Party.

There appear to be two primary paths to the national legislature in Tokyo. (These paths have been described in Gerald L. Curtis' book *Election Campaigning Japanese Style.*) One method is to go to Tokyo early in one's career as a bureaucrat, journalist, businessman, or lawyer to develop ties and influence with the men at the top. Once this is done, the transition into the party becomes a lateral move utilizing the established ties as stepping stones to success. The other path is to succeed at the local level, be recognized by local party officials, and be called to Tokyo later in one's career. Individuals within this group are local politicians, owners of regionally oriented businesses, and their representatives or lobbyists.[25]

Endorsement of a candidate in the LDP is based on a recommendation from the prefectual chapters to the national level. There is much informal "crosstalk," however, so that often prefectures nominate individuals recommended to them by Tokyo. This situation occurs most frequently when an individual who is known only at the national level seeks endorsement. In a sense, he uses his Tokyo base to introduce him at the local level. The reverse happens when local officials try to see that their candidate receives a favorable reception on the national level.

There are 130 election districts in Japan that return a total of 511 representatives to the lower house. Thus, it is primarily a multimember district system, with three to five members from almost every district. It is very difficult for a candidate to get himself added as a third LDP candidate in a district where the LDP has historically held two seats. The two incumbents and their affiliated faction leaders will fight the addition of a third candidate because it might possibly cost one of the incumbents his seat. (More will be said about factions in later chapters.)

Curtis identifies three typical strategies for a person aspiring to a Diet seat. Since there are no primary elections, and so much depends on the recommendations of incumbents, one strategy is to become closely associated with a Diet member. Working on the local level the candidate tries to further the cause of his patron in hope of a favorable political testament. With the best of luck, he may be able to inherit the political organization and support base of the incumbent.

There are obvious risks to such a strategy. A potential candidate might spend years waiting for his turn, only to be disappointed because of changing political circumstances. One of those circumstances could be a "second-generation" candidate; the idea of sons replacing fathers is looked upon as good strategy by the party to give the LDP a more youthful image. It has obvious merits as far as support groups are concerned, even if it does not contribute to the ideal image of representative democracy.

A second, and equally risky strategy would be to register and run in the election as an independent and if victorious at the polls, present one's incumbency to the party as reason enough for endorsement in coming elections. Of course, if the initial attempt at victory as an independent fails, the party leadership will consider the matter closed and congratulate themselves for not having backed a loser.

The third route identified by Curtis is the one most frequently used by former bureaucrats. They form close associations with national figures who can endorse a candidacy. This alliance overcomes incumbent reluctance based on fear of splitting the party vote. A variant would be for a candidate to become so strong at the local level that he could overcome an incumbent's opposition on his own—a difficult and rarely accomplished feat.

The Executive Board of the Prefecture LDP Chapter, consisting of approximately 100 prefectural assemblymen, and other party activists from the entire prefecture must choose between all potential candidates. This can be as contentious as a local church selecting a new minister in the United States, and usually involves the interplay of all local factions and interest groups of the various election districts in the prefecture.

Once the prefectural committee has selected certain candidates, a list of the endorsed persons goes to the Election Policy Committee of the National LDP. This committee consists of fifteen members: the LDP president, vice-president, secretary general, and twelve members chosen by the president of the LDP. (The twelve members are essentially the faction leaders or their representatives.) The number of candidates to be endorsed is established by the president and the secretary general. This is a critical decision, since too many candidates from the LDP in any one district could weaken all candidates and result in a no-win situation for the LDP. Therefore, the condition of the party must generally be taken into consideration as well as the politics of the specific districts. It is a difficult line to tread; desire to increase party strength in the Diet must be shrewdly balanced against political reality.

According to Curtis, the Election Policy Committee is guided in its deliberations by five principles:

1. endorse only those candidates who can win;
2. never endorse more candidates in a district than there are seats for that district;
3. endorse on the principle "incumbent first";
4. do not endorse persons being prosecuted for criminal offense; and
5. give serious consideration to Prefectural Chapter's recommendations.[26]

As the Election Policy Committee goes through the recommendations of the forty-seven prefectural chapters, it announces its decision in three lists. The easiest ones are announced first. A list of readily agreed-upon incumbents and candidates is issued first; the next two lists represent the outcome of hard bargaining and the realities of political struggle, faction leader against faction leader. Candidates are sometimes removed from the list of recommendations forwarded by the prefectural chapters if the national party officials feel dilution of LDP strength is a probability.

Once the candidates are identified by the party, an official announcement is made of the election date, always a Sunday, and the campaigning period. (Campaigning is limited to a hectic three to five weeks!)

There are other aspects of the Japanese system that distinguish it from the American free-for-all. For example, election posters with a picture, party name, and slogan are strictly limited as to number and size. Only minimal use of radio and television is permitted, and no telephone campaigns or parades are allowed.[27] The one exception to these limitations are sound trucks, which are allowed to roam the district with speaker volume "maxed-out." Inside a van the candidate or his assistant makes life particularly uncomfortable for all but the most deaf voters. Frequently, these trucks will take up positions in front of busy subway stations where the candidate, bedecked with a flower in his lapel, will try to look like a friend of the people.

As the election approaches, the candidate will try to obtain the biggest *Daruma* possible and go through the ceremony of painting in one eye. (The Daruma is a Buddhist doll with the eyes left unpainted. When a wish is made—in this case, success in the election—one eye is painted. If the wish comes true, the other eye is painted.) If the candidate wins shouts of *"banzai"* will echo throughout the halls. (*Banzai*, or "ten-thousand years" in this particular setting, would be equivalent to the British "hip, hip, hooray!")

The support base for a candidate will often depend on his locale, his party, and his own temperament. Since World War II the *koenkai* (or public support group) has been the traditional way to marshall and keep support. The *koenkai* is organized to give the citizens access to the candidate, and vice versa, and serves as a means of informing the candidate about the needs of his supporters. Even births or deaths in a *koenkai* member's family can be acknowledged in the appropriate manner by the Diet member. The *koenkai* may include youth groups, women's groups, and elderly supporters and serves as a social center on many occasions. Alternate names for these support groups, like cultural associations or educational study groups, are used so that the candidate or Diet member can address followers during the noncampaign periods without running afoul of the election law.

These support groups can sometimes be difficult to maintain in urban areas the size of Tokyo or Osaka, and in such regions politics tends to become oriented more toward issues. In any event, due to the existing multimember district system, it is essential for candidates from the larger parties to get their names before the public. Name recognition by the voter can mean the difference between success or failure, for in Japan votes tend to go to individuals rather than parties; this makes the *koenkai* even more necessary.

CHAPTER SEVEN

The Political Framework: Major Institutions

The constitution of Japan was promulgated in November 1946 and became effective six months later on May 3, 1947. The third of May is celebrated as *Kenpo Kinenbi* (Constitution Anniversary Day) and comes two days after the Emperor's Birthday and two days before Children's Day. This holiday season is known in Japan as "Golden Week" because of the extremely well-placed holidays. While the popularity of the basic law of Japan does not depend on its celebration during this period, the date of the celebration underlines the fact that the constitution finds its strength in the people.

The 1947 constitution reveals its difference from the Meiji constitution in its preamble, which introduces and legitimizes the doctrine of popular sovereignty:

> We, the Japanese people, acting through our duly elected representatives in the National Diet, determined that we shall secure for ourselves and our posterity the fruits of peaceful cooperation with all nations and the blessings of liberty throughout this land, and resolved that never again shall we be visited with the horrors of war through the action of government, do proclaim that sovereign power resides with the people and do firmly establish this Constitution. Government is a sacred trust of the people, the authority for which is derived from the people, the powers of which are exercised by the representatives of the people, and the benefits of which are enjoyed by the people.

In clear, unmistakable terms sovereignty is placed in the hands of the people and removed from the emperor, who was the fount of all power in the Meiji constitution. The role of the emperor is addressed in the first chapter of this rather brief document. He is made the "symbol of the State" but given no powers in relation to the government itself. Article 7 identifies certain perfunctory duties that the emperor is to perform for the people on advice of the cabinet. Such duties include, but are not limited to: "promulgation of . . . laws, cabinet orders and treaties; convocation of the Diet; dissolution of the House of Representatives; . . . awarding of honors; . . . receiving foreign ambassadors and ministers." In essence, the emperor is made a constitutional monarch similar to the British monarchy.

After the enunciation of the ceremonial functions of the emperor and imperial household there follows one of the most remarkable statements of intent ever to appear in a national constitution. Chapter II is entitled simply "Renunciation of War"; Article 9 reads:

> Aspiring sincerely to an international peace based on justice and order, the Japanese people forever renounce war as a sovereign right of the nation and the threat or use of force as a means of settling international disputes.
>
> In order to accomplish the aim of the preceding paragraph, land, sea, and air forces, as well as other war potential, will never be maintained. The right of belligerency of the state will not be recognized.

This article has tended to stir controversy within Japan because of the difficulty of conducting the national defense under such restrictions. The issue has not been settled and remains a point of contention about which more will be said later.

The British model of government is reflected again in the parliamentary system chosen for the roles of the legislative and executive branches of government. Specifically, the constitution places superior legislative power in the lower house (the House of Representatives), combines executive and administrative duties in a cabinet, and makes the cabinet responsible to the Diet. The judiciary reflects the American model, existing independently of the other branches and holding the right of judicial review.

More attention is given to the detailing of civil rights and duties of the people than to any other subject in the constitution. An admonition like the one in Article 25 that "all people shall have the right to maintain the minimum standards of wholesome and cultured living" may seem normative at first, but it is strikingly similar to our right to "life, liberty, and the pursuit of happiness" as presented in the Declaration of Independence. The concept of local autonomy is also introduced in the new basic law, and provisions are made for constitutional amendments. The constitution has not yet been amended, but there is good reason for this; it is extremely difficult to accomplish. Chapter IX states specifically that amendments are to be initiated by the Diet and require the concurrence of two-thirds of the membership of both houses. Once an amendment has been successfully introduced by the Diet, it then must go to the people for a special referendum in which a majority of all votes cast is required for approval of the measure.

Not all aspects of the constitution have been universally acclaimed by the Japanese body politic. For many years conservative forces have called for some revision of the constitution. Areas such as the right to national defense, the role of the emperor, and greater control over local governments have been singled out, as well as measures to change the amendment procedure itself. In 1956 a Constitutional Inquiry Commission was created by the Diet; the Socialists chose to boycott the commission. After extensive hearings, it reported its findings in 1964. It recommended revision of Article 9, but it did not deem any change in the emperor's role necessary.

The movement for constitutional revision is kept alive by splinter rightist organizations on the fringes of political legitimacy and by a few Liberal Democratic Diet members who address the subject with less and less frequency. For all practical purposes it is a moribund matter in the world of political reality.

Article 9 and its relation to the Japanese "Self-Defense Forces" has been of intermittent interest to the Japanese judiciary since 1947. In fact, on three occasions the question of the constitutionality of the defense forces has been presented to the courts. In the first case in 1952 no judgment was made because the court found no adversary, no "dispute between specific parties."[1] The so-called Sunakawa case of 1959 provided an adversary—and a bit of crisis—when a district court judge found the U.S.-Japan Security Treaty unconstitutional under Article 9. The Supreme Court subsequently held that a treaty was not subject to review once the Diet and cabinet had endorsed it and that it fell "outside the right of judicial review . . . unless there is a clearly obvious unconstitutionality or invalidity."[2]

In the recent Naganuma case, a district judge in Sapporo found that the self-defense forces were based on unconstitutional laws and were therefore extralegal.[3] The decision sent shockwaves through the Japanese government before it was overturned in August 1976 by a

One of the ceremonial functions of the Emperor. Here the Emperor and Empress listen to New Year lectures at the Imperial Palace. (Source: *Japan*, Vol. XV, No. 1, Tokyo: Ministry of Foreign Affairs, 1977.)

higher court, which stressed the political nature of the question. Evidently the role of judicial review—having been a rather dormant aspect of the Japanese governmental system—is still in its formative stages.

The constitution remains basically a foreign (American) injection into the Japanese political scene, but defenders of the document point to the fact that it was debated in the Diet and altered before its promulgation. It may not be perfect, but the political parties of the Left stand resolutely in the way of any changes. They maintain that once a precedence for change is established, the protections and guarantees preventing a return to oligarchic rule will be placed in jeopardy. The LDP platform still "aims at establishing an independent constitution,"[4] but former Prime Minister Miki stated: "I have never thought of constitution revision to date."[5] It will, most likely, remain unamended for years to come.

THE EMPEROR

The emperor of Japan is the "symbol of the state and of the unity of the people." In essence, his role is similar to that of other constitutional monarchs who perform those duties we in the United States often associate with the chief-of-state functions of the president. The emperor performs ceremonial duties, receives ambassadors, promulgates laws and treaties, announces certain lists of national award winners, and appoints the prime minister and chief judge of the Supreme Court. All these acts he does with the advice and approval of the cabinet, and, though he may be doing functions analagous to those of a chief of state, he is nevertheless the "symbol of the state" and nothing more. His position is somewhat weaker than that of the British monarch because there are no provisions for making his political opinion known to the cabinet, even superficially.

The emperor himself is subject to the Imperial House Law of 1947. Under its provisions only a male heir may succeed to the throne. An Imperial Household Conference or Council sets basic policy for the imperial household. This council is made up of elected officials from the Diet and judiciary plus other representatives of the imperial family and Imperial Household Agency. The Imperial Household Agency is part of the prime minister's office.

The emperor provides the stability and unity necessary for a nation to continue its identity with the past as it seeks the future. He acts on behalf of the entire nation, representing people from all walks of life as he takes part in official functions. One of the most successful endeavors was Emperor Hirohito's visit to the United States in October 1975. According to various public opinion polls, from 63 to 68 percent of all respondents thought the visit was "good" and "of service for making U.S.-Japan friendly relations still closer."[6] His visit to the United States was so successful that Japanese newspapers began to question why "the people have no memory of direct contact with the emperor" except for a short time after World War II.[7] Such pressures led to a formal press conference with the emperor and empress on October 31, 1975, that was generally assessed in a positive manner. One account noted that "from the emperor's attitude of speaking falteringly, choosing his words carefully, the people must have sensed anew a charming humanity."[8] Not everyone endorses the current role of the emperor, however. The Japanese Communist Party's platform calls for an end to the emperor system.[9]

Of frequent interest is the possibility that the emperor might abdicate in favor of his oldest son, Prince Akihito. It appears, however, that the current emperor will not consider this option because it does not appear in the constitution. He intends to serve out his natural reign, after which his son, born in 1933, will succeed him in the usual fashion.[10]

THE NATIONAL DIET

The National Diet is a bicameral body that consists of the *Sangi-in* (House of Councillors) and the *Shugi-in* (House of Representatives).

The National Diet Building—heart of the Japanese representative system. (Source: *The Japan of Today*, Ministry of Foreign Affairs, 1976.)

Real power is located in the House of Representatives, but the House of Councillors shares some important roles with the lower house. Under the Public Offices Election Law, passed in July 1975, the lower house consists of 511 members. Members are elected from 130 multimember districts for a four-year term unless the lower house is dissolved earlier. The multimember districts are represented by three to five members each. There are some problems with these districts due to demographic changes that have occurred in Japan. Thus, some rural areas return three members to the Diet who each represent slightly more than 79,000 people, while some urban members represent approximately 395,000 apiece.[11] Electoral reform has been requested, but the reforms suggested so far seem to favor the major parties at the expense of the small. Thus, there is little likelihood of immediate reform.

The House of Councillors, in some respects, is similar to the U.S. Senate. That analogy must be made quite cautiously, but the 252 members do serve a specified term of six years, with one-half of the Councillors being elected every three years. One hundred of the Councillors are elected in nationwide constituencies; the remaining 152 are elected in prefectural constituencies or districts. The national constituency has been criticized primarily because of the inordinate expense of running a successful race on a nationwide basis. Reforms centering on proportional representation have been advanced, and will be discussed later in this book. The forty-seven prefectures are all assured of two members (another similarity to the U.S. Senate).

The House of Councillors cannot be dissolved; however, under Article 54 of the constitution, when dissolution of the lower house occurs, the upper house closes but may be recalled by the cabinet "in time of national emergency." All measures accomplished by an emergency session are subject to lower house confirmation within ten days of the next session or they become null and void. Emergency sessions have only occurred twice in the past. In 1952 one was called to nominate members for the Central Election Management Council, and in 1953 the upper house passed a provisional budget and other important measures after Prime Minister Yoshida called a member of the opposition a "fool" in the Diet and the cabinet resigned en masse.[12]

As mentioned previously, although the House of Representatives holds ultimate power, there are some items that require concurrence of the House of Councillors. For example, any constitutional amendment must have a positive vote from two-thirds of all members of each house. Furthermore, the cabinet is responsible to the Diet— not just the lower house—and legislative power is shared between both Houses, except for those measures covered by Article 61, budgets and treaties. "The decision of the House of Representatives shall be the decision of the Diet" in those matters. In regard to all other legislation, the lower house prevails over the upper house if it passes a bill by two-thirds of the members present.

Normal or ordinary sessions of the Diet last 150 days and must be convened "once per year." Sessions are convened in December and can be extended once.[13] An extraordinary session can be convened by the cabinet in an attempt to have the Diet consider particularly important bills left over from an ordinary session. Such a session can also be convened if one-fourth of either House votes for it. A third kind of Diet session—the special session—must be called "within thirty (30) days from the date of . . . (an) election."

The Diet Law provides for presiding officers in both Houses. They are not impartial in the British sense, but are charged with maintaining order, adjusting business, supervising administration, and representing their respective Houses.[14] They have the right, in the event of a tie vote, to cast the deciding ballot. As of January 1977 the president of the House of Councillors and the Speaker of the House of Representatives were both from the Liberal Democratic Party. The vice-president of the upper house was also LDP-oriented, but his counterpart in the lower house was from the Japan Socialist Party. Kono Kenzo, the President of the House of Councillors, severed his formal membership with the LDP on his own initiative.[15]

The internal business of each House is directed by the Diet Steering Committees generally composed of senior party officials. The various party Diet Strategy Committees form a position on bills before they are brought to the chambers for consideration in plenary session. The House Steering Committee then attempts to establish daily agendas and only if an impasse results is an appeal made to the Secretaries General of the political parties. If no progress is possible through this avenue, the heads of both Houses have the authority to establish an agenda.[16] Because these individuals are usually somewhat partisan— and likely to be members of the majority party—the desires of the prime minister are adhered to more often than not.[17]

The House Steering Committees have some similarity to the U.S. House Rules Committee, in that they decide what matters will be considered, when, and how long noncontroversial matters will be dealt with. All parties take part in creating the agenda, placing great emphasis on participatory decision making.[18]

It is when controversial matters appear that this friendly decision-making process breaks down. Officials resort to LDP majority rule, and charges of the tyranny of the majority are heard. On these occasions the decorum of the Diet collapses. However, the norm is cooperation rather than overt competition.

When the majority decides it must act, the opposition may resort to delaying actions. One of the most colorful ways a distraught Diet member can vent his unhappiness at being forced to vote on an issue he thinks has not been adequately discussed is to adopt the tactic of *gyuho senjutsu,* or "cow-walking." The use of this tactic varies slightly depending on the House. In the lower house the opposition votes first. As the clerk reads the roll, the representatives pick up their ballots (white chips for, blue chips against) and head for the receptacles on a raised dais. As they get to the box, they stop. The resulting traffic jam is not dispersed until LDP representatives create enough back-pressure to clear the aisle.[19] In the upper house the tactic takes a slightly different form because the opposition casts votes last. In this case, like actors from a Japanese No play, the representatives move to the ballot box one step at a time, as if walking on a path of robin's eggs. Reaching the ballot box and casting a vote become dilatory at worst, artistic at best. What is normally accomplished in fifteen minutes can take as long as three hours.[20]

There are other, more formal, parliamentary tactics for slowing progress when the opposition feels that adequate *hanashiai* (discussion) has not been permitted. In short, the Diet can be a most exciting and colorful place.

Committee Structure

The discussion on the Diet thus far has concentrated on the plenary sessions of the lower and upper houses, but as in several other national legislatures substantial work is done in committees. The Diet in Japan is no exception, and mirrors the U.S. system in this regard.

There are sixteen standing committees in each house of the Diet. They are: Cabinet; Local Administration; Judiciary; Foreign Affairs; Finance; Education; Social and Labor Affairs; Agriculture, Forestry and Fishery; Commerce and Industry; Transportation; Communications; Construction; Audit; Discipline; Budget; and the Diet Steering Committee. In the seventy-seventh regular Diet session of 1976 all standing committee chairmenships in the lower house were held by members of the LDP. For the most part they had been elected to the Diet four times (two had been elected five times and one ten times) and were senior LDP representatives.[21] In the same session, LDP members chaired the following committees in the Upper House: Cabinet; Local Administration; Foreign Affairs; Finance; Education; Agriculture, Forestry and Fishery; Commerce and Industry; Budget; and House Steering Committees. Japan Socialist Party members chaired the following Upper House committees: Audit; Construction; Social and Labor; Disciplinary; and Communications. The

Komeito chaired the Judicial Affairs and Transportation Committees.

Most of the standing committees were established to handle problems and issues that would be dealt with by government ministries of the same name, and a close relationship has been established between the government bureaucracies and the Diet committees. There are also special committees established at the beginning of each Diet session to address issues of more short-term interest. (Some, however, have amazingly long lives, and are reinstituted at the beginning of several Diets.) In 1977 the special committees consisted of: Okinawa and Northern Problems; Lockheed Problem; Price Policy; Public Offices Election Law Revision; Disasters Counter-measures; Traffic Safety Measures; Public Nuisances Control Measures and Environment Preservation; and Science and Technology Development. During the course of the year it was decided to establish another special committee dealing with defense matters. The name, appropriately, is the Defense Special Committee. The opposition parties generally provide more chairmen for the Special Committees than does the LDP.

All Diet members are obligated to have at least one committee assignment unless they are holding posts as members of the cabinet or are parliamentary vice-ministers.[22] The assignments are evidently not relished by Diet members unless they can secure a chairmanship. As indicated earlier, that is unlikely for newly elected members. The reason for such a dilatory attitude will become clearer as we examine the inner workings of the party system. At this point suffice it to say that because of party positions and the existence of party discipline, the Diet committees are not arenas for individual initiative, at least not within the LDP.

Factionalism pervades the Japanese political system and the balance that is so important to the creation of a government is reflected in the Diet chairmanship posts. In the 1976 Diet, the affiliation of standing committee chairmen in the lower house was as follows: Ohira faction, 4; Nakasone faction, 3; Tanaka faction, 1; Miki faction, 3; Mizuta faction, 2; Funada faction, 1; Fukada faction, 1; Shiina faction, 1. We will examine this interesting aspect of Japanese politics in more detail later on.

Each committee of the Diet is aided in its deliberations by one specialist and six to eight staff researchers. Specialists, who supervise the researchers, are usually drawn from the the ministry most closely associated with the work of the committee. They are senior bureaucrats and provide a vital link tying government ministries to

Prime Minister Fukuda's second cabinet. This is the traditonal photo taken on the steps of the Prime Minister's official residence. (Source: Information section, Embassy of Japan, 1978.)

the legislative process of the Diet.[23] See Figures 7.1 and 7.2 for a representation of the steps a bill follows from its introduction to its enactment as law.

The Diet has adopted a modified "Question Time" system from the British House of Commons. In open meetings of the Budget Committee (both upper and lower houses), where agendas have been previously coordinated between the appropriate steering and budget committees, questions can be addressed to cabinet ministers and other members of the government. Officials asked to be present at these question periods are required by law to appear. The sessions serve as invaluable forums for the opposition parties, and because they are frequently televised, they provide a measure of public information on Diet and governmental happenings.[24]

THE CABINET

Eleven articles of the 1947 constitution are devoted to matters relating to the cabinet. They specifically provide that the prime minister and the other ministers must be civilians, that a majority of the members must be chosen from the Diet, and that "the Prime Minister may remove the Ministers of State as he chooses."[25]

The last statement makes the prime minister appear to have a great deal more power than he actually does. Appointments to the cabinet are under a great number of constraints and restrictions that limit the prime minister's authority in actuality. We have not yet discussed the internal workings of the ruling Liberal Democratic Party, and it should be noted that the prime minister is the party president—or has been since 1955 when the party was formed—and owes his position to the formation of a successful coalition of various factions within the LDP. The number and size of factions in the party may change, but when choosing his cabinet, the prime minister must first and foremost reward the factions that supported him (mainstream factions) with appropriate cabinet posts. He must also make enough cabinet appointments from the other LDP factions that did not support him (anti-mainstream forces) to keep them from bolting the party. In his very perceptive account of the LDP, Nathaniel B. Thayer calls this kind of cabinet a "cabinet of strong men"—one with factional balance. If a prime minister finds himself in an exceedingly strong position, he can give all cabinet posts to the factions that supported him. This kind of cabinet has become known as a "one-lunged cabinet" and occurs less frequently than the "cabinet of strong men."[26]

FIGURE 7.1

FROM BILL TO LAW IN JAPAN

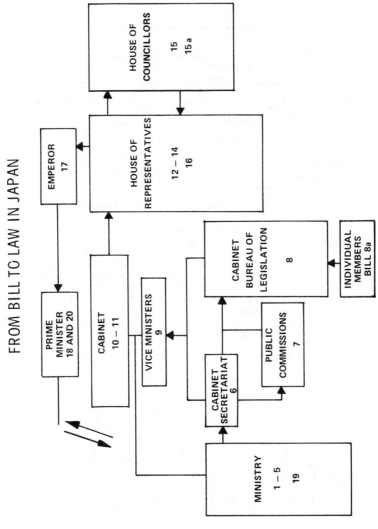

FIGURE 7.2

FROM BILL TO LAW IN JAPAN

Government-Sponsored Bill

Ministry

1. Section drafts
2. Bureau examines, revises
3. Documents Section of Secretariat examines, revises
4. Parliamentary Vice-Minister examines
5. Minister examines and refers
6. Cabinet Secretariat records, refers
7. Public Commissions to hold hearings, make recommendations (sometimes)
8. Cabinet Bureau of Legislation confers with representatives from one or more ministries - final drafting occurs.
9. Vice Ministers study bill
10. Cabinet receive bill from Deputy Chief of Secretariat
11. Discussion and decision passed to parliament
12. House of Representatives Speaker records bill, refers to proper committee
13. Assigned to Committee - ministers or deputies questioned; testimony heard. Committee makes its recommendation.
14. Voted on in House of Representatives
15. House of Councillors may assign to proper committee, but may have held joint meetings with House of Reps committee. House of Councillors has 60 days to act or House of Reps can vote the bill into law with 2/3 majority. Treaties and budgets become law in 30 days if passed by a House of Representative majority. A constitutional amendment requires 2/3's of all members of each house.
15a. Passage, amendment or defeat.
16. Speaker of House of Reps reports passage of bill to Emperior.
17. Emperor signs.
18. Prime Minister signs.
19. Ministers countersign.
20. Law published in Kampo (Official Gazette).

Individual Members Bill

8a. Bill must be endorsed by at least 20 other members in the House of Reps for non-money bills. If bill involves money, 50 members must endorse the private member's bill. In the House of Councillors a private bill must be endorsed by 10 other councillors unless it is a "money" bill. Money bills require 20 other councillors. Private bills follow the same path to law from step 8 as government sponsored bill.

Our thanks to Professor Allan B. Cole for providing the data reflected in this chart.

The constitution requires that a majority of the cabinet be members of the Diet. For all practical purposes this has come to mean lower house as opposed to upper house. In the first Miki cabinet of 1975, only two members were from the upper house. Ueki Mitsunori was in charge of Okinawa Development and Kimura Mutsuo was Minister of Transport. One individual, Nagai Michio, the Minister of Education, was not a Diet member at all, but a well-known educator.

The cabinet is basically made up of ministers with portfolios (those who head one of the twelve ministries) and ministers of state or individuals who head a department as yet lacking full ministerial status. The twelve ministries are the following: Agriculture and Forestry; Construction; Education; Finance; Foreign Affairs; Health and Welfare; Home Affairs; International Trade and Industry; Justice; Labor; Posts and Telecommunications; and Transport. Seven or eight state ministers head the remaining agencies and commissions, bringing the total cabinet to twenty ministers plus the prime minister. The state ministers oversee organizations such as the Administrative Management Agency, the Defense Agency, the Economic Planning Agency, the Environment Agency, the Hokkaido Development Agency, the National Land Utilization Commission, the Okinawa Development Agency, the Prime Minister's Office, and the Science and Technology Agency. There are twenty-four agencies in all, not including the prime minister's office.[27] The director for Cabinet Legislation, though not a state minister, is also considered part of the cabinet.

As there are obviously more posts than ministers, one person frequently fills more than one post. For example, in the first Tanaka cabinet of July 1972, the construction minister, Kimura Takeo, held four additional posts.[28] In 1975 Home Affairs Minister Fukuda Hajime was also the director general of the Hokkaido Development Agency.

According to Thayer, a Diet member usually does not become a cabinet member until he has been elected five times.[29] This figure will probably change, but cabinet rank is reserved for those who have shown the political power to deserve it. (Interestingly enough, the faction leaders are the ones who recommend Diet members to the prime minister for inclusion in the cabinet.) In the first Miki cabinet of 1975, only one person, Foreign Minister Miyazawa Kiichi, had less than five elections to his credit (he had three). Most had been elected more than five times.[30]

The lofty position of cabinet minister is much sought after by the average LDP Diet member. Serving in the government can be extremely useful for reelection purposes, especially if one of the four most prestigious posts can be secured—Foreign Affairs, Finance, Agriculture, or International Trade and Industry.[31] Diligence and patience is usually rewarded, for the average official life of a minister is only one year. The terrific turnover of ministers has led to the charge—not unjustified—that Japan mass produces her cabinet ministers. Imagine a one-year-period as head of a vast administrative department; continuity becomes a myth that ultimately favors the career bureaucrat.

The rapid cabinet turnover and almost yearly creation of new cabinets under the same prime minister has been seen as detrimental to Japanese foreign relations.[32] Japanese observers have lamented the situation, placing responsibility at the feet of the LDP system of intraparty factions. Of course generalization fails to account for the other impelling factors that cause frequent cabinet shuffles. For example, the constitution requires that a cabinet must resign: (1) if a no-confidence vote is passed; (2) after general elections for the lower house; and (3) when a new prime minister is selected. Political factors can also cause turmoil, as did the resignation of Prime Minister Tanaka. In any event, a number of factors contribute to the frequent maneuvering by ministers. This has tended to weaken the system, but not to an unacceptable degree.

What does the cabinet do? It prepares the annual budget and oversees the submission of legislation to the Diet, acting as a final screen between the LDP structure and the legislature. It sets foreign, economic, and general domestic policy and has considerable power as head of the extensive bureaucratic system. Collective responsibility is followed with the cabinet, and dissident voices are heard only within the confines of closed meetings or after resignation of a dissatisfied minister. In essence, the cabinet is responsible for guiding the ship of state. If the Diet finds the cabinet's course unacceptable, the cabinet may collapse in the wake of a no-confidence vote. After such a vote, the constitution stipulates that the cabinet must either resign or must dissolve the House of Representatives and call for new elections, which would also result in the formation of a new cabinet. As long as the LDP can maintain party discipline and a majority in the Diet such no-confidence votes are for speculation only.

A series of interdependencies exists between the Diet and the cabinet, but ultimately, due to its size and the availability of gross patronage, the cabinet with the prime minister at its head can be considered as the principal repository of political power in the Japanese system. How it is subject to further controls by the bureaucracy and other elements of the Japanese body politic will become clearer as we proceed.

THE JUDICIAL SYSTEM

The seven articles of the 1947 constitution that set forth the framework of the Japanese judiciary introduced the legal precepts of the Anglo-American rather than European tradition to Japan. In fact, Article 81 established the concept of judicial review, giving the Supreme Court the power to "determine the constitutionality of any law, order, regulation or official act."[33] Completely independent of the executive and legislative functions, the court system of post–World War II Japan is significantly different from that set up by the Meiji oligarchs.

The current judiciary is headed by the Supreme Court.[34] When sitting as the Judicial Assembly it is charged with the administrative responsibility of supervising the entire system and has access to funds in the national budget. The Supreme Court consists of fifteen justices, one of whom is the Chief Justice. The Chief Justice is appointed by the emperor after recommendation by the cabinet; the fourteen associate justices are appointed directly by the cabinet. Of special interest is the provision for popular review of these appointments. The original appointments are subject to voter approval in the following lower house general elections and at ten year intervals thereafter. Justices must retire at the age of seventy.

The Supreme Court divides itself into four bodies in order to better organize the work of the court. The Grand Bench consists of all fifteen justices with the chief justice presiding. A quorum is obtained by the presence of nine justices. The Grand Bench considers cases in which the constitutionality of laws, ordinances, regulations, or dispositions is being contested. To find for unconstitutionality, at least eight justices must concur.

Besides the Grand Bench, there are three petty benches known simply as the First, Second and Third Petty Benches. A petty bench consists of five judges (three are required for a quorum). They can issue decisions on constitutionality if the Grand Bench has provided a precedent. In practice the three benches have come to divide cases according to criminal, civil, and administrative areas. All cases are seen by the concerned petty bench before being passed on to the Grand Bench for consideration.

In addition to aspects of adjudication mentioned above, the court has responsibilities in the administration and training of personnel for the entire court system. When dealing with issues of general administrative policy, the court sits not as the Grand Bench, but as the Judicial Assembly. The actual administrative functions are carried out by the Secretariat General, which also provides judicial assistance to the court. As in the United States, the Supreme Court has become overburdened with cases and faces a continuous backlog.

Lower courts are organized into four general categories: high courts, district courts, summary courts, and family or domestic courts. There are no juries in the Japanese court system, and the courts function in either a collegiate manner or with single judges. High courts are collegiate, requiring three judges, but district and domestic courts can sit as either three-man collegiate or single-judge bodies. Summary courts are always single-judge courts. The number of judges is determined by specific law when severe penalties are involved or when appeals are being heard.

There are eight high courts. They serve as appellate courts except in the case of insurrection when they are the court of original jurisdiction.

Next in importance are the fifty district courts located, for all practical purposes, on a prefectural basis throughout Japan (Hokkaido has four). These are the courts of first instance for major crimes like grand larceny and theft.

Five hundred and seventy courts handle minor offenses, misdemeanors, and crimes involving claims of less than an established sum. No prison sentences are given by this level of jurisdiction, since it handles only minor cases.

A court system unique to Japan is the family or domestic court system. There are 50 courts with 235 branches. Seventy-eight of these branches are collegiate courts and 157 are single-judge courts. They handle such things as family disputes and the protection of juveniles, including crimes by adults against juveniles.

Trials must be conducted open to public scrutiny unless the nature of the case is unanimously adjudged by the court to be dangerous to public order or morals. However, all issues of a political nature related to the press or involving the constitutionally generated rights of individuals must be conducted in public.

With the introduction of common law principles, the overall impact of Anglo-American legal tradition has been made manifest in Japan. The Supreme Court has not taken the same dynamic role that the U.S. Supreme Court takes in relation to the consitutionality of laws, but there are indications that young judges increasingly view the court's role to be more activist than in the past. The 1976 decision that declared the electoral system unconstitutional underscores this changing attitude.

LOCAL GOVERNMENT

Prior to World War II local government at the prefectural and municipal level followed the basic unitary models used by several European states. In Japan's case, the prefectural governors (a prefecture is roughly the same as a *départment* in France) were appointed officials. In fact, these individuals held posts considered to be at a level just below that of vice-minister. Their powers were extensive, including the determination of the prefectural budget and the right to override decisions of prefectural assemblies. As officials appointed by the emperor, the governors also acted as agents for several key ministries of the central government. The Home, Finance, and Education Ministries were three ministries that had extensive dealings on the local levels. Often these ministries would use the prefectural system to execute their directives; certain prerogatives over governors were enjoyed in order to insure adequate policy implementation.

Occupation authorities in the immediate post–World War II era sought to induce aspects of home rule into these lower levels of government, which the United States has long considered nurseries for democracy. Service at the lower levels, was thought to allow individuals to acquire the experience and capabilities to actively engage in higher levels of national government.

The new constitution provided for the election of "the chief executives of all local public entities." It also explicitly stated, "Regulations concerning organizations and operations of local public entities shall be fixed by law in accordance with the principle of *local autonomy.*"[35] However, although the constitution framers made those stipulations, they did *not* enumerate or specify responsibilities or powers to be reserved for the local entities. Rather, the court defined their rights as being within law or as "fixed by law." Such a law, the Local Autonomy Law, was passed in 1947, and the central government set out the responsibilities of local government. The following areas were left open to local government involvement:

1. maintenance of public order
2. protection of health and safety
3. establishment and management of parks, playgrounds, canals,

irrigation and drainage waterways, electric plants, water plants, sewerage systems, gas plants, public transportation systems, docks, piers, warehouses, schools, libraries museums, hospitals, asylums for the aged, jails, crematories, cemeteries, disaster relief, protection of minors, indigents and the inferior, land reclamation, identification and registration of inhabitants, and zoning
4. coordination of activities with other bodies
5. levying and collecting taxes[36]

The only difficulty with the long list of items for local attention is the fact that the central government, can, when it deems necessary, also enter these areas and pass laws that cannot be contravened by local levels.

In essence, we can consider the local governments as agents for the central government in designated areas and as autonomous—enacting their own measures—in other areas delegated to them. Due to the requirements of the central government and the inability to collect sufficient taxes, the local governments are forced to request grants-in-aid and subsidies from the Tokyo government. With each request comes the inevitable bureaucrat to oversee the program. Thus, even though "local autonomy" is incorporated into the constitution, the Japanese system is basically a unitary one, and because of several very compelling reasons—among which are size of the country, its homogeneity, and the thrust of its traditions—it will probably continue as such for some time to come.

THE BASIC ORGANIZATION

There are forty-seven prefectures in Japan. This level of government comes immediately under the central government. In 1977 there were prefectures for the metropolitan area of Tokyo (*Tokyo-To*) and the district (*do*) of Hokkaido, as well as two urban prefectures (*fu*), Osaka and Kyoto, and forty-three rural prefectures (*hen*), including Okinawa. Boundaries of these units are established by the central government in such a manner as to keep prefectural boundaries from overlapping in major urban areas. Certain major cities, called *seirie toshi*, or designated cities, have a special status removing them from prefectural oversight and control. To be so designated, the areas must have populations in excess of 500,000; most are over 1 million. These cities include: Tokyo, Kyoto, Osaka, Nagoya, Yokohama, Kobe, Kita Kyushu, Kawasaki, Sapporo, and Fukuoka.[37]

Each of the forty-seven prefectures has an elected governor and a unicameral assembly. The term of office for both is four years, but the executive is subject to votes of no-confidence by the assembly. For example, if two-thirds of an assembly is present and three-fourths vote no-confidence, the governor must step down, or, more likely, dissolve the assembly and call for new elections. When the newly elected assembly returns, if a simple majority still votes no-confidence, the governor must resign.

The governor must not only please his assembly, but must also satisfy the requirements of the central government ministries that are involved in local affairs. If he proves incapable of complying or refuses to comply with the directives of the central government, he may be removed from office by the prime minister.

In addition to the forty-seven prefectures there are the municipal governments. This level of local government is known as the *shichoson* level. The name comes from the Japanese for cities, towns, and villages, which make up this level of government. They all have an elected head—a mayor—who serves a four-year term with an elected council. The same kind of no-confidence relationship exists in the *shichoson* assemblies as in the prefectural assemblies. The basis for determining status is primarily population. Cities require a population over 50,000; towns over 30,000; and villages must be under 30,000.[38] Other determinants are percentage of "urban" inhabitants and the availability of public facilities.

Only the national Diet can pass laws. All the other assemblies, from prefecture to the smallest village, can only enact "by-laws" on subjects permitted by the Local Autonomy Law.[39]

As we have seen, then, the local autonomy of the Japanese system is somewhat constrained. Financing has been one of the primary reasons for local government dependence on the central government, and in this respect we can see similarities with the American system. The local level's inability to tax adequately leaves real power in the hands of the central government ministries, which establish standards that must be met. In many cases, the only way these standards can be realized is to use money provided by the central government. Professor Frank Langdon points out that approximately "80 percent of local administration operates in behalf of the central authorities; this state obviously leaves little leeway for independent local action."[40] A general trend toward consolidation of villages and towns has also added to the loss of local autonomy. These mergers have been justified in the name of economy, which is probably fair, but they have had the effect of removing village assemblies from some areas.

CHAPTER EIGHT

Political Dynamics

POSTWAR RECREATION OF POLITICAL PARTIES AND THEIR SUBSEQUENT DEVELOPMENT

As discussed in Chapter 5, the prewar parties, though unsuccessful in establishing themselves as part of the decision-making structure, did much to lay the foundation for their successors in postwar Japan. In the prewar milieu, the constitutional deck was stacked against them. Various weaknesses in the Meiji constitution permitted the oligarchs or their immediate organizational successors to keep the parties in the public eye but out of the true councils of decision making. If the parties were impotent, the very visibility that they had was useful in producing an expectation on the part of the people that parties did have a legitimate role in government. After the war, this expectation was fulfilled, and the parties became not only symbolic, but substantive participants in government.

Political parties reemerged after the war with the help of the Occupation during autumn of 1945. After the period of dormancy enforced by the IRAA, they returned to life demonstrating many of the characteristics that had made them inefficient during the Taisho and early Showa periods. For example, more than sixteen of the revived parties initially vied for the conservative label.[1] However, this time there was a difference: the new constitution established the principle of legislative supremacy, and the parties were offered an opportunity to be primary actors. The cabinet answered to the Diet.

The upper house no longer contained peers or other appointees, but consisted of elected representatives as in the lower house. The lower house was given clear superiority over the upper house in fiscal matters and—when permitted by the Occupation—review of treaties entered into by the executive. In short, the political parties were no longer to be on the periphery of the Japanese government; they were to form its core.

One feature that characterized party organizations immediately after the war was the absence of many former politicians who were subject to the purge that lasted in varying degrees until 1951. This void was largely filled by bureaucrats-turned-politicians, and some of the more interesting political battles fought during this period were intraparty struggles between factions as depurged politicians returned and attempted to regain their former prominence.

The first party to reemerge after the war was the Japan Communist Party. It was followed in rapid succession by the Japan Socialist Party, Japan Liberal Party, and Japan Progressive Party.

The Japan Communist Party (JCP)

The Japanese Communist Party began its initial postwar activities on October 10, 1945, only six days after most of its leadership were released from prison by Occupation authorities. A call to action appearing in the party newspaper, *Akahata (Red Flag)*, stressed that the new "democratic revolution would attempt . . . to overthrow the Emperor system, . . . eliminate militarism, and police politics, . . . confiscate 'parasitic' and idle land, . . . establish free labor unions, . . . abolish the old security laws, . . . remove the military and bureaucratic cliques from power, and . . . set up a national assembly based on universal suffrage for all Japanese over eighteen years of age."[2] This appeal was accompanied by polemical attacks on both the Socialist and Liberal Parties: the Socialists were denounced as "the Social Emperor Party" and the Liberals were called "lackeys of the monopoly capitalists."[3] The party itself advocated peaceful revolution through the vehicle of a united front.[4] The early JCP policy of cooperation with the U.S. Occupation in order to strengthen the party was continued until 1950-51. By that time, the domestic political environment had shifted decidedly to the right, the cold war had settled in internationally, and the Americans were denounced as having brought the Japanese people "only chains and slavery."[5] The concept of a peaceful revolution was declared a deception, and the JCP took a decided turn to the violent left.[6]

The Japan Socialist Party (JSP) and
The Democratic Socialist Party (DSP)

On November 2, 1945, the Nihon Shakaito, or Socialist Party of Japan, was formed. Preferring not to incur the wrath of the Occupation, the founders chose to use the name Social Democratic Party of Japan as the official English translation. The action program or platform, announced by the newly formed party included only three aims: "democracy, socialism, and eternal peace."[7] It would have been appropriate to identify these objectives as goals for JSP internal affairs, for as events soon revealed, the socialists were in need of eternal peace within their own party. The JSP did not begin quiescently, nor has its history been tranquil. Basically, during the early postwar years, the right wing of the party maintained control over policy in the face of a vociferous left wing. During this period, the right wing cautiously led the party away from the inviting but dangerous "shoals of JCP collaboration."

In the first postwar election of April 1946, the socialists campaigned on a simple slogan of "socialism or capitalism" and did well at the polls. By April 1947 the socialists had obtained a plurality in the lower house. Shortly after this election, the socialists formed a government with conservative forces, agreeing that left wing members would not be eligible for cabinet posts. Such tactics did not help the cause of party unity, but they did result in Socialist leadership of the first government formed under the new constitution. Katayama Tetsu became the prime minister.

Katayama, in late 1947, dismissed his own minister of agriculture and forestry, a left-socialist, causing the right and left wings of the party to become more polarized. After the fall of the Katayama government, which had the unfortunate happenstance to preside over Japan during the worst inflationary period to date, the socialists agreed to work with the conservatives and formed a government under the leadership of Ashida Hitoshi of the Japan Democratic Party.[8] This coalition was formed in the face of increasing opposition from left wing socialists. It was clear to the nation that factionalism was reducing the organizational vitality of the party, and in the 1949 election for the lower house the socialists fell from 143 seats to 48.

Internal debate over "correct" policy options continued to mar the party until finally in 1951 the right and left wings split over what policy to follow on the peace treaty and the U.S.-Japan Security Treaty. The left wing opposed both treaties; the right wing favored the peace treaty but opposed the security treaty.

The left- and right-wing socialists maintained separate parties until 1955. In the election of that year they campaigned on identical platforms, and after winning one seat more than one-third of the lower house total, the socialists reunited.

This unity lasted until 1959 when the two wings split apart once again, never-as-yet to return. Right-wing leader Nishio Suehiro, citing JSP subservience to radical labor demands, led thirty-three Diet members out of the JSP to form the Democratic Socialist Party. Reasons for this parting of the ways were many. The primary reasons, however, seemed to be arguments over ideology and socialist losses in the 1959 election. It appeared that mass appeal had waned. The nature of the party, the identity of the socialist revolution, interaction with the JCP, and foreign policy issues—especially the security treaty issue—were also factors in the separation.

Since 1959 the right-wing DSP has tended to move toward more centrist positions on issues; the JSP, the larger of the two parties, has remained more ideologically committed to the rhetoric of class struggle and close association with the largest labor federation, Sohyo. The DSP has offered a moderate socialist alternative and also has attracted certain union support to its banner, principally the labor federation Domei.

The Conservatives: The Japan Liberal Party
and the Japan Progressive Party

Successor to the Seiyukai of pre–World War II days, the Liberal Party, was formed on November 9, 1945, by Hatoyama Ichiro. In the same month former Minseito members joined with one faction of the Seiyukai and organized the Progressive Party. The Liberal Party espoused continuation of the emperor system and retention of an updated Confucian ethic; the Progressives were oriented toward reformed capitalism and widened social welfare measures.[9]

Initial election results in 1946 gave the Liberal Party 24 percent of the vote and the Progressives 19 percent. Purges by Occupation authorities began in early 1946 and, as might be expected, affected the conservative parties rather severely. Hatoyama, leader of the Liberal Party, was purged and was succeeded by a former bureaucrat, Yoshida Shigeru. Yoshida served as prime minister until May 1947 when a period of coalition governments occurred, involving Katayama and Ashida Hitoshi. Yoshida and the Liberal Party returned to power in 1948 and remained the dominant conservative party until 1954. The Progressive Party had assumed a new name in 1947, the Japan

Democratic Party, hoping to project a new and winning image. By 1949, though, the Liberals had obtained 44 percent of the vote and the Democrats only 16 percent.[10]

Hatoyama, the former leader of the Liberal Party, now "de-purged," returned to challenge Yoshida for party leadership in 1952, and the conservatives fell into factional warfare. Under pressures from industrial supporters, the conservatives finally formed one party in 1955 after the Socialists temporarily had settled their internal struggles and presented a potential threat. The Liberal and Democratic Parties united under Ishibashi Tanzan as the Liberal Democratic Party (LDP). This conservative coalition remained intact until June of 1976 when a young Diet member, Kono Yohei, led a secession of six members to form the New Liberal Club. The LDP has ruled Japan since November 15, 1955, and though it has been plagued by innumerable factional struggles and one successful "mutiny," the spectre of losing power has kept the conservatives together. In the face of a continuing decline in percentage of popular vote, it has become a party seeking internal reform and rejuvenation.

CONTEMPORARY POLITICAL PARTIES: PARTIES IN AN ERA OF CHANGE

The Liberal Democratic Party: The Ruling Party

Since 1955 and the beginning of governmental control by the LDP, it has been customary to call the Japanese party system a one-and-one-half party system. This is testimony to the strength of the LDP and the collective weakness of the opposition parties.

Party structure. The Liberal Democratic Party is headed by a president who becomes prime minister by action of the LDP members in the Diet. Inasmuch as the LDP has been the majority party since 1955, the vote to elect the prime minister has been pro forma. However, the election for president can be very exciting and is far from predictable. Until 1977, elections for the top party post occurred at a national party conference at which each LDP Diet member had one vote. A delegate from each of the party's forty-seven prefectural federations was also enfranchised bringing the number of total electors to approximately 500.[11] The vote, taken by secret ballot, was closely tied to the party factions. Faction leaders directed their followers to support a particular candidate.

The president has the power that comes with being the chief executive of the government, but there are other party positions that are important because of their influence over the LDP itself.

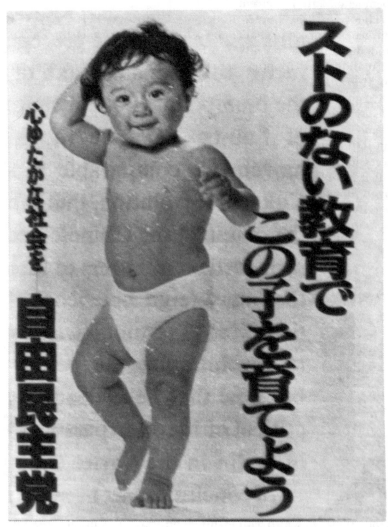

An election poster for the Liberal Democratic Party. The appeal on the right of the picture says: "Bring up this child with a strike-free education." The notation on the left says: "For a society with heart—Liberal Democratic Party."

Following the president of the party in order of importance is the secretary general, and the chairmen of the Executive Council and the Policy Affairs Research Council. At times there is also a party vice-president. The secretary general is, for all practical purposes, the primary executive in the day-to-day running of the party. He has a great deal of power over party finances and appointments to party and Diet posts. Depending on the individual, this position can be used to increase the incumbent's chances for president and prime minister. The chairmen of the Executive Council and Policy Affairs Research Council have considerable influence over party policy and are usually very senior members of the LDP who have been elected some ten or more times to the Diet.

The situation does not, however, approach "bossism." There are many restraints on party leaders. Both the secretary general and the president rely on a factional alliance of party leaders who demand proportionate shares of party posts, party contributions, and input into party policy as the "price" for their continued support.

Although the party is fairly well organized at the national level, until 1977 it lacked substance at the base. The LDP was not a popularist-oriented organization. It had offices in the prefectures and districts away from Tokyo, but the support base that existed (*koenkai*) was oriented more toward individual Diet members or candidates than toward the party as such. Indeed, the LDP ruled in conjunction with the Japanese leadership triad, business and bureaucracy, and paid little attention to popular support. Events of 1977 may have significantly altered this stance.

Factionalism. The party demands strict discipline on votes in the Diet, but the parliamentary party—those members actually elected to the Diet—still has to deal with factionalism. Much criticism of the LDP, warranted or not, is aimed at the role played by factions in party organization. Diet member factions have as many as ninety or more members. The factions are based not on ideological differences, but on a relationship between leader and members that is closely akin to financial dependence.

By their very existence and efficiency the factions spared the party the trouble of developing a monolithic party organization. Indeed, the dynamics of Japanese politics since 1955 has been centered in the intraparty factional struggles of the LDP. Major factions have a membership of forty or more, and the possible movement of Diet members from one faction to another makes the political world buzz with excitement. LDP factional strength as it existed just prior to the 1976 elections is shown in Table 8.1.

TABLE 8.1
Liberal Democratic Party Factions (Prior to the
1976 Elections)

Faction	Total	Number of Members Lower House	Upper House
Tanaka	92	47	45
Fukuda	82	55	27
Ohira	65	42	23
Miki	45	37	8
Nakasone	43	37	6
Shiina	20	17	3
Mizuta	14	13	1
Funada	12	8	4
Ishii	8	8	0
No Faction	24	15	9

Nathaniel B. Thayer, in his classic *How the Conservatives Rule Japan,* has detailed the character of LDP factions, stressing the importance of the faction leader's relationship to his followers. The traditional *on-giri* reciprocal relationship is formed between leader and followers, and has as its core essential duties performed by the factions such as providing money, choosing the party president, determining party and governmental posts, aiding candidates in elections, and satisfying psychological needs of the Dietmen.[12] Factions also act as the means for an individual to obtain official party sponsorship or endorsement to run as an LDP candidate in elections. Paramount to the existence of factions is the average Diet member's desperate need for financial aid. The faction leader is able to provide financial assistance through access to huge sums of extragovernmental money. He distributes funds to followers, and, in return, receives a degree of fidelity any Western political whip would envy.

Party Financing. One paradox has existed in Japan for years. Constituents expect almost personal attention from their Diet representatives. Flowers for the opening of new stores, weddings, and funerals, and other such incidentals are expected whenever the occasion warrants. These expectations place a grave financial burden on Diet members that far exceeds normal government pay. When

TABLE 8.2
Funds Contributed to the Major Political Parties (In
millions of Yen)

Date	LDP	JSP	JCP	DSP	Komeito
1960	1890	219	207	186	---
1965	3382	260	1271	120	728
1974	18879	1134	10074	856	4956
1975	11493	1714	11958	779	6536

SOURCE: Kishimoto, p. 75.
NOTE: In 1975 there were about 300 yen to the dollar.

such daily expenses are added to organizational and reelection costs—
which approached $560,000 per member in the 1974 election—the
ordinary representative, even on a salary of approximately $5200 per
month, is living beyond his means. Thus, dependence on the faction
leader who has access to money from his patrons in business has
become the norm.

Table 8.2 indicates the large contributions the various parties were
handling up to 1975, and these were only the funds reported. Sub-rosa
monies would undoubtedly inflate these figures considerably. Also
note that the major fund raiser in 1975 was the Japan Communist
Party.

The Election Control Law of 1975, which in its revised form
became effective in January 1976, has placed very definite limits on
contributions from individuals and organizations to political parties
and affiliated support groups. An individual, for example, is limited
to a total of 20 million yen per year to parties and another 10 million
to factions, or koenkai. Corporations, unions, and the like are
constrained to a maximum determined by their size. However, the
figures run from a low of 7.5 million yen to a high of 100 million yen
for the giants of Japanese industry and labor. Contributions from
these kinds of groups are also limited to "other political associations"; the spectrum runs from 3.75 million yen to 50 million yen.[13]
Factions and individuals can receive a maximum of 1.5 million yen
from any one donor, and all donations of 10,000 million yen or more
must be made in public.[14]

The strict controls on financial contributions plus the backlash
arising from the Tanaka and Lockheed scandals, have had a

measurable impact on the ability of the LDP faction leaders to obtain the large sums necessary for business-as-usual. A lack of funds was reported as the LDP prepared its war chest for the summer 1977 upper house elections.[15] Coupled with the reluctance of donors to keep the funds flowing at the old rate the new law has had a significant effect.

Policy Formulation. Factions may play an important role in determining the power structure of the party, but when it comes to policy formulation and internal decision making, they have less of an impact. Factions in the LDP are organized not for ideological purposes but for very pragmatic reasons relating to financing and controlling leadership positions. When it comes to policy formulation, the LDP Diet member tends to associate with different groups on an issue-by-issue basis. (At times superfactional discussion groups are created to meet Diet members' need for association with individuals of shared ideological persuasion.) How then does the party arrive at agreed-upon positions that can be presented to the Diet as a proposed legislative program?

The Organization of the Decision-making Process in the LDP. The LDP decision-making structure is multitiered, as illustrated in Figure 8.1. The Policy Affairs Research Council (PARC), with its numerous commissions and committees, is on the bottom level. Each Diet member must belong to one of the commissions or committees. There are fifteen main areas of concentration. The actual councils often parallel the organization found in the governmental ministries and cover such subjects as foreign policy and science and technology. To maximize efficiency several committees with overlapping jurisdiction will often meet jointly to discuss subjects of common concern. It is at this level that ideals and policy are thrashed out. Individual Diet members debate the issues and carefully consider expert testimony from representatives of the various ministries and businesses. Gradually consensus is achieved, and proposed legislation is sent up to the next layer for consideration.

Once a basic position has been worked out through *hanashiai* (or conversation), it is forwarded to the Deliberation Commission, which consists of sixteen to twenty members carefully selected to insure knowledgeable individuals and factional balance. From here, the proposal is passed on to the five PARC vice-chairmen and then to the chairman.[16]

Once policy is formulated by PARC it is recommended to the

FIGURE 8.1
Policy Formulation Structure in the LDP

CABINET

EXECUTIVE COUNCIL
34 Members

CHAIRMAN
Policy Affairs Research Council

VICE CHAIRMEN
Policy Affairs Research Council
5 Members

DELIBERATION COMMISSION
16-20 Members

POLICY AFFAIRS RESEARCH COUNCIL
LDP Members
15 Areas of
Concentration: Committee and
sub-committee structure.

Note: The process is upward.

Executive Council of the LDP. This body has members from the upper house and lower house, and takes into consideration the geographical area represented by a Diet member. Total membership is around thirty-four, with eight members appointed by the party president. Since all party policy goes through the Executive Council prior to submission to the cabinet for consideration by the Diet, it is often seen as the last point of appeal within the LDP for those who oppose a proposal.

The entire system is permeated by the spirit and reality of consensus. Not until most members are satisfied with a measure under consideration does it move to the next level. This requires a great deal of time but it insures that practically all members are satisfied that their views are heard and, most often, heeded. Rarely does one of the higher levels of deliberation reject a proposal from a subordinate level.

LDP Party Platform. Besides being conservative and committed to the capitalist system, the Liberal Democratic Party lacks a strong ideological commitment and often tends to be extremely pragmatic, responding to developing issues as do the "umbrella" parties in the United States. The election pledges made just prior to the general election in November 1976 are representative of a typical election platform. The party promised: elimination of party factions; reform of the election process for party president; creation of an election system that would reduce campaign expenditures; creation of a social security system; better education, labor conditions, and housing through a "life-cycle plan"; efforts to reduce taxes; and a total review of the tax system. In addition, the LDP pledged maintenance of the U.S.-Japan Security Treaty, conclusion of the Japan-China Peace and Friendship Treaty, increased aid to developing nations, and an improved defense posture. Because the party was under intense criticism in the wake of the Lockheed scandal, the platform also contained frequent reference to ethics and called for a "fresh party reformation."[17]

Campaigning on these issues and its record of success and stability, the party did relatively well in the 1976-77 elections, in spite of forebodings to the contrary. LDP strength after the 1976 lower house elections and the 1977 upper house elections is shown in Tables 8.3 and 8.4 respectively. The tables demonstrate the gradual decline in percentage of the vote being won by the LDP. With the advent of the New Liberal Club that trend should continue, but the overall vote for the conservative parties should remain strong.

TABLE 8.3
1976 Lower House Elections

Party	Seats	% of vote	Total Votes (In millions)
LDP	249	41.7	23.6
JSP	123	21	11.7
CGP	55	11	6.2
DSP	29	6	3.5
NLC	17	4	2.4
JCP	17	10	5.9
IND	21	6	3.2

TABLE 8.4
1977 Upper House Elections

Party	Local Constituency	% of vote	National Constituency	% of vote	Total	New Upper House Composition
LDP	45	39.5	18	35.8	63	124 (+3)*
JSP	17	25.9	10	17.4	27	56
CGP	5	6.2	9	14.2	14	28
JCP	2	9.9	3	8.4	5	16
DSP	2	4.5	4	6.7	6	11
NLC	2	5.7	1	3.9	3	4 (+1)
Minor	1	3.5	2	6.2	3	3 (−1)
Ind	2	4.8	3	7.4	5	9 (−3)
Vac						1
TOTAL	76	100.0	50	100.0	126	252

*New Upper House strengths demonstrate the independents and other small party
members that changed parties after the election.

The 1977 Reforms. The accumulated effects of years of political power are beginning to take their toll on the LDP. Events like the revelation in late 1974 of financial misdealings by former Prime Minister Tanaka Kakuei[18] and the gradual unfolding of the Lockheed scandal that began in February 1976,[19] contributed to a general lack of interest and faith in the political system and in the LDP specifically. It might be noted that the Lockheed scandal engendered popular involvement and revulsion similar to that experienced by the U.S. electorate during Watergate. Past success was also reflected in the LDP age profile. Candidates sponsored by the Party in the 1976 general election averaged 57.9 years of age, highest for all parties. In fact 51 LDP candidates were over 70 years of age.[20]

The problems of longevity and corruption were compounded by an economy that had not rebounded from the 1973 oil crisis as dynamically as many had hoped, and by increased pressures from external sources to moderate Japan's trade policies. The era of rapid economic growth had ended, and the LDP was searching for an alternative method to capture the imagination of voters.

In such a political environment, it was recognized that, short of a miracle, reform of the party was needed. A succession of party leaders spoke about the need for a commitment to reform, but were unable or unwilling to do more than assume reform posture. Having worked without success for change from within the LDP, Kono Yohei broke with the party in June 1976 to establish the New Liberal Club (NLC), a conservative alternative. At first, the LDP leadership thought it could deal with the secessionist group of six by nonsupport in the general election, but the newly formed group appealed to the people and scored initial gains that were impressive.

In the face of NLC success, discussions of reform in the Liberal Democratic Party became more meaningful. Areas most often raised as needing reform were those of party factions and the method for electing the party president. Under increasing pressure from the success of the NLC, and finding it difficult to attract suitable candidates for the 1977 upper house elections, the LDP convened in April 1977 and enacted reforms aimed at projecting a new image to the Japanese voter.

The 1977 reforms were certainly significant; prior to 1977 the most radical reform of the LDP occurred under Prime Minister Sato Eisaku in 1971, when the party president's term was lengthened from two to three years. The new reforms were announced by LDP President and Prime Minister Fukuda Takeo. If they turn out to be more than cosmetic efforts to placate voters, the nature of the Japanese political milieu could change dramatically, and the steady decline in LDP appeal at the polls could be reversed.

One of the reforms concerned the procedure for electing the party president. Hereafter, a primary election will be conducted in which all LDP members in good standing will be invited to participate. Nominees for the post of LDP president will be selected by a body of twenty Dietmen and will be submitted throughout the nation to party members in good standing for a vote. The top two candidates will then be voted on by the LDP parliamentary party, that is, only Diet members will vote. This change allows the old guard to have its say, but in the final analysis, it widens participation in the process; would the old guard overturn the wishes of the members?

Another important reform measure was aimed at eliminating all intraparty factions. These small groups, regarded as the "root of all evil" by some observers were supposedly disbanded.[21] Whether this will actually happen depends on the LDP's ability to provide Diet members with adequate funding to replace the funds now received from faction leaders. Factions have been central to the operation of the party, the election of the president, the selection of cabinet members, and the endorsement of candidates, and they are such a part of Japanese culture that any successful reform will affect all aspects of party life. An LDP spokesman commented on the past importance of factions, stating that: "The Diet members' activities have been at the ratio of six by factions and four by party hitherto"; as a result of faction dissolution, it is hoped that the ratio can be altered to "seven by the party and three by factions."[22]

Although the factions have been disbanded by the 1977 reforms, their complete dissolution is doubtful, given their past strength. In fact, most factions have reorganized as policy study groups with much the same leadership and personal association as before. The only major difference may be the leaders' inability to provide funds at the same level as in the past. It was reported in 1974 that candidates for the upper house election were obtaining money from the Tanaka Faction Headquarters in "paper bags containing bank notes amounting to tens of millions of yen . . . in a free and easy manner."[23] Such amounts were clearly illegal in 1974, but possible. In 1977 there was reluctance on the part of big business to make such sums available. Whether or not the funding will continue at present levels is a matter of pure speculation.

In her sociological study *Japanese Society* Chie Nakane pointed out quite succinctly that the desire to eliminate the factions (*habatsu*) has been a long-term goal. However, they would have to be replaced with interpersonal organizational forms that have so far been unsuccessful in Japan.[24] In fact no sooner were the factions disbanded than the "policy research councils" were formed encompassing former factional memberships.[25] Of these policy groups, some were newly created and others were older suprafactional policy groups that received a new lease on life. Whether these new bodies can replace the old factional form and become the "foundation of new conservative politics" remains to be seen.[26] Of the two reforms, the election of the party president carries the most significant democratic implications.

The *Tokyo Shimbun*, in some very good political reporting, has examined the nine policy groups that became active immediately after the April 1977 declaration. The groups included: the 36-member Hirakawa Society headed by Miyazawa Kiichi; the 55-member Free Society Research Association headed by Takeshita Noboru; the 125-member A-A Ken (Afro-Asian) headed by Kimura Toshio; the 25-member Yamanaka Group under the leadership of Yamanaka Sadanori; the 17-member Shimpu Group (New Breeze) headed by Kosaka Takusaburo; the 18-member Seirankai led by Nakao Eiichi; the 25-member Group 21 chaired by Nikaido Susumu; the 50-member Chiyoda Society headed by Kosaka Zentaro; and the 26-member Shinsei Club led by Fujinami Takao.

The groups' objectives varied quite a bit. For example, the Shinsei Club and the Free Society Research Association were reported as attempting to hasten the departure of the older leaders of the party in order to make way for those in their late fifties. Several groups saw fostering the political future of their respective leaders as their main purpose. The Hirakawa Society, the New Breeze Politics Research Society, and the Yamanaka Group were each hoping to see their leader assume the party presidency. The Afro-Asian Research Group (A-A Ken) and the Seirankai espoused foreign policy objectives at opposite ends of the political spectrum. One association, Group 21, hoped to lead the revival of conservative politics. The Chiyoda Society was primarily concerned with opposing Fukuda.

Practically all groups require dues from members, and little, if any, money has changed hands from leaders to members.[27] What, then, did the Diet members do in July 1977 when the upper house had elections? The "former factions established their respective 'illegal election measures headquarters' and actively supported their own candidates."[28] Obviously the system to distribute money has not changed significantly. Unless the financial needs of the candidates are met by some suprafactional or party source, the old-time factions will remain "sunk below the water surface, . . . but not collapsed."[29] To add emphasis to this interpretation, in mid-October 1977 the

Tanaka faction began holding what amounted to factional meetings of the old style under a new title, the New Over-All Policy Study Association.[30] With the resumption of factional activities by the Tanaka group, others will probably be close behind.

The nature of the Fukuda cabinet of November 1977 underlined the fact that factions cannot be eliminated by a simple declaration. In announcing the composition of his new cabinet, Prime Minister Fukuda revealed a perfectly balanced cabinet with his supporters (mainstream factions) getting seven portfolios, or ministerial positions, and his detractors (antimainstream factions) receiving the other five positions.

However, if we look at the new study groups rather than the old factions, some innovative functions can be found. Several groups, especially the New Breeze (Shimpu) and Group 21, have established contacts with middle-of-the-road parties, the Komeito and the Democratic Socialist Party. If and when a coalition is appropriate, some important working relationships will have been developed.

Another reform that came out of the New Liberal Club secession was more a change of emphasis. It called for seeking out younger candidates for the 1977 upper house elections. The increasing frequency of second generation candidates, sons replacing aging fathers, is also helping the LDP project a somewhat more youthful image.

In 1978 party officials have begun making final plans to implement establishment of a Liberal People's League. The concept entailed organizing LDP supporters to accomplish two goals. The new league is intended to strengthen the Party organization by giving it some grass roots, and it should ease the financial issue somewhat through its 1,000-yen membership fee.[31] Whether this will bring in enough money to actually fill the gap caused by the elimination of factions is very doubtful; it may not even be enough to elect one candidate. One observer of the Japanese political scene stated in an interview that these funds would just cover two lunches apiece and are insignificant.

It seems reasonable to predict that the role of Japanese factions will be reduced somewhat, but the small group is extremely important in Japan, as is the relationship between patron and client. The more meaningful reforms of 1977 are related to the manner of selecting the party president, infusing younger blood into the party, and slowing the overzealousness of some of the factions. The Liberal Peoples' League may play some small role in the collection of money, but their major role will be in the greater democratization of the party through participation in the election of the president.

Regardless of the outcome of the party reform movement, the LDP will likely remain the primary party well into the 1980s. One reason for this expectation is the development of the New Liberal Club. Votes at one time siphoned off by the progressive opposition parties as protest votes can now go to the NLC. In essence, its arrival on the scene may bring stability to the system that seemed to be eroding in the mid-1970s.

Although the LDP is not excessively committed to the importance of ideology, the opposition parties are. In fact, if one were to place blame for the failure of the opposition parties to approach parity with the LDP, it would rest on their inability to overcome their ideological differences and form effective coalitions. Little needs to be said about opposition party leadership structure, for all party organizations are relatively alike.

The Japan Socialist Party

"Always a bridesmaid, never the bride"—such might be the lament of the Japan Socialist Party since the 1955 union of the Liberal and Democratic Parties. Some observers have called the JSP the "one-third party" because it has reached that figure in Diet strength but has never surpassed it. In fact, the JSP has been experiencing a gradual decline in the percentage of the total vote, much like the LDP. The JSP reached its highest share of the vote in the 1963 election when its polling rate was 29 percent. After that the rate gradually declined to near 21 percent in 1976.[32]

Factions. Though centered around some key individual, JSP factions are more caught up with ideological differences than LDP factions. Although the number of factions and their leadership has varied, a left-right political dispute has been inherent in the JSP since its creation. Of course ideological groups can and do change beliefs frequently; our discussion here deals with current orientations.

The Shakaishugi Kyokai/Sakisaka faction and the Sangatsu-kai represent the most doctrinaire leftist groups in the JSP. They are not overly strong in the Diet, where they have influence with 40 to 50 members, and derive most of their strength from local assemblies and party activists. Of the total JSP membership of about 48,000, some 20,000 are Shakaishugi Kyokai members. In 1962 party convention rules were modified; JSP Diet members did not automatically become representatives at the JSP convention. Representation was based on one delegate for every 100 party members at the local level. Due to the

An election poster for the Japan Socialist Party. The statement to the right says: "Politics that rewards your efforts!" The name of the party appears at the bottom of the poster.

Shakaishugi Kyokai's superior organization at the grass-roots level, the conventions became more and more controlled by leftist groups. Because the party convention elects the Central Executive Committee of the party, that committee gradually became dominated by the extreme leftists also. Forty percent of the delegates belonged to the Shakaishugi Kyokai. This group, plus allies at the convention, provided the margin of control.[33] The Shakaishugi Kyokai is so orthodox when it comes to Marxist-Leninist doctrine that they have outflanked the more flexible Japan Communist Party and today are the group most closely following Marxist-Leninist tenets.[34]

The remaining factions—the Shakaishugi Kenkyu-kai (Socialist Research Group), the Gendai Shakaishugi Kenkyu-kai (Modern Socialism Study Group), Atarashii Nagare no Kai (New Current Group), and the Seisaku Kenkyu-kai (Policy Research Group)—are chiefly composed of Diet members, are more oriented toward China in the Sino-Soviet dispute, and advocate a moderate policy of gradual reform toward socialism within a parliamentary democratic framework.[35]

An intense, almost all-consuming, struggle has been joined between the Shakaishugi Kyokai and anti–Shakaishugi Kyokai forces. The moderate groups have joined forces to oppose the main program advanced by the leftists. The leftist factions wish to:

1. see their ideology, strongly Marxist-Leninist in orientation, become the only one for the party;
2. place greater emphasis on rigid party organization;
3. emphasize class orientation of the party with closer ties to labor unions;
4. form a united front with the Japan Communist Party;
5. place greater emphasis on ties with the Soviet Union;
6. stress theory within practical day-to-day activities;
7. make Diet members adhere more closely to policies emanating from the party convention; and
8. maintain their tightly controlled organizations, called "parties within the party" that parallel the party structure.[36]

The factional struggle has not ended. The Shakaishugi Kyokai was formed in 1951 and keeps growing through its intense organizational efforts at the local level. While the convention organization now reflects membership at the local level and Diet membership, its strength will continue to grow. As a direct result of this intraparty debate, three JSP Diet members left the party during its 1977 convention, and eventually formed a new party—United Social Democrats (USD).

The defections at the national convention were serious enough, but a far graver challenge to the socialist cause occurred in March 1977 when Eda Saburo, one-time vice-chairman of the JSP, seceded from the party and established a new group called the Socialist Citizens' League. His purpose was to create a new organization less dedicated to ideological purity that would catch the imagination of the floating, or noncommitted voters in Japan. By May 1977 Eda's group was prepared to enter six candidates in the upper house election of July 1977. This was seen as a serious move by the JSP because Eda was proposing close cooperation between his new group and the Komeito, or Clean Government Party.[37] However, on May 22, Eda died and the driving force behind the Socialist Citizens' League was removed. Eda's son stepped in and won impressively in the July election, but the initial hopes for the party did not materialize and it merged with the USD.

With members of the right wing continuing to leave the JSP, the need to resolve the ideological dispute is paramount. A center group does exist between the two extremes, but it has increasingly supported the Left. Until this situation can be resolved, the JSP will not even be the "one-third party" it once was.

A significant portion of the JSP support comes from the labor federation Sohyo, which gives the federation power to act as mediator in this struggle. Fifty-five percent of JSP Diet members in 1976 were former labor leaders. The union, concerned about the intraparty ideological dispute, has periodically prodded the party toward a more flexible structure, asking it to pay more attention to political challenges outside the party and less to ideological purity. In one party-union meeting in late May of 1977, JSP leaders promised the union leadership that they would try to eliminate internal factions.[38] This promise will be difficult to keep.

Policy Orientation. Although the JSP has not had the opportunity to run the government for thirty years, it has been effective in its role as the "loyal opposition." Some have accused the party of being anti-LDP, opposing whatever the LDP proposes. Such is not the case, for cooperation in the Diet is the norm. However, on some issues the JSP and the LDP are poles apart. It is on matters like foreign policy that the two diverge. The JSP, for example, advocates "unarmed neutrality" as Japan's defense policy.

As the strength of the LDP has declined, many opposition parties have called for creation of a coalition base, and renewed debate on the "correctness" of unarmed neutrality has arisen within the JSP. JSP Diet member Narazaki Yanosuke, in December 1975, revealed a plan for the gradual dissolution of the U.S.-Japan security structure with gradual reorganization of the Self Defense Forces. Although this position has not been accepted by the JSP majority, it marks a radical departure from the official position of abrogation of the U.S.-Japan treaty and disbandment of the security forces.[39]

JSP domestic policy is to "eliminate money-power politics and protect parliamentary democracy," oppose any military alliance, revise the anti-monopoly law, and correct social inequality.[40] Some of the pronouncements deal with time-sensitive or fleeting issues, but the policy commitments are representative of the historic JSP orientation.

The future success of the JSP will depend greatly on the outcome of the right-left ideological struggle and the coalition arrangements that can be realized with other opposition parties. If the left-wing members of the Shakaishugi Kyokai or Sangatsu-kai have their way, the JSP will propose a united front with the JCP. If the right-wing factions prevail, an alliance could be consummated with the two centrist parties, the DSP and the Komeito. If the LDP is at a significant crossroads in its history, so too is the JSP; the next several years may reveal whether the JSP is capable of running a government.

The organizational crisis of the JSP brought on by vitriolic factional struggles temporarily abated when JSP Chairman Narita Tomomi resigned and through astute maneuvering convinced Asukata Ichio, long-time mayor of Yokohama, to assume leadership of the party. Asukata, for his part, refused to become chairman as long as debilitating factional strife continued. He also demanded from the JSP leadership that party rules be altered so that he could be elected chairman by vote of all party members. Accordingly, on December 5, 1977, all factions disbanded, including the leftist oriented Sangatsu-kai, and shortly thereafter, by action of an extraordinary party convention, Asukata assumed the position of chairman.[41]

Present information does not indicate that anything has occurred to remove the deeply felt ideological differences that exist throughout the party. Factions have been disbanded, but, as with the LDP, that action can be considered superficial at best. Until the basic issues that have comprised the historic left-right split are resolved, party fissures will recur.

The Democratic Socialist Party

Originating with Nishio Suehiro's 1959 departure from the JSP, the Democratic Socialist Party has attempted to offer the Japanese electorate a nondoctrinaire socialist alternative. It has been said that the DSP exhibits a characteristic of realism minus dogmatism,[42] which has been the DSP's strong point. The party has been oriented toward bridging the gap between the LDP and the other *kakushin,* or revisionist, parties. The party's policies are moderate in tone, often leading to DSP-LDP collaboration in the Diet. In fact, so closely do the two parties cooperate that the DSP sometimes receives the title, "the other LDP."

In the general election of 1976, the DSP celebrated a victory of sorts by increasing Diet membership from nineteen to twenty-nine seats. The party convention of March 1977 reflected an air of satisfaction and success; however, the victory was not as substantial as the DSP might have desired. The DSP's share of the vote decreased from 6.98 percent of the total to 6.29 percent with 110,000 fewer votes being cast for the party. This decrease probably occurred due to a reduction in the number of candidates sponsored in the election. Only fifty-one candidates were nominated by the party, down from 65 in 1972.[43]

To strengthen its support base the DSP has worked to improve relations with the "moderate" labor union Domei and with several religious groups like the Rissho Kosei Kai and World Salvation Religion. These groups may be able to provide the increased support needed to develop the party's viability.[44]

The DSP looks to the future with optimism. Party leaders feel that fragmentation of the LDP will continue, and they hope that the more liberal LDP Miki faction will withdraw from the party and enter a coalition made up of the JSP, DSP, Komeito, NLC, and other LDP splinter groups.[45] The DSP believes that Japan will soon enter an era of coalition politics, and it plans to be ready when the time comes.

Komeito (Clean Government Party)

A comparative newcomer to the political scene, the Komeito first contested local elections in 1955 and moved up to national involvement by 1964. The first general election it participated in was in January 1967 when 25 of its candidates were elected to the lower house. Originally, the party was closely and openly associated with the Soka Gakkai (Value Creating Society) Buddhist movement, but the intimacy of the relationship detracted from the possibilities of the Komeito becoming a broadly based mass party. In mid-1970 a formal uncoupling of church and party occurred; however, little real difference has resulted in party membership or leadership, and in 1975 90 percent of its 110,000 members still belonged to the Soka Gakkai.[46]

As a result of the 1976 election, the party emerged as a national party. Until then it had primarily been strong in major cities; after the election it boasted of successes throughout Japan. Komeito's share of the vote rose from 8.46 percent to 10.91 percent, and the party's Diet membership increased from 30 to 55 seats. Interestingly enough, many youthful voters were drawn to the Komeito banner.[47] Party espousal of the "middle way" (*chudo*) and leader Takeiri Yoshikatsu's advocation of a three-party coalition involving the JSP, Komeito, and DSP may have increased its attractiveness.

Party Orientation. The policy program advocated by the Komeito includes "firm maintenance of the three Constitutional principles of peace, human rights, and democracy, . . . perfect equidistant neutral (foreign) policy based on the principle of lasting peace, . . . consolidation of the welfare of inhabitants through local autonomy and sound local finance, and . . . stabilization of commodity prices and the tiding over of the depression under such an economic structure as to give preference to the people's livelihood."[48] The Party's foreign policy incorporates the abrogation of the U.S.-Japan Security Treaty. However, it has included in its objectives the wording "abrogation of the . . . Treaty will not bring about new tension and confrontation between Japan and the U.S."[49]

The party has also come out against any electoral reform that would create a small constituency system for lower house elections or a system of proportional representation for the national constituency in the upper house. It is believed that such reforms would benefit the LDP and JSP at the expense of the smaller parties.[50]

In 1975 a surprise ten-year agreement was signed between the Soka Gakkai and the Japan Communist Party. Because the Soka Gakkai is the religious base for the Komeito, this ten-year political "nonaggression pact" came as a shock to the political world. It was soon made clear by Komeito Party Chairman Takeiri that cooperation with the JCP would not be possible as long as the JCP commitment toward the three principles of the constitution—peace, democracy, and human rights—was obscure. He made it clear that the agreement was made by the religious men of Soka Gakkai, not the political men of Komeito.[51]

Attempts by the party to enhance its national image and encourage growth are based on efforts to broaden the membership base and attract uncommitted voters. They can only be attracted if the party continues to popularize its image and subdue its Soka Gakkai association.

The Japan Communist Party

The Japan Communist Party gained respectability during the late 1960s and early 1970s as a party calling for ecological reforms and efficient government. Under the leadership of Miyamoto Kenji, it enjoyed years of increasing voter attractiveness, but in the 1976 election the party suffered a major setback. Although the party obtained 10 percent of the vote, the number of Diet members selected fell by twelve to a total of seventeen. There are several possible reasons for this sudden drop. The election law was revised in 1975 and some redistricting resulted. The law also imposed strict controls on leaflet distribution, a method of voter contact heavily used by the JCP.[52]

In his perceptive analysis of the 1976 election, Shiratori Rei identified other reasons for the JCP losses. The most striking factor was the JCP's apparent failure to maintain its percentage of the uncommitted voters. Previously it had attracted 26 percent of this sizable bloc. In the 1976 election it received only 20 percent of this group's vote. Shiratori suggests that one of the reasons for the loss might be the policy line currently advocated by Miyamoto and the JCP.

The Miyamoto Line was adopted on July 30, 1976, and reflected many of the innovative aspects of the Italian and French Communist parties. As early as 1973, however, movement toward a more moderate line had caused the phrase "dictatorship of the proletariat" to be replaced by "proletarian regency." In the Manifesto of Freedom and Democracy adopted in 1976, "Marxism-Leninism" was replaced by "scientific socialism" and even "proletarian regency" became "workers' power."[53] Still incorporated into JCP policy is the nationalization of key industries held by big business. However, only the "major means of production" were slated for nationalization. A multiparty system is guaranteed, as is "freedom of speech, the press and other expressions."[54] The JCP's opposition to the U.S.-Japan Security Treaty was reaffirmed by the 1976 policy line.

As might be expected, relations with the two centers of world communism could be better. Ideologically, the JCP follows and independent path of "nationalistic legalism." Relations between the JCP and the USSR are almost "correct," but China has insisted on conformity to a Peking policy line.[55] Miyamoto has not been quick to respond to Chinese or, for that matter, Soviet prodding.

The JCP has approximately 300,000 members, but as a proletarian movement it must rely on individual appeals for support. Seventy percent of its finances are obtained from the highly successful party newspaper *Akahata,* which has sales approaching three million copies per week.[56] The party does not have the support of the large union federations, but not having to respond to such groups allows it greater political latitude.

Until 1973 when severe economic readjustment was necessary, the JCP was able to ride the tide of the environmental movement in Japan. As a critic of unrestrained industrialism, it also received what might be called protest votes from many of the white collar bureaucrats who felt themselves not really represented by the LDP and the "old" politics of factionalism and money. Now that the conservatives have introduced an alternative, the JCP is finding it more difficult to attract voters. The future success of the Party may disappoint adherents of the Miyamoto line. It would appear that the JCP has entered a period of consolidation and introspection. Any forward movement must await a significant modification of the current political situation.

The New Liberal Club (Shin Jiyu Club)

On June 13, 1976, Kono Yohei and five other members of the LDP announced their intention to leave the LDP and form a new party. LDP executives attempted to dissuade them, but to no avail. On June 14 at a formal press conference, Kono launched what has since become known as the New Liberal Club (NLC). The new party, born out of the group's impatience with LDP steps toward party reform, represented the first formal break from the LDP since its formation in 1955. Five of the Diet members were from the lower house and one was from the upper house.

Upon secession from the LDP, the group had little in mind concerning policy except to demonstrate by their actions their intense displeasure with the LDP. Party reform had not progressed fast enough and the lingering aftershocks of the Lockheed affair were still being felt. Kono and the band of five decided to "strive for the resuscitation of the conservative forces" by starting a new party.[57]

The dissidents officially broke away on June 25, 1976. They were led by the charismatic Kono, who stated that: "Inasmuch as the LDP's decline and senility can no longer be held in check, we have decided to secede from the Party, with the awareness that the LDP has already played the role demanded by our time and with a pathetic desire to create a new conservative politics. . . ."[58]

Instead of meeting defeat at the polls as many had predicted, seventeen of the NLC candidates were elected along with two who were recommended by the party—a total of nineteen. The party garnered 4.18 percent of the vote, which was outstanding for a first time out.[59]

Party Orientation. The NLC party platform has developed considerably since those emotional outbursts calling for action first, discussion later. Current policy objectives call for creation of a "free society with justice and vitality," a new "free-economy structure," and new national goals based on conservative political philosophy. They also call for creation of an "overall security structure" and the formation of "a stable, international order." The NLC hopes to restore the trust and faith of the Japanese nation in the democratic system.[60]

Some additional characteristics of the party have made it quite distinct. There is an age limit of fifty-five for the head of the party and the secretary general. This stress on youth is also found in the decentralized nationwide party organization from which delegates are sent to party conventions in Tokyo. Delegates to the national convention cannot exceed fifty-five years of age. Nonmembers of the parliamentary party are to form a Political Morals Committee to oversee the party's Diet members, and a junior member system has been created for individuals below twenty years of age.[61]

The establishment of the NLC is a manifestation of political discontent in Japan, a phenomenon that affects many industrial societies. Its overall impact will take time to assess, but at the moment, it has a conservative tenor. The NLC may move toward closer collaboration with the LDP, but it might also start a new trend in Japanese politics.

The Potential for Coalition Government

With public support for the LDP declining, there has been much speculation about what the nature of the parties in power will be after the long era of one-party rule has ceased. The JSP, like the other opposition parties, would like to form its own one-party government, but the decline in JSP strength has even exceeded that experienced by the LDP. Thus, a post-LDP government will probably have to be some kind of party coalition. That alliance, based on many recent statements by party leaders, will most likely be centered on the LDP and the DSP. The DSP has increasingly sided with the LDP and, in fact, during a Diet impasse caused by the Lockheed scandal, it was and LDP-DSP arrangement that permitted legislative business to be transacted. Although the LDP has disavowed any formal intention to ally with the DSP, based on past ability to coexist and similar defense policy orientations, this coalition is most likely.

It would also be possible for the NLC to ally with the LDP. The price would be more ministerial posts than Kono could get if he were leading only one faction of the LDP. This prospect seems less likely than an LDP-DSP coalition, because over the next several years the NLC will be attempting to create its own identity unique and distinct from the LDP. Nor could the NLC easily join forces with the party it has castigated with such great abandon. Perhaps after the LDP reforms have taken root and become less of a "money-is-everything party," the NLC could afford renewed proximity. At any rate the similarity of their political ideology makes it likely that the NLC will vote with the LDP on most critical issues.

If serious losses of support weaken the LDP and a revisionist coalition becomes possible, it would most likely include a JSP-Komeito-DSP grouping. A variant of this three-party coalition would be the much talked about "E-Ko-Min" possibility. In this case, a right-wing splinter group of the JSP (named "E" after the late Eda Saburo, its former leader) would unite with the Komeito (the "Ko") and the Democratic Socialist Party (Minshato in Japanese). This middle-of-the-road coalition would require the garnering of many votes by the group to even come close to being a collective majority.

The JSP advocates an alliance between all opposition parties. This would mean that a JSP-JCP-Komeito-DSP (perhaps NLC) alignment would take control of the government. However, since the Komeito, DSP, and NLC refuse to enter into any united front arrangement with the JCP, this alliance is unlikely.

Perhaps the least probable alliance would be a JSP-JCP coalition. Both parties are stagnating. The JCP has lost most of its attractive issues and the JSP has serious internal divisions. The possibility of a completely leftist government is remote at best. Both parties would need to increase their respective strengths by a factor of two to gain control, which is highly unlikely.

CHAPTER NINE

Other Major Actors

Up to this point, our examination of Japanese political behavior has been focused on political parties, but there are other major actors that also have a significant impact on Japanese policy decisions or, in the special case of the bureaucracy, policy formulation and execution.

THE BUREAUCRACY—ITS SPECIAL ROLE

The Japanese bureaucracies are far more extensive than their United States counterparts. Ministries have only two or possibly three politically appointed posts; the other positions are held by career bureaucrats. These professionals have a very clear perception of their unique role in the process of government in Japan. They are part of a proud tradition of government service that goes back to the time of the Meiji Restoration when the higher civil servants served the emperor and not the people. During this period many ex-samurai were integrated into various government services, and the saying *kanson mimpi* became common. "Honor the officials, despise the people" generally characterized the relationship between the bureaucracy and the people. Once the national universities like Tokyo Imperial University were established, a special relationship developed between the universities and the bureaucracies. Most of the top graduates filled positions in the new ministries, and before long Tokyo Imperial was the route to a high civil service position and service, in theory, to the emperor.

Since the war and the democratization of the nation, the power of the bureaucrats has not declined; if anything, it has increased. Basically, political leadership of a ministry is only a perfunctory position for most LDP ministers due to the complexities of today's governmental tasks. Also, the LDP's self-imposed burden of frequent cabinet shuffles produces a variant of musical chairs in the ministries. Because LDP political leadership is only pro forma in nature, the importance of the bureaucrats is compounded. Bureaucrats are asked to write 80 to 90 percent of all bills introduced in the Diet and they provide a large portion of the information requested by LDP research committees and Diet standing and special committees.

The importance of Tokyo University as a source of higher civil servants is a fact of special significance. As of 1974, 83 percent of the senior positions in the twenty-one ministries and agencies in Tokyo above the rank of bureau chief were held by Tokyo University graduates.[1] This startling fact can be placed in better perspective if one considers that in the United States, Harvard graduates accounted for only 11.2 percent of higher civil servants in 1940, and in 1959 the largest proportion of federal career civil service executives were from George Washington University, and that figure was only 3 percent.[2]

The pressure to gain admittance to Todai (Tokyo University) in order to ensure a government job is extraordinary. It does not start with the examinations for Todai; it starts as the Japanese child enters kindergarten. From that point on, life is one long series of preparations for examinations to get into a "good" elementary school, a "good" junior high school, and a "good" high school. To those countless souls who fail the Todai examinations (or fail to enter several other national universities), the options are preparatory school to study for next year's exams, attendance at a lesser college, or, sometimes suicide. This process has received a very fitting name, "examination hell."

An indication of the keen competition that awaits the graduate at the end of this process is provided by figures released in August 1977 comparing the number of people taking the government examinations to the number of available jobs. Some 53,602 applicants vied for 1,300 openings, a rate of 41.3 to 1. There were 23,400 applicants for the science and engineering examinations, 23,052 for the law exams, and 7,150 for the agricultural exams. Once these examinations are over, additional testing, and personal interviews follow. The total process requires approximately four months.[3] The Japanese bureaucracy clearly approaches the ideal of a meritocracy.

The picture drawn thus far depicts powerful government

executives coming from one principal training center to assume a disproportionate share of government power. They have special access to information, and usually focus their efforts on one or two ministries at most. Their assignments are generally long term, they are involved in drafting legislation and providing witnesses to party and Diet legislative committees, and they take part in administering the law. But Kakizawa Koji, a Japanese bureaucrat turned political critic, feels that bureaucrats are not actually that powerful. Writing in one of Japan's sophisticated monthly magazines, Kakizawa charged that politicians have come to meddle too much in the bureaucrat's business. Speaking of recent political trends he states:

> Yearly the politicians stepped up their interference with the bureaucracy. By and by, they came to meddle even in the delicate and intricate regulatory powers of bureaucrats. As a consequence, the bureaucrats gradually lost their power of resistance.[4]

According to Kakizawa, questioning by Diet committees in session has left the bureaucracy debilitated and has diverted it from more important tasks. One of these tasks is long-range planning, a traditional bureaucratic function that he asserts cannot be accomplished by politicians. It is best to let Kakizawa describe in his own words his opinion of the bureaucracy today:

> The prewar bureaucrats were aglow with pride and a sense that it was they who had steered the course of the country. They found their life worth living as they consecrated themselves to their own task. They were, so to speak, patriotic bureaucrats.
> However, present-day bureaucrats philosophize differently. "We are mere office clerks, or administrative officials at best."[5]

Kakizawa finally calls for bureaucrats to be no longer "subordinate to the politicians."[6] Thus, it is clear some individuals do not perceive the current bureaucracy as being the principal apex of a governmental triad. Nor do they recognize the value of legislative control of the power of bureaucrats. With such commentary fresh in mind it may be possible to say that the democratization of Japan succeeded.

The criticism above notwithstanding, bureaucrats do have important input into the process of policy formulation and policy implementation. In the Japanese decision-making process, it is very evident that bureaucratic input is frequent and crucial.

The Marunouchi district of Tokyo. This area is the center of the Zaikai. (Source: *The Japan of Today*, Ministry of Foreign Affairs, 1976.)

THE ECONOMIC COMMUNITY

The Zaikai

There are a few words in Japanese that have been absorbed into the English, or at least American, language. Such words as tsunami, taifu (typhoon), ikebana, kabuki, and geisha have become, if not household words, parts of speech recognizable to a large portion of the public. There is another word, *zaikai*, which should join this group. It can be easily translated as "economic world"—in this case, the Japanese economic world.

No commentary on the Japanese domestic political environment would be complete without covering the manner in which the economic world is organized and how this organization interacts with its political counterparts. Many studies examine this Japanese phenomenon in far greater depth than can be accomplished here; we are primarily concerned with outlining the structure of this community and its special access, if any, to the political/governmental structure so that interests can be articulated and acted upon.

Organization of the Zaikai

The zaikai is generally described as having four principal components: Keidanren, Nissho, Keizai Doyukai, and Nikkeiren. According to Thayer these components are augmented by the "leaders of basic industries and large financial institutions, . . . representatives of industrial federations and the leaders of small- and medium-sized enterprises."[7] An idea of the overall thrust of the zaikai can be gained by a closer look at the four major components.

Keidanren. The powerful Federation of Economic Organizations was established in August 1946 to represent big business. It excludes small and medium firms from membership, but includes large government corporations.[8] Over 800 of the nation's largest corporations are members of this group.

Nissho. The Japan Chamber of Commerce and Industry is the oldest of the major economic organizations. It was founded in 1878 and has grown to a federation of 445 local and regional chapters. Eclectic in nature with all facets of the business community represented, it generally expresses the views of corporate enterprises somewhat smaller than those of the Keidanren.[9]

Keizai Doyukai. The Japan Committee for Economic Development was founded in April 1946 by rather young executives who had as a universal goal the rebuilding of the then shattered Japanese economy. The drive to revitalize capitalism remains a hallmark of this group. Keizai Doyukai is committed to policies that encourage full employment and increased productivity.[10]

Nikkeiren. The Japan Federation of Employers' Association was founded in April 1948. It had as its initial goals the achievement of peace between industry and labor and the realization of increased productivity. Although not completely an oppositive task, it soon became known as "fighting Nikkeiren" for its drive to neutralize labor offensives. It became, and remains, the headquarters for management labor policy. Over 30,000 companies are members of this group, which has come to promote productive cooperation between management and labor.[11]

These organizations have "cooperative" relationships with certain government ministries. Keidanren, for example, has especially close ties with the Ministry of International Trade and Industry (MITI), and its 1977 chairman, Doko Toshio, has, on occasion, traveled abroad to represent semi-official government interest.

Access to the political decision makers is fostered by the very proximity of the organization's national headquarters to the Diet. Of course, contact is encouraged between ministries and business concerns—often former bureaucrats become leading members of the various zaikai organizations. The access born of long-term friendships within the bureaucracy pays handsome dividends in providing continued "crosstalk." Since most government legislation that is introduced into the Diet is written in the various ministries, the ability to influence at this level is critical.

The impression should not be given of pressure flowing in only one direction from business toward government decision makers. This is far from reality. Probably the best way to demonstrate how government and business work as responsive entities is to review briefly the economic planning accomplished by the government of Japan.

Government Economic Planning

Since 1955, five-year plans have been the primary method of coordinating government and business toward a general goal. The Economic Planning Agency is charged with the overall requirement of plan development, but all ministries involved in some aspect of economic affairs have an input. Thus, policy contributions might be provided by the Finance Ministry, Ministry of International Trade and Industry, the Transportation Ministry, Agriculture-Forestry Ministry, Construction Ministry, the Labor Ministry, and the Medium and Small Enterprise Agency. Although business has various degrees of access to these ministries through advisory councils and other avenues, a formal mechanism has been established to insure that the prime minister receives the "advice" and cooperation of the zaikai. This particular body is called the Economic Deliberation Council, which has a formal membership of approximately 30, but more than 500 if subordinate committees are included.[12] Goals are devised in very general terms and then made more specific by the individual ministries concerned. For a better idea of the product of the Economic Deliberation Council, refer to Appendix A, where an abridged report of the December 1975 "Economic Plan for the Second Half of the 1970s" can be found.

Once the goals are established, the supportive governmental apparatus goes into operation. Industries adjudged no longer "growth-oriented" or contributing to the overall attainment of a new five-year plan will find loans and import licenses more difficult to obtain and other obstacles will be put in their paths. The reverse would be the case for industries declared valuable to the plan.

Besides studies and reports for the Economic Deliberation Council, the various organizations of the zaikai turn out a continuous flow of critical assessments of business trends, establishing some economic goals and some normative social goals. Appendix B is an example of a report produced by Keidanren that outlines future expectations for the various prime industries of Japan. Such words as "readjustment" and "integration" imply industries facing severe competition from other nations' industries; possible government policy in regard to such Japanese industrial concerns is proffered in the text.

In June of 1976, the Keizai Doyukai issued a report entitled "Renovation of Management under a Low-Rate-Growth Economy," which also touched on the problems faced by Japanese business. It concentrated on management aspects that needed to be addressed and contained many highly normative items. It was written by the Management Renovation Subcommittee of the Management Policy Deliberation Council and is the third in a series. The chairman of the subcommittee was the vice-president of a large investment company. In essence, the report proposed that business follow seven principles as management techniques. These seven admonitions are listed in Appendix C.

Another example of the way the economic community assesses the health of business and makes recommendations for possible government action is a resolution from a general meeting of Nissho. The primary areas of concern for this organization can be understood by examining the contents of this particular document. Such items as the government budget, public projects, fiscal discount rates, income tax reductions, size of wage increases, expansion of workmen's benefits, and effects of illegal strikes on industry are covered. Refer to Appendix D for the text.

Economic cooperation between government and business is not new in Japan. During the Meiji era entire industries developed by the reform-minded Meiji bureaucrats were sold at subsidized prices to Japanese commercial interests. The capability of the Japanese system to react to gross changes in the world economic environment and still achieve marked advancement of the gross national product tends to indicate to other states that they might look to Japan's example for some answers to the demands of development. The Japanese five-year plans do not carry with them the heavy-handedness of many socialist systems; they work through a series of financial incentives and subtle pressures. Industries to be encouraged are given government assistance; industries to be discouraged find increasing governmental reluctance and are encouraged to adapt to the changing scene.

IS THERE A JAPANESE MILITARY-INDUSTRIAL COMPLEX?

If such close cooperation does exist in Japan between government and the business world, can it be said that a military-industrial complex also exists? Before answering that question, let us examine the defense sector of the Japanese economy.

The Japanese defense budget in 1976 stood at 1,512.4 billion yen. Let us put these figures into perspective. Government expenditures in the same year for education and science promotion were 3,029.2 billion yen and for social security some 4,807.6 billion yen. At an exchange rate of 300 yen to the dollar, the amount spent on defense was approximately five billion dollars. This is not a small sum; it ranks about tenth among all nations.[13] However, the portion of that $5 billion that went to the Japanese defense industry was not large. In fact, 56 percent of the entire sum was spent on costs related to personnel. Only 16.4 percent, or approximately $800 million, went for the purchase of new equipment such as tanks, planes, and ships.[14] It appears likely that the upward pressure of personnel cost will continue, placing Japanese defense-related industries in a very difficult situation.

The Defense Production Committee of Keidanren stated in a proposal to the government of Japan in May 1976 that if this trend continues, "capital expenditures will fall to the 12 percent level in fiscal 1981 and the SDF (Self-Defense Forces) will change into "bamboo-spear units.' "[15]

This is a classic example of overstatement for effect, but there is some cause for concern. For example, there is only one manufacturer of small-caliber ammunition in all of Japan. In 1975 it produced 20 million bullets and used only one-third of its capacity. It has let two-thirds of its employees go to other jobs and is trying desperately to expand into civilian related products.[16]

Other defense industries are in better condition, but not much. In a survey of the entire defense production industry, using 1972 as the base of 100 points, Keidanren reported the following capacity utilization of industries: aircraft and engines, 80.9; warships, 72.1; and weapons, 75.7.[17]

There are several organizations that speak for the defense industry. The Defense Production Committee of Keidanren represents approximately eighty companies in defense production. It is very active, especially in contact with the LDP, and speaks with an authoritative voice; Kono Fumihiko is its chairman as well as being a consultant to Mitsubishi Heavy Industries, a leading defense producer.

Another organization that articulates the defense industry point of view is the Japan Weapons Industry Association, which is chaired by Tsuchiya Yoshio of Daikin Industries. Approximately 100 companies belong to this group, which keeps close account of the members' defense contributions. It typically calls for rearmament and takes a much more "hawkish" posture than the Defense Production Committee.[18] A report issued by this association showed that a total of eighteen companies took part in the production of aircraft in Japan; fifty-seven companies were involved, to some degree, in manufacturing missiles, guns, and ammunition; forty-five were involved in producing defense related electronic goods; fifteen companies produced ships; and sixteen firms manufactured tanks, combat vehicles, and trucks.[19] Of course, some of these firms contributed to more than one category.

Although sharing of available defense contracts is often attempted by the Japanese firms, several have come to be associated with certain kinds of weapons. Mitsubishi Heavy Industries and Kawasaki Heavy Industries, for example, are associated with naval vessels; Japan Steel with cannons and other weapons; and Mitsubishi Electricity Machinery with communication equipment.

What keeps these giants so weak when other sectors of the Japanese economy are enjoying relative prosperity? Basically, government policy limits military exports to almost nothing (only trucks, uniforms, and some communications equipment),[20] forcing the domestic producers to be dependent on national defense needs only. It is plain to see that as the amount for capital expenses decreases, the problems of the defense industries will increase.

Although 80 firms belong to one organization and 100 to another, as recently as 1969 Paul Langer found that the top ten producers controlled about 65 percent of the total business.[21] Less than 10 percent of Mitsubishi Heavy Industries' total business is related to the military.[22] If the proportion of military business is so small, and decreasing yearly, why do the eighty or so firms in the defense production industry stay in the field? One reason is national duty, but another, very important reason can be found in the normally small allocation to research and development by Japanese industry. In the defense industries, technological transfer is often involved in the production of new equipment. This makes the involvement technologically profitable, if not in the short-term financially rewarding. Sophisticated electronics and aircraft avionics have been the subject of such transfers in the past. The benevolent eye of the government might be expected to turn toward such a firm when other contracts, not defense related, are being let.

The government of Japan has followed three principles when dealing with weapons. No exports of weapons are permitted to communist countries as specified by the Coordinating Committee with Japan, U.S., and NATO membership. No exports can be made to states undergoing United Nations sanction, e.g., Rhodesia, and no weapons can be exported to countries involved, or about to be involved, in conflict. These three principles are adhered to within a framework of a total embargo of lethal weapons from Japan. This is accomplished under the authority of the Foreign Trade Control Ordinance administered by the MITI.

Japan's weapon-exporting policy could be changed by government decision, but change seems highly unlikely. In the winter of 1976 when the world-wide recession and depression were driving unemployment beyond the one percent level, Keidanren, Nissho, and the Japan Aeronautics and Space Industry Association called for "approval of weapons exports,"[23] but the policy was not altered even then.

To return to our original question, does Japan have a military-industrial complex? If judged by its overall impact on the economy, no. If judged by its competitive strength internationally, no. If judged as a successful lobby for a change in export policies, no. If judged as an embryonic defense industry whose leaders maintain extensive contacts with the Defense Agency and the Liberal Democratic Party, yes. This latter category is essentially meaningless in the context of Japan's current defense policy, but has possible future implications.

THE IMPACT OF THE ORGANIZATION OF THE ECONOMY ON SUZUKI-SAN

To this point we have concentrated on highlighting the role played

TABLE 9.1
Rank and Share of the Ten Leading Defense Contractors in Total Defense Procurement
For FY 1969 (April 1969 through March 1970)

	Name of Firm	Contracts in Billion Yen	Percent of Total Defense Procurement
1.	Mitsubishi Heavy Industries	70.13	31.0
2.	Kawasaki Heavy Industries	21.41	9.5
3.	Ishikawajima Harima Heavy Industries	19.17	8.5
4.	Mitsubishi Electric	11.36	5.0
5.	Nippon Electric	5.90	2.6
6.	Toshiba Electric	4.75	2.1
7.	Hitachi	3.82	1.7
8.	Komatsu	3.64	1.6
9.	Nihon Aviation	2.82	1.3
10.	Ito Chu Trading Company	2.38	1.1
	Total	145.38*	64.4

Source: Nihon no anzen hosho, 1971, p. 104, as found in Japanese National Security Policy--Domestic Determinants, Paul F. Langer, Rand, R-1030-ISA, June 1972, p. 66.

*Out of a total procurement of 226.36 billion yen.

An automated steel rolling mill. The sign in Japanese is an admonition calling for safety. (Source: *The Japan of Today*, Ministry of Foreign Affairs, 1976.)

by the zaikai in interest articulation. We have seen that large organizations have ready access to the government bureaucracy and the ruling party (LDP). Let us now turn to a brief description of another often overlooked element of the economic world, the average worker. The employed work force in Japan in April 1977 numbered 51.33 million out of a population of 113 million. Of those employed 32.42 million were male, and of the total, some 13.43 million were engaged in manufacturing. The figure of unemployed workers during the same period stood at 1.22 million, or 2.3 percent.[24] If the worker's lot becomes such that he can no longer attain his goals and desires, radical alteration in the political system could result.

Permanent Employment, Labor, and Labor Unions

One of the characteristics of the Japanese work force has been the feature of lifetime employment or permanent employment. Upon graduation from college or high school, workers enter into a relationship with an employer that lasts until retirement. Not only is the tenure long-term, but practically all the needs of the employees are looked after by the employer in a most paternalistic fashion. For example, when the male employee reaches an age where he could take on the responsibilities of married life, the company might act as an intermediary to provide a suitable bride as well as the facilities for the ceremony, reception, and honeymoon. Housing would probably be provided at a highly subsidized rate. Other aspects of permanent employment include subsidized transportation to work, lunches, recreation facilities, and bonuses twice a year amounting to a total of perhaps five to eight months' salary. While a worker's average take-home pay might be less than that of his U.S. counterpart, his needs are less and his security greater. During times of poor economic conditions, the firms usually do not release the workers but continue to carry them on the payroll. In a sense, welfare becomes the responsibility of the firm. Adjustments might be made by encouraging vacations, reduced work days, or temporary sabbaticals.

Unfortunately, as may be deduced from the 2.3 percent unemployment rate, not all workers enjoy the security and paternalistic benefits of permanent employment. At the top of Japan's multitiered industrial system are the large internationally-known corporations. These firms offer permanent employment to many but not all of their personnel. Next come the smaller firms that do subcontracting for the largest firms during times of an upturning economy. They can offer most benefits except life-time employment; in time of recession, these industries and commercial concerns have to rationalize their employment policy with the fact that they do not possess the resources to keep large numbers of underemployed personnel on the payroll. Finally, there are the small, family-size enterprises that may or may not possess the benefits associated with permanent employment. Chances are, they do not. During depression and recession their lot is difficult indeed. In all probability, the great bulk of the unemployed came from these small enterprises where tenure can be tenuous indeed.

Advancement in Japanese firms is usually based on seniority. There is great expectation on the part of the employee that, if faithful service is rendered to the company, in time his wages and benefits will increase. Loyalty to the company is stressed to such a degree that when asked about his employment, rather than say he is an accountant, sales manager, or lathe operator, his first response will identify the company. This is especially true if the company happens to be one of the prestigious giants of the zaikai.

This identity with one corporation primarily and a specific trade or duty secondarily leads to another positive aspect of the Japanese industrial scene. Very few employees of the larger corporations fear technological unemployment. If a mechanical innovation is introduced, the laborer has little to fear, for once the transition is accomplished, he will be trained to fill a new position. This in-plant mobility leads to the identification of some employees as generalists. Such personnel are trained in all aspects of the production cycle involved in their company's product. This kind of organization provides the company with a measure of diversity not often found in the United States or Great Britain.

Labor Organization

For U.S. or British labor union organizations, the company generalists would present a problem. They would be crossing the prerogatives of various unions and, chances are, there would be pressure for individual union members to do each job. That is because unions in the United States and Britain are trade unions. Plumbers belong to one union and electricians to another though they may work side-by-side in the same factory. This, of course, is a gross oversimplification, but it leads to one main point—in Japan labor unions are generally organized around a company not a trade.

For example, a worker in Japan joins the union encompassing Mitsubishi Heavy Industries; he can be transferred to any job within the MHI Union without crossing into a jurisdictional dispute with another union. Besides allowing the company great flexibility, this setup insures that every employee in the union is also, first and foremost, a member of the same firm.

This arrangement brings into play the reciprocal loyalties and obligations of *on* and *giri*. These obligations operate in the company labor unions, but in their truly classic nature they involve a degree of conflict. On the one hand, union members owe allegiance and loyalty to the union and the union leader. On the other hand, there is the obvious duty to the company and its president. How can this conflict be resolved in a noncontradictory fashion?

Typically the union, perhaps in a spring labor offensive (when all unions normally put pressure on management for increased wages or other benefits), will call for a strike or slowdown to underscore the demands it is making on management. However, when a settlement has been reached, the employees may work extra diligently to make up the lost production. Above all, the union understands that continued employment depends on the continued economic viability of the firm. The desire is to improve wages and benefits, not destroy the company.

Labor Federations

With the unions in Japan company- or enterprise-oriented, how are political issues of interest to labor articulated on the national scene? Generally, but not always, company unions join federations that represent groups of similar unions.

Federations such as Tekko Roren (the National Federation of Iron and Steel Workers Unions), Goka Roren (the Japanese Federation of Synthetic Chemical Workers Unions) and Zosen Juki Roren (the National Federation of Shipbuilding and Heavy Machinery Workers Unions) are typical of the numerous national federations in Japan. The largest of these umbrella organizations is Sohyo (the General Council of Trade Unions in Japan). It consists of unions in the public and private sectors and has a membership approaching 4.5. million.[25] It has been dominated by unions representing the large government concerns such as the National Railroads. In 1974 and 1975 it backed a move by one of its major members, Korokyo (the Council of Public Corporations and Government Enterprises Workers Unions) to gain legal sanction for government employees to strike. The efforts failed, but the attempt brought its primary political spokesman, the Japan Socialist Party, into confrontation with the LDP. The LDP looked within itself and found the political strength to oppose the strike and the then prime minister, Miki Takeo, issued a call for an end to the walkout. Korokyo ended the strike two days later without obtaining the prize that it sought.[26] The issue of the right-to-strike by public employees remains part of the platform of Sohyo.

The Korokyo strike can also be used as an example of the fragmented nature of the Japanese union movement. While Sohyo was backing the moves by Korokyo saying that it "naturally has the right to strike," another national federation, Domei, was classifying the strike as illegal.[27]

Domei is the second largest of the umbrella national federations and consists of approximately 2.5 million members, mainly from private industry unions.[28] This organization is much more moderate than Sohyo and has formed a political alliance with the middle-of-the-road Democratic Socialist Party. Together they called the 1974 strike illegal and even called for government punishment of strikers.[29]

One of the major concerns in Japan's labor movement today is that of the ultimate unification of all unions. The two principal federations, Sohyo and Domei, having different political alliances and different opinions on substantive issues such as the right-to-strike for public employees, as might be expected, propose different concepts for the unification of the Japanese labor front. Sohyo maintains that all unions should be unified simultaneously, while Domei calls for the unification of private industry workers unions first.[30] Since so much is at stake both politically and in the union movement itself, no early resolution of this issue should be expected.

The total number of union members in Japan approximates 12 million, which places Japan close to West Germany and ahead of the United States in percentage of unionized labor force. The accomplishments of the Japanese unions are impressive indeed. In 1973, for example, the spring wage struggles in Japan resulted in an average 22 percent increase and in 1974 a record 30.5 percent increase.[31] Goals for similar labor offensives in 1977 were lowered to 13 percent to reflect the recession and the slowing inflation rate.[32] Union leaders generally recognize the slowing of the super high rate of economic growth experienced in recent years. At a meeting of the Keizai Doyukai in 1977, the leader of Sohyo, known for his ofttimes militant stances, noted that "labor-management relations are entering an age of 'cooperation' from that of 'confrontation.' "[33]

An institution called the Industry-Labor Consultive Council was created to help facilitate this transition. It is composed of the leading members of the Japanese government, management, and labor. Sessions are held regularly in the form of breakfast meetings where *hanashiai* ("conversation") can be encouraged in a friendly environment. This is not a decision-making body, but , as is the case with many of Japan's close leadership ties, it helps the nation establish general priorities.[34]

Whether an idyllic state between management and labor is reached in Japan, the political scene will continue to have demands placed on it by the unions through their political spokesmen the JSP, DSP, and JCP. Parties without formal labor ties will attempt to attract labor's vote to keep pace with changes in the Japanese political system.

The future will not necessarily be one of cooperation. Developments like the continuing decrease in the size and nature of the work force will put strains on certain aspects of life-time employment. The seniority system will come under increasing fire as youth enter in force into the job market. Issues such as increased security to cover those not part of the permanent employment system, a national minimum wage, improved annuities, improved welfare, and decreased income tax will serve as the basis for increased labor-management confrontation.[35] The role of unions will continue to be critical to the effective articulation of workers' goals and aspirations, and as such will continue to contribute positively to the Japanese political system.

Issues and Problems

One of the most revealing developments that has occurred recently in Japan is the apparent disaffection of many Japanese citizens with the existing political party structure. In March 1977 a public opinion survey showed that 72.7 percent of all respondents were not satisfied with politics. The percentage of voters not identifying with any political party reached 23 percent for all respondents; among the twenty-year-olds the rate rose to a startling 32.4 percent, as compared to 16.5 percent for those aged sixty or more.[1]

Such figures lead to the conclusion that the next ten years will be transitional in nature. Politics of the old style will need to be adaptive to restore public esteem, particularly among the youth of the nation. Fiascos like the Lockheed scandal and "money politics" may result in a dynamic restructuring of the political community. However, the great political negativism of the past several years might subside if the parties are in any way successful in implementing their public pronouncements of revitalization.

Real external challenges to the two major political parties materialized in the 1976-77 period with the formation of the Kono-led *Shin Jiyu Club* (**New Liberal Club**) **and the Eda-led Socialist Citizens' League.** The same poll that revealed the growing disaffection with the old LDP and JSP indicated that such splinter groups as the NLC may serve as catalysts for new citizen-oriented movements now strong at the local and prefectural levels of government. However, the existing parties may revise their own images and programs to accommodate the movements for increased citizen involvement. One-issue groups often find their cause incorporated by the astute politics of the old school.

Revision of the electoral system, especially in view of population changes, is another issue that must be dealt with adequately. Even after the Public Office Election Law Revision of 1975, which increased the number of seats in the lower house of the Diet to 511, there were gross imbalances in the number of votes required to be elected. In the 1976 elections one-hundred-thousand votes apiece were not enough to bring success to ten candidates in certain districts, while in others, fewer than 50,000 were sufficient.[2]

The April 14, 1976, finding of the Supreme Court that the current electoral system was unconstitutional promises future corrective action.[3] The form this revision takes will be critical to the viability of several of the political parties. During Prime Minister Tanaka's administration, a single-member election district like the ones used in the United States was proposed, but it met with little support from the smaller parties, which would be adversely affected.

Recommendations for reform of the lower house election system have usually been tied to moves for upper house reform. However, in 1976, the LDP decided to back the incorporation of a restricted proportional representation system. Under this system, the parties determine the precedence of their respective candidates, and voters cast for parties only. The seats are then proportionally distributed among the parties depending on the votes received.[4] The LDP and JSP would probably fare well under this system, but the minor parties are opposed to this and similar plans.

Bringing a true one-man, one-vote system to Japan will take time and would probably weaken the LDP to some degree, since any system of realignment would take seats from party strongholds in rural areas and give them to urban areas where other parties are strong contenders. Under those circumstances, it is likely that the LDP will try to forestall forward movement on this critical issue.

Economic Growth

From the early 1960s to 1973, the LDP could claim as one of its prime accomplishments the ever-rapid increase in the GNP (about 10 percent increase each year). Since 1973 and the oil embargo, the Japanese economy has been developing at approximately 5 percent per year. This lower rate of economic growth will continue to plague the LDP. The Japanese will also be faced with increasing reluctance on the part of the world economic powers to permit unrestricted import of Japanese products into the European Common Market and the United States. Growing trade protectionism throughout the world will have to be dealt with by any successful Japanese government.

Embryonic efforts at "labor diplomacy" and attempts to increase awareness of Japan's special export/import needs among the unions of the industrialized world may bring the LDP closer to operating relationships with unions in Japan. The resulting awareness of mutual problems will be a positive development and may create an environment for further constructive relationships between the LDP and Japanese labor.

Closely related to Japan's efforts to expand exports is the need to meet the costs of rising oil imports. A program for growing energy independence must be a principal concern for Japan, and the degree to which it is successful will have certain repercussions on the domestic political scene. By 1977, Japan had become dependent on Saudi Arabia alone for 30.7 percent of its crude oil imports and on the Middle East in general for 79.3 percent.[5] Such outright dependency is viewed as unwise, and efforts are underway to increase imports from China, Indonesia, Venezuela, Rumania, the USSR, and other oil-producing states. Attempts to exploit off-shore oil will be hastened in areas of increasing promise.[6]

The same kind of one-source dependency has been present to an even greater degree in U.S.-Japanese enriched uranium supply exchanges. Complete reliance on the United States will give way to some degree when the Japanese complete their domestic capability based on the centrifugal enrichment process. Construction began in the autumn of 1977, and a product enriched to power-reactor levels will be available in the 1980s.[7] Other advancements such as a domestic reprocessing capability and research in nuclear fusion have been given emphasis by the Japanese government. After a long series of tense negotiations, the Japanese were permitted by the United States to process spent nuclear fuel from Japanese reactors in the Tokai Mura Reprocessing Facility. American acquiescence in the operation of the facility was required by international agreement; U.S. faith in the good intentions of the Japanese government was reflected in the outcome of the negotiations and helped the Japanese search for methods of energy independence to continue.

Coal, the only major source of energy besides hydropower found in Japan, may once again be mined in significant amounts. A goal of 20 million tons a year has been mentioned frequently but would require government emphasis and more labor. In any event, increased diversification of sources will be sought through increased imports from Canada, Australia, and the United States.[8]

The Ministry of International Trade and Industry hopes to pursue these avenues and seek further energy relief through alternative sources like geothermal and solar heat. How well Japan is able to meet and master the issue of energy will play a significant role in her future and that of the world.

The Japan Self-Defense Forces and the Era of the Basic Standing Force

Until recently, one of the most contentious issues in Japanese politics was that of national defense. However, as the exposed nature of their archipelago has become more apparent to the Japanese, the divisive nature of "defense" has changed. A series of events beginning with the enunciation of the Nixon Doctrine and including the return of Okinawa to Japanese control, the near normalization of relations between the United States and the People's Republic of China, the withdrawal of U.S. forces from South Vietnam and the Southeast Asian peninsula, the continuing withdrawal of U.S. forces from the Republic of China (Taiwan), the reduction of U.S. ground troops in South Korea, and the increasing activity of Soviet air and naval forces around the periphery of Japanese territory have tended to modify the nature of the defense debate. In fact, the defense issue received the lowest marks for electorate interest just prior to the July 1977 upper house elections. Only 2.2 percent of respondents to a *Yomiuri* poll indicated that defense was of interest to them.[9]

Although the electorate may seem to be nonplused over defense issues, the political parties and opinion leaders in Japan are showing much greater interest in defense, especially regarding the reduction of U.S. forces in Korea. Plans have been advanced to form a special committee in the Diet to discuss defense related matters.[10] Although a consensus by no means exists, even the Japan Socialist Party engaged in an intraparty dialogue on defense issues in 1976 in which several of its members made a proposal that would have reversed the party's age-old policy of unarmed neutrality. The opposition parties have gradually modified their positions on the U.S.-Japan Security Treaty so that only the JSP and JCP now call for immediate abrogation or termination. The party shifts and a reported 80 percent public support for the Japan Self-Defense Force[11] have placed the Japanese defense establishment in the most positive position they have enjoyed in recent times.

Although awareness of the necessity for the JSDF is growing, there is a parallel reluctance to support increases in funding for it. This is reflected in the so-called peace barrier which holds funds for the JSDF below 1 percent of Japan's gross national product. With such a small proportion of the GNP, the JSDF has been forced to concentrate on the purchase of sophisticated weaponry with very little logistical backup.

Increases in defense capabilities were previously incorporated into five-year defense plans. The Fourth Five-Year Defense Build-up Plan lasted from October 1972 to March 1977. The level of expenditures was some $16 billion over the five-year period. This became difficult to realize due to the oil embargo of 1973 and the double-digit inflation of the following period. The actual accomplishments of the plan are outlined in Table 10.1.

In the 1976 Defense White Paper, it was recognized that a rational basis for defense equipment levels must be established. That level was announced as the Basic Standing Force and incorporated the concept of qualitative as opposed to quantitative increases in defense capabilities. The force, as desired, would have an operational capability to "deal quickly and appropriately with indirect aggression, violations of territorial air and other types of illegal military acts."[12] The Basic Standing Force was seen as a "basis for a smooth expansion and reinforcement to a necessary level, if and when a political decision should be made to that effect in response to changes in the international situation."[13]

The entire plan is an attempt to place more emphasis on the personnel programs of the JSDF and to improve the balance between combat and support functions without increasing the size of the total force. Several new weapons systems are seen as necessary for the future, such as the F-15 interceptor for air defense and improved antisubmarine capability via the PC3 patrol aircraft. However, due to the Lockheed scandal, procurement of new systems will be exposed to much greater public scrutiny, a change which will strengthen the political process.

By deciding to hold the size of the JSDF constant at approximately 230,000 men, the government of Japan has helped to take the agency out of the political realm for the immediate future. Any attempts to cross the 1 percent barrier or accomplish a major expansion would reestablish the JSDF as a major issue. The U.S.-Japan Security Treaty continues to provide the base-line of defense for any major confrontation with Japan's neighbors in Northeast Asia. Before ending our summary glance at issues facing the Japanese political system, we should look at areas of possible confrontation that

TABLE 10.1
Accomplished Strength of Main Items in 4th Defense
Plan (Estimate)

(As of Dec 30, 1975)

	Item*	At end of 3rd Program	At end of 4th plan Planned Goal	Estimated Actual Strength
GSDF	Tanks	Apx 660	Apx 820	Apx 790
	Armored Veh	Apx 650	Apx 650	Apx 640
	Self-propelled guns	Apx 60	Apx 140	Apx 80
	Combat Aircraft	Apx 310	Apx 350	Apx 330
	(helicopters)	(Apx 280)	(Apx 320)	(Apx 310)
	Ground-to-air Hawk missiles	5 groups	8 groups	8 groups
MSDF	Ships	Apx 210 (Apx 174,000 tons)	Apx 170 (Apx 214,000 tons)	Apx 150 (Apx 193,000 tons)
	Destroyers	48 (Apx 97,000 tons)	54 (Apx 121,000 tons)	49 (Apx 109,000 tons)
	Submarines	15 (Apx 21,000 tons)	15 (Apx 27,000 tons)	12 (Apx 22,000 tons)
	Combat Aircraft	Apx 170	Apx 200	Apx 190
	Antisubmarine aircraft	Apx 160	Apx 190	Apx 180
ASDF	Aircraft	Apx 880	Apx 770	Apx 770
	F-4EJs	Apx 80	Apx 120	Apx 120
	RF-4Es	--	14	14
	T-2s	4	Apx 60	Apx 60
	FS-T2s MOD	--	Apx 60	26
	C-1s	4	Apx 30	Apx 30
	Ground-to-air Nike J missiles	4 groups	6 groups	5 groups

Source: Defense of Japan, 1976, p. 93.

*GSDF - Ground Self-Defense Force; MSDF - Maritime
Self-Defense Force; ASDF - Air Self-Defense Force.

exist in Northeast Asia.

INTERNATIONAL ISSUES

Japan's closest neighbors are Korea, the Soviet Union, the People's Republic of China, and the United States. With each power she has some degree of discord that ultimately puts pressure on the Japanese political system. Understanding these pressures will aid in following political developments and assessing the Japanese future.

The USSR

The USSR's capture of the South Sakhalin peninsula (Kurafuto) and the islands of Etorofu, Shikotan, Kunashiri, and the Habomais in the twilight of World War II has plagued Japanese-Soviet relations ever since. The Japanese insist on the return of all four islands before a peace treaty can be signed between the two countries. The Soviet Union has offered to return two of the islands, but the Japanese, including even the JCP, have insisted on the return of all the territory.

This particular dispute may seem minor, but it assumes rather major significance when fishing zones are being negotiated in and about northern Japan. The issue came to a recent peak during the 1977 fishery negotiations between the two states in the wake of the USSR's unilateral declaration of a 200-mile limit commercial zone and Japan's subsequent declaration of a 12-mile territorial limit. Since 1946 over 1,300 fishing boats have been captured by Soviet authorities in the contested waters, and the issue's volatile nature continues. A series of visits by Japanese and Soviet dignitaries has not moved the dispute one centimeter closer to solution. The Soviets, because of the precedent involved, are adamant and contend that further negotiations over the matter would be futile.

Since the early 1970s the more important and less emotional issue of joint development of Siberian resources has been discussed frequently by representatives of the two states. Gas deposits of Yakutsk, oil of Tyumen, Yuzhno-Yakutsk coal, and Sakhalin continental shelf oil and gas have been the subject of discussion and some investment by the Japanese. The years immediately after the 1973 oil embargo saw significant progress toward joint ventures, but as detente between the U.S. and the USSR began to cool, Japanese investment in Soviet enterprises became more cautious. Ultimately, it would appear that Japan will need coal, oil, and gas more than it will need the islands off Hokkaido and the fish thereabouts. The Soviet Union and Japan could assist each other and may do so as long as the

Japanese put commercial interests first. Soviet overtures for Japanese participation in the construction of a number of atomic power plants and offers to supply enriched uranium have been received with interest by the Japanese. Increasing pressures for energy sources have had a serious impact on this issue. Progress toward a formal peace treaty between the two powers, however, will be slow. The 1956 agreement still functions, and relations are not overly hampered by the absence of a formal treaty. There is every reason in 1978 to assume that the current cordial but correct relationship between the two states will continue.

The People's Republic of China

The "abnormal state of affairs" that had existed between Japan and China for years was "terminated" on September 28, 1972. At that time, the two countries exchanged a communique that:

1. ended the state of war;
2. established the PRC as the "sole legal government of China";
3. affirmed Japan's understanding of China's claim to Taiwan;
4. established diplomatic relations;
5. renounced China's claims for war indemnities;
6. established the principles of peaceful coexistence as the basis of relations between both states;
7. stated that neither country would seek hegemony in the Asian-Pacific region;
8. announced that negotiations for a treaty of peace and friendship would begin; and
9. stated that negotiations for other agreements would be held.[14]

The communique was a diplomatic breakthrough accomplished in less than 100 days by the then prime minister, Tanaka Kakuei. The years shortly thereafter saw an increase in trade, the formalization of many agreements, and a period of adjustment as Taiwan became an economic entity. (Table 10.2 shows the treaty's impact on trade.) As time passed, however, relations cooled and progress toward signing a Peace and Friendship Treaty came to a halt.

Negotiations for the treaty were largely blocked by what has been called the hegemony clause. The Chinese insisted that such a statement be included, while the Japanese kept introducing ways to clarify its intent. Both sides were aware of negative Soviet reaction to the clause and acted to aggravate or dampen the consequences.

The death of Mao and Chou and the purge of the "Gang of Four"

TABLE 10.2
Japanese Trade with China and Taiwan

Year	Japan-China	Japan-Taiwan
1970	$ 823	$ 868
1971	$ 901	$1,073
1972	$1.100	$1.418
1973	$2.014	$2,252
1974	$3,289	$3,059
1975	$3,793	$2.506
1976	$3,033	$3,546
1977 (Jan-Jun)	$1,500	$1,762

Source: Sankei, August 26, 1977.

on the Chinese side also hampered negotiations. The Tanaka "money politics" situation, followed by the Lockheed scandal, tied the hands of the Japanese. As the late 1970s approach, it seems likely that areas of continuing disagreement will be resolved and a more stable Sino-Japanese relationship will evolve.

One area of possible conflict is the energy resource field, for the Japanese desire to explore certain continental shelf areas claimed by the PRC, Korea, Taiwan, and Vietnam. One such area is the Senkaku Islands off the southern region of the Ryukyu chain. This area has great oil potential but is claimed by the Republic of China, the PRC, and Japan. Japan maintains possession and indicates sovereignty by operating an unmanned weather station on one of the islands. How these territorial issues are resolved will in large part set the tone for the entire spectrum of Sino-Japanese relations for the next decade.

The United States

Relations with the United States have been at a high point every since the departure of Secretary of State Henry Kissinger, whose diplomatic maneuverings made the Japanese painfully aware of their diplomatic "adulthood." U.S. overtures towards the PRC, monetary and import policies, and the soybean embargo were ill received by the government of Japan even though Kissinger had indicated they had a certain intrinsic value. Stable U.S.-Japan relations have been encouraged by increased acceptance of the U.S.-Japan Security Treaty as necessary for the stability of NEA. As recently as 1960 such consensus would have been thought impossible.

Mutual security interests have become easier to solve, but the success of Japanese exports, especially televisions, cars, electronics, and steel, have placed strains on the U.S.-Japan alliance. In 1977 a trade imbalance of eight billion dollars in Japan's favor caused the United States to put increased pressure on the Japanese to import more U.S. goods. As the yen increases in value against the dollar, the attractiveness of Japanese products will lessen, and the Japanese government will have to take measures that will further reduce the imbalance.

U.S. reluctance to allow the Japanese to gain a domestic plutonium reprocessing capability was understood by the Japanese as a worldwide position adopted by the Carter Administration, but it was hardly appreciated coming as it did only months after Japan's ratification of the nuclear Non-Proliferation Treaty. The issue was resolved by the U.S.'s astute diplomatic recognition that some concessions to Japan were warranted if the U.S. expected that country to continue as the cornerstone of U.S. policy in the Pacific.

Such problems have placed strains on the Japanese political system, but they are insignificant when compared to the close relations achieved between the two Pacific states. Trade in historic amounts, interchange between citizens and scholars, and life-styles that are continuously being brought closer together serve as bonds of major significance. U.S.-Japanese relations have entered a period of mutual trust and admiration with the end of the client-patron relationship between the two states. Only in matters of defense does the government of Japan seem to be reluctant to assume a major burden. With the United States drawing back its ground forces in Korea and leaders of the PRC reportedly calling on the Japanese to rearm, this posture will be increasingly difficult to maintain. It will certainly have an impact, however, on the manner in which Japan performs in her immediate zone of interest, northeast Asia.

Japan in Northeast Asia

The deterioration of the Sino-Soviet Alliance has left their former protégé, North Korea, in a less-than-desirable position. In addition to North Korea's uncomfortable political relationships, the northern power of the Korean Peninsula has encountered serious economic problems and has had to default on numerous foreign loans.

In contrast, the South Korean regime of Park Chung-hee, certainly not a bastion of liberal democracy, has developed a system that is relatively free and economically prosperous, though not without problems, and it enjoys a continued U.S. pledge of assistance in the event of North Korean aggression.

Japan enters this dynamic picture, more as an interested observer than an eager participant. As the U.S reduces its forces (but not its commitment) in South Korea, the Japanese have begun a national security dialogue of a nature unique since World War II. The outcome depends on the Japanese perception of U.S. intent to honor its commitments to defend the region in the event of conflagration. This debate is so dependent on U.S. policy that it is impossible to estimate its outcome.

As can be seen, the NEA political, economic, and military milieu is as dynamic as the seas that impatiently tear at the shores of the nations involved. Japan, a member of this political region by grace of nature, realizes that her destiny is inseparable from the relationships of the surrounding states. The path Japan chooses will be founded on the domestic political system that has evolved since World War II. It is this system that provides confidence that Japan's choices will be consistent with the precepts of a mature democratic society.

PART THREE

KOREA

CHAPTER ELEVEN

The Two Koreas:
Which Model To Follow?

The Korean peninsula is dominated by two strong personalities, Kim Il-sung in the north and Park Chung-hee in the south. Any study that attempted to describe the democratic processes and participatory aspects of either state would be hard pressed to get beyond the impact of these two individuals on their respective systems. That is not to say that differences do not exist; the systems are substantially different. Nonetheless it is a fact that the democratic process in South Korea has never deprived the ruling party of political control. Political change has always been accomplished by "either popular uprising or military coup."[1] North Korea has not even enjoyed that much political "choice." The lack of a meaningful franchise and the existence of strong-man rule in both countries have repeatedly been justified in terms of the threats to national security faced by both nations. Both leaders have a great deal in common; they have extended their unique systems of control on the justification of an all-consuming reciprocal military threat. In essence, each needs the other to assure the continuation of their respective regimes.

NORTH KOREA

The North Korean regime was established officially under the patronship of the Soviet Union on September 9, 1948.[2] Kim Il-sung immediately became premier and began the long-term process of power consolidation and elimination of potential political rivals.

Kim Il-sung had been introduced to the people of P'yongyang on

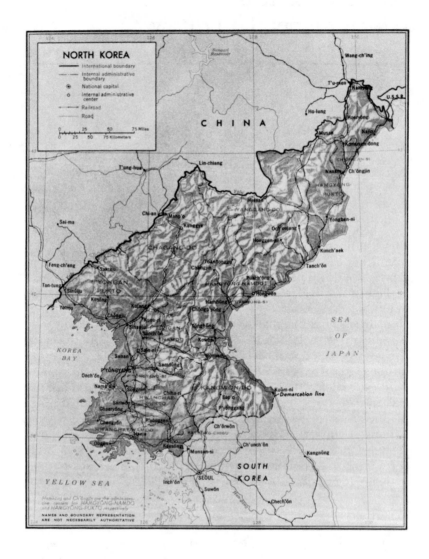

October 14, 1945, at a political rally. His mentor at the public meeting interestingly enough was a Russian general. Kim, who gained fame as a leader in the anti-Japanese struggle, called for the establishment of a "democratic, autonomous and independent" Korea.[3] At that time he was thirty-four years old and a "general" of the Special Military Operations Corps, a group of Koreans that had fled or been driven into the Soviet Union during the era of Japanese mainland expansionism. Kim himself had fled to Russia in 1942.

He was not the immediately unchallenged ruler of the North Korean regime. In December of 1945 he gained the first secretary position of the North Korean Communist Party. Over the next few years the elimination of rival power centers, or the "disappearance of factionalism" as it is sometimes referred to was to consume much of Kim's political energy.[4] He successfully dealt with non-Communist North Korean Christians, the ultranationalist followers of the "Teaching of the Way of Heaven," the North Korean Democratic Party, the North Korean Youth Fraternal Party, members of the northern native Communist factions, and South Korean Communists. He also eliminated several other Communist factions (Yenen and Soviet factions) that had previously supported him in his Machiavellian maneuvers to reduce or eliminate the other groups. It took Kim until 1958 to emerge as the unchallenged ruler of North Korea, but after that he was able to enforce a rigid official ideology, supported by a personal popularity of cult proportions. The principal tool Kim used to achieve such preeminence was the clique of former partisans from Manchuria.[5]

Governmental Structure

As of 1977 Kim Il-sung held the official titles of president and general secretary of the Korean Workers' Party, president of the Democratic People's Republic of Korea, prime minister and chairman of the Military Affairs Committee, and supreme commander of the Armed Forces.[6] Regardless of the structure, Kim is an autocrat in a Communist system. As in all Communist states, the principal management mechanism is based on the concept of "democratic centralism."[7] In essence, during the formation process policy is the subject of considerable debate, allowing ideals to proceed upward. Various representative organs then debate and recommend reform or new initiatives. However, once policy is decided upon by the government or party, it flows downward and must be supported by all, majority and minority alike.

The primary source for policy input into the system is the Korean

Workers' Party which serves to "exercise the dictatorship of the proletariat."[8] The more than 1.7 million members of this party (about 11 percent of the total population) form a most significant link between policy formulation and policy execution.

North Korea is a unitary state. Basically all governmental functions are accomplished or initiated from the capital, P'yongyang. The highest legislative body is the unicameral Supreme People's Assembly. It has a body of 541 deputies who are elected for a four-year term. Sessions are held twice yearly. When the Assembly is not in session, basic functions can be accomplished by its Standing Committee. The Supreme People's Assembly has never voted down a government measure presented to it.[9] Such a record is hardly the hallmark of democracy; however, it is probably the envy of certain beleaguered Western parliamentarians.

The negligible power of the Supreme People's Assembly was weakened by the 1972 constitution. The constitution removed the title of national president from the chairman of the Standing Committee of the Supreme People's Assembly and added it to the myriad responsibilities of Kim Il-sung. The assembly was further weakened in 1972 by the creation of the Central People's Committee, which was cited in the constitution as being the "highest leadership organ of state power."[10] It acts as the formal union of party and government, since important party figures are members.

The committee formulates, implements, and reviews policy. Elected to office by the Supreme People's Assembly for four years, its members have extensive power to oversee the thirty ministries and ministry-level committees that are officially responsible to the State Administrative Council (the organ that had been called the cabinet under the old constitution). Although formally responsible to the Supreme People's Assembly, it has yet to be called to task by that largely ceremonial body.

Under the 1972 constitution, the State Administrative Council is recognized as the highest administrative arm of the government; it has considerable power in developing and implementing Korean economic plans. Constitutionally the State Council is also charged with foreign affairs, national defense, and public order. When meeting as a body with Kim Il-sung it can perhaps live up to its charter. The unanswered question is how often the premier chooses to use this council instead of the newly established Central People's Committee. It probably does not make much difference as long as Kim Il-sung maintains absolute authority.

The judicial system is three tiered: the Central Court acts as a supreme court, the provincial courts serve as appellate bodies, and the local people's courts serve as the courts of first instance. The courts are used to protect the interests of the state as well as those of workers and peasants. Judges at the top two levels serve for four years; people's court judges serve for two. All are elected by representative bodies or the standing committees of such groups.

On the local level North Korea's unitary system closely monitors the progress of government in 9 provinces, 2 cities with provincial equivalent status, 18 regular cities, 36 urban districts, and 151 counties. Each local government entity has a people's assembly that serves a ceremonial function much like the national assembly. Day-to-day activities are placed in the hands of people's committees, which delegate much to local administrative committees. Their primary function is to implement government policy passed along from equivalent or higher levels.[11]

Political Dynamics

Although a governmental structure exists, as in most communist states real political control and activity rests in the hands of the state communist party. The Korean Workers' Party (KWP), headed by Kim Il-sung, is the state party of North Korea, but all government agencies, in fact, officially exist as "the faithful executors of the general line of the Party."[12] The party provides the necessary connections between people and government. Approximately 11 percent of the population belongs to the party, and virtually all aspects of life are touched if not controlled by party input.

The party is organized much like the government, down to and including the villages. The Party Congress, as in other communist systems is the highest party organ. It elects a Central Committee and is supposed to meet every four years, although nine years came between the Fourth and the Fifth Congress, which was held in November 1970. Membership in the Party Congress approaches 1,800, and the Central Committee, which has roughly 170 members, is a more appropriate policy-making body. However, real leadership is exercised by the Party Political Committee, which consists of approximately 20 members including Kim Il-sung.

This nerve center of the KWP is charged with "policymaking, coordination, and supervision"[13]—quite a task for any body of twenty individuals. Various groups have been created to assist the Political Committee; the Central Committee Secretariat is the most important. As might be expected, this body is also headed by Kim Il-sung, who oversees the efforts of thirteen secretaries in charge of administrative departments that manage specific party responsibilities. The more important departments are: the Organization and Guidance Department; the Central Auditing Committee; the Central Inspection Committee; the Liaison Bureau (with South Korea); and the Military Committee.

At the other end of the organization/management spectrum are the myriad party cells. The individual party members or candidates serve as the motivators for the entire system. Active participation is required at least once a week. Self-criticism, group study, and policy review are conducted in these meetings. Revolutionary zeal is maintained through the meetings, which Kim considers one of the most important tools for developing the spirit of *chuch'e*, or self-reliance, the most pervasive and overriding concept of the Korean Workers' Party.

Policies and Issues

The party, through the constitution, establishes three principal goals for North Korea: "to achieve the 'complete victory' of socialist construction in North Korea; to force the withdrawal of foreign troops from South Korea; and to reunify Korea 'peacefully on a democratic basis.' "[14] Two principal precepts form the ideological basis for this rather ambitious program: Marxism-Leninism and *chuch-e sasang*. Marxism-Leninism, of course, provides the economic framework necessary to achieve "true" socialism, and the policy of *chuch'e* provides an ideological rationalization for reality. *Chuch'e* is nothing more than a call for governmental and individual self-reliance.

Under Kim's direction, the party continually calls for advancement along three revolutionary fronts: ideological, technical, and cultural. On the ideological front, an attempt is being made to create revolutionary awareness as well as produce a working class mentality throughout all classes. The technical revolution is oriented toward meeting the challenge of providing North Korea with modern agricultural and industrial capabilities. Interestingly enough, included in the objectives of the technical revolution is a stated desire to "free" women from housework to make them available for "more production" chores. The desire to "improve" the lot of women obviously corresponds with a very severe manpower shortage. In the cultural area the Korean Workers' Party has been attempting to reduce the inequities that exist between the urban and rural communities. The party wants to transform culture, improve education, and generally mobilize and transform Korean society.

The concern for national defense and national reunification pervades all programs. Expenditures for defense reached the extremely high figure of over 20 percent of the gross national product for the years between 1967-70.[15] Since then they have declined to a level between 5 and 10 percent,[16] but the issue of defense and eventual reunification serves as a standard rallying point for the party. It is also a convenient and accurate reason for the failure of North Korea's economy to meet some of the goals established by various economic programs.

During the years of Japanese colonialization, the northern part of Korea received the lion's share of Japanese capital investments. The southern part of Korea was designated the "rice bowl"; significant industrialization efforts were focused on the north. These gains and those of the period between 1946 and 1949 were largely eliminated during the course of the Korean War. Since then a series of plans have been implemented to restore vitality to the economy. First was a three-year plan (1954-56) that primarily concentrated on a restoration of the war-damaged industrial base. The second was a five-year plan implemented over the years 1957 to 1961. It continued reconstruction efforts but also included goals for increased industrial and agricultural progress. Some imbalances to the economy resulted from overzealous achievers, and some dislocation of effort occurred in connection with the collectivization of agriculture. Heavy foreign assistance from Communist states, however, helped achieve many of the goals.

The third plan was a seven-year plan that extended from 1961 to 1970. It was affected by the general dispute that occurred in the Communist camp during those years, but especially the Sino-Soviet dispute. By 1966 industrial output had actually suffered a setback and the plan, which had as its goal "full-fledged industrialization," had to be extended until 1970.[17] Even with the extension, plan achievement was not complete.

A subsequent six-year plan stressed continued modernization of industrial plants, but allowed for the importation of necessary technology from non-Communist sources like Japan. As this plan ran its course, new goals were established for a follow-on effort: objectives were set for production of 100 million tons of coal, 12 million tons of steel, 5 million tons of chemical fertilizer, and 20 million tons of cement.[18] All-in-all, these plans have resulted in an economy that is more than 90 percent state owned. Agriculture is completely collectivized, and 95 percent of all manufactured goods (by value) are produced by state-owned enterprises.[19]

The continued achievement of goals like those identified in the new plan will depend on the continued political mobilization and motivation of the membership of the KWP, as well as continued access to capital and credits in the world. The North Korean regime has defaulted on massive amounts of loans, and there is reason to doubt the country's economic viability. The availability of credits will be dependent on the capital-exporting states' perceptions of North Korea's economic viability. North Korea will invariably be compared with South Korea which we will look at next.

SOUTH KOREA

The current South Korean government goes back to the era of military government that lasted from 1961 to 1963. A military coup headed by Major General Park Chung-hee took over from Dr. Chang Myun, who had assumed power in July of 1960 after the strife connected with the concluding days of the government of Syngman Rhee. Syngman Rhee had dominated South Korean politics from creation of the state on August 15, 1948, through the crisis years of the Korean War (June 25, 1950 to July 25, 1953), and into 1960. The election of March 1960 was marked by irregularities that went to unusual extremes to return Dr. Rhee to office. Even though Rhee was running unopposed (his opponent had died one month before the elections), the overzealous home minister, Choe In-kyu, specified to local officials the plurality by which Rhee and the Liberal Party were to be returned.[20]

The predictable results were not well received by the public. The entire process was decried by the opposition Democratic Party, and massive student protests broke out on April 19, 1960, leading to the utter collapse of the Rhee government. By July 1960 Dr. Chang Myun, mentioned above, assumed the position of prime minister, and the Democratic Party coincidentally gained undisputed control of the Parliament.

While Chang attempted to practice democratic ideals, his ability to lead the country came into question. Student activism continued unabated, and the Democratic Party, interested more in opposing the defeated Liberal Party than new programs, began to disintegrate. One faction of "Old Guard" Democrats rallied around the president, Yum Po-sun; followers of Chang became the new faction. Soon these factions began to subdivide and what Henderson describes as an age-old Korean pattern—"that the unity and cohesion of groups must yield to the demands of individuals or subgroups for access to

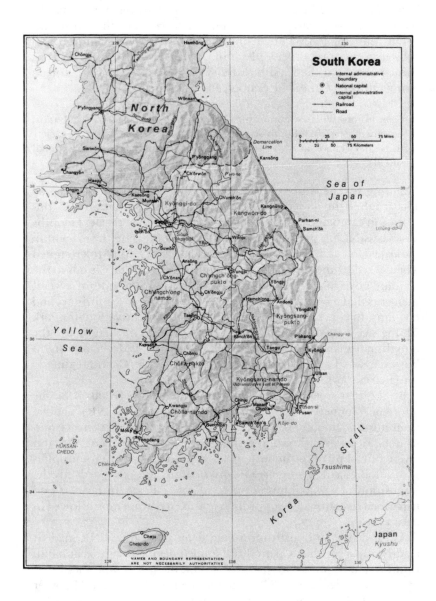

South Korea

- Internal administrative boundary
- National capital
- Internal administrative capital
- Railroad
- Road

power"—began to recur.[21] In October 1960 the Old Guard established
the New Democratic Party. Students increased attempts to foster
North-South reunification, and on May 13, 1961, demanded that the
nation begin negotiations to that end. Three days later the coup came.

On May 16, 1961, Park Chung-hee and Lt. Col. Kim Jong-pil
moved to restore order.[22] Leading a group of junior officers,
principally from the Eighth military class of 1948-49 of the Korean
Army Officers' Candidate School, Park declared:

> Compromise with the Communist Party is the beginning of defeat. It must
> be remembered that the advocacy of territorial unification with the society
> in a state of chaos, as it was under the Chang regime, is the way to national
> suicide.[23]

Planning for the coup had, by one account, started as early as May
1960. Eight lieutenant colonels met to discuss the initiation of a "pu-
rification campaign" against corrupt generals. Over the next months
a succession of generals resigned under pressure from within
the armed forces. In February 1961 Lt. Gen. Ch'oi Kyong-rok resigned
when asked by the Chang government to divert military funds to the
civilian government. This turned out to be only one of several
incidents that resulted in growing antipathy between the military and
civilians. In fact, supposedly one of the primary motivations for Park
Chung-hee's involvement in the coup was "a revulsion for the
bungling legislature of the Second Republic."[24] More important,
however, was Park's despair at the inability of the Chang regime to
initiate reform for the rural areas.

By the first week in May 1961, measures had been taken by the
Supreme Council for National Reconstruction (SCNR) against
Communists, hoodlums, beggars, smugglers, black marketeers, and
usurers; rice was rationed at restaurants, movies were censored, and
severe punishment for unauthorized disposition of military supplies
was announced. Park's rural orientation was reflected in the
imposition of a maximum 20 percent interest rate for farmers and
fishermen in contrast to the ordinary 60 to 80 percent rates allowed in
urban areas.

As for democratic institutions and democracy, the SCNR made it
readily apparent that a period of "guided democracy" was at hand.
Coining a new phrase for an old concept, the junta announced that
the state would follow a path of "administrative democracy." In order
to assure that this period of tutelage was seen through to the end, a
security apparatus, the Korean Central Intelligence Agency (KCIA),

was created on June 19, 1961. Headed by Kim Jong-pil, a leader of the coup, the KCIA soon proved its value to Park by routing out "counterrevolutionary" figures. By February 1963 only Park remained in a position of authority. The other key instigators and their factions had been overcome by the efficiency of the KCIA.

Another unique accomplishment of the SCNR, later to become a hallmark of Park's rule, was the formulation and implementation of a five-year economic plan. Plans had been drafted by both Rhee and Chang but the implementation of Park's plan was entirely new. The plan called for $2.5 billion in investments from all sources, aiming for an annual growth rate of 7.1 percent. The goals were to be achieved primarily by public corporations. They were to manage the government-sponsored industries without the need to induce forced accumulation of capital. A model of guided capitalism emerged. It looked significantly like the capitalism followed by Japan during the Meiji period when trying to catch-up economically with the Western world.

During the interregnum of military control, a new constitution was placed before the people. In a referendum of December 17, 1962, the Korean people approved a revised constitution by a mandate of 78.8 percent, once again giving significant power to the president and drastically weakening the legislature, which was made unicameral. The president was given unchecked power to appoint a premier and cabinet and to ratify treaties, command the armed forces, issue ordinances, and institute marital law. In an effort to bring stability to the national legislature, all candidates for office had to be members of a political party.

In order to run for president in the promised October elections, Park retired from the Korean Army in August 1963 and built up the junta-sponsored Democratic Republican Party. He defeated the former president of the Second Republic, Yum Po-sun by a scant 181,126 votes from a total of more than 11 million. Due to the diversity of the civilian opposition, his 46.7 percent of the vote was sufficient to win, and on December 17, 1963, Park Chung-hee was inaugurated as the third president of the Republic of Korea.

Political Activity and Governmental Organization in the Third Republic

In the space alloted here it would be impossible to give a detailed account of constitutional development since the first constitution was promulgated in 1948. There were amendments in 1952, 1954, 1960, 1962, and 1969. In 1972 the existing document incorporating the fundamental law of South Korea was suspended and finally, on November 29, 1972, was replaced with the Yushin, or reform constitution. This constitution removed the limit placed by previous constitutions on the number of terms a president can serve and placed executive power in the president's hands. It also provided for his indirect election by the National Council for Unification, a body of 2,359 delegates. (In 1972 Park was elected by a vote of 2,357 to 0 with two invalid votes cast.)

Under the Yushin constitution the legislature is unicameral and consists of 219 members elected for six years. Two-thirds of these delegates are elected under universal suffrage; the president appoints the rest based on approval of the National Council for Unification. Power rests in the hands of the president; the government he heads cannot be held responsible by the National Assembly. In fact, on especially critical issues, the Yushin constitution provides for the president to bypass the National Assembly altogether and go to the people for a referendum.

Most of these constitutional reforms were accomplished by the Park government under the rationale of "national security." The threat of subversion and overt attack from North Korea was held to be so grave that special procedures had to be taken. In light of the Pueblo crisis and the Blue House raid of 1968, the attack on a U.S. aircraft, the fall of Vietnam, and the discovery of militarily-useful tunnels in and about the Korean demilitarized zone (DMZ) some cause for concern existed. However, most of the immediate reforms were said to be necessary to improve the bargaining position of South Korea during negotiations with the North that began in early 1970.[25] As Park said in 1972:

> We must urgently make a readjustment of our political institutions in order that the difficult but invaluable South-North dialogue can most effectively be backed up by these elements of vigor and vitality and that we can positively adapt ourselves to the vast changing international situation.[26]

After the 1972 constitution was promulgated (it had been preceded by a declaration of martial law), a period of reaction to Korean Central Intelligence Agency excesses occurred. However, in January 1974, Presidential Emergency Measure Number 1 made it a crime punishable by up to fifteen years of hard labor to advocate revisions to the Yushin constitution. This measure was followed by others that restricted human rights; the repression did not abate until August 1974 when the measures were repealed in the face of domestic and foreign pressure. This situation continued until the visit of President Ford to Korea.

By May 1975 and the fall of South Vietnam, the Park regime had reinstated most of its controls on expression of popular discontent. The most oppressive of these decrees was Emergency Measure Number 9; under this decree, individuals could be punished by prison terms of one to fifteen years if they:

- advocated or petitioned for revision or repeal of the martial-law constitution (Yushin Constitution);
- broadcasted or published any news reports of any opposition to the martial-law constitution;
- staged any student demonstration or assembly that "interfered" with politics;
- moved any Korean-owned property out of the country with intent to perpetuate a property flight;
- publicly opposed the new emergency edict, or reported on any such opposition.[27]

Trial by civil court was provided, which was an improvement on the 1974 decrees, but "detention, search and seizure without warrant" continued.[28]

The constitutional history of the sixteen-year rule of Park Chung-hee has been marked by: a coup to take power; a shift to an elected president with a limited term of office; a constitutional amendment to increase the maximum number of terms from two to three; a disavowal of the constitution; the creation of a new constitution allowing unlimited six-year terms for the president; and a series of unilateral presidential decrees permitting "heavy-handed roundups and suppression."[29] One can only conclude that the basic law of Korea is exactly what President Park desires it to be.

Political Activity

With Emergency Measure Number 9 of 1975 as a backdrop, political activity in South Korea is somewhat subdued. However, on occasion political activity has been acute. The Kim Dai Jung affair became the cause célèbre for many who opposed Park but held their criticism out of fear of the KCIA or concern for national security.

In the 1971 election—the last election genuinely contested between two major parties—Kim Dai Jung ran against Park and received 44 percent of the popular vote. He almost defeated the former general and remained a formidable opponent. When Park declared martial law in October of 1972 to deal with North Korean unification negotiations, Kim was by happenstance in Japan. From there he carried on a campaign against the "military dictatorship and tyranny" of the Park regime.[30] He became a rallying point for critics of the South Korean government in the United States and Japan. In the midst of his campaign (August 8, 1973), he was abducted from his hotel room in Tokyo and reappeared several days later in Seoul. Opposition parties were incensed, and the debate in the National Assembly became intense. Government suppression of public outbursts was increased and Kim was finally charged with violations of the presidential and National Assembly election laws in 1967 and violations of the presidential election law of 1971.[31] He was found guilty and sent to prison. The affair had several repercussions: the Japanese were angry at the violation of their sovereignty; the world was amazed at the omnipresence of the KCIA; and the utter weakness of the South Korean opposition parties was demonstrated once again.

The political parties that do exist in South Korea must, of course, function in the shadow of the KCIA and within the narrow confines of applicable presidential decrees. They are thus somewhat subdued. However, parties like the New Democratic Party and Democratic Unification Party do possess enough strength to win seats in the National Assembly. The New Democratic Party obtained fifty-two seats in the 1973 election, while the Democratic Unification Party returned only two delegates. The Democratic Republican Party, formed as Park's vehicle to elected office in 1963, is the strongest party, and due to KCIA influence will likely remain so under the current constitutional situation. It garnered 146 seats in the 1973 election and thus can carry out its supportive role efficiently.

In the main, the parties are ineffective because of the president's power. One might say that "South Korea has bipartisan politics."[32] Such was the comment in August 1977 of the leader of the New Democratic Party, Yi Chol-song after a modus operandi was made with Park. This feature, combined with a constitution that can be manipulated almost at will and a strong military presence, assures that Korean democracy will continue to be somewhat different from the democracy of Western states.

Policies and Issues

While neither North nor South Korea gain high marks for political freedom in their respective systems, under President Park South Korea has achieved a record of economic achievement that is enviable.

TABLE 11.1
Foreign Investments in the Republic of Korea: The
Share of Japan, 1967-1974 (Approval basis)

Year	Total Approved from Japan (In millions of dollars)	Share of Japan in Total Approved by South Korea (In percentages)
1967*	1.3	6.3
1968	4.5	18.4
1969	15.4	54.6
1970	14.1	22.9
1971	23.3	51.6
1972	75.0	67.9
1973	246.4	93.1
1974	94.8	67.8

Source: Republic of Korea, Bureau of Foreign Investment Promotion, Economic Planning Board, Status of Foreign Investment: Approval Basis, in Korean (Seoul: 1975) as found in Nat White's "Japan's Interests in Korea," IDA, unpublished study, 1975, p. 28.
*Year in which Japanese investment in South Korea began according to official ROK statistics.

From the beginning years of the Third Republic (1963), to 1974 the GNP has progressed at a rate averaging approximately 10 percent per year. Since the 1973 oil crisis, the rate has hovered between 7 and 8 percent. This prosperity has been largely based on several key industries: textiles, electronics, machine tools, plywood, metalworking, and petrochemicals.[33]

The stable political environment provided by Park has helped secure foreign investment capital to meet the requirements of the five-year plans. Japan and the United States have provided about 60 percent of such funding (see Table 11.1). This economic success story has insured South Korea a living standard reportedly "far higher than that in North Korea."[34] Much of the prosperity is based on a willingness to settle old differences with Japan and establish a new working relationship. This accomplishment is due largely to President Park who normalized relations in the face of considerable domestic opposition.

The Park regime is also oriented toward positive relationships with
the business community. It has established a working environment
that fosters increased output. For example, the Yushin constitution
constrains collective bargaining by unions to that "between labor
and management . . . to 'ensure the improvement of productivity.' "[35]
The constitution also provides that collective action by workers in
support of a dispute "is restricted by a clause that says workers who
exert a 'strong influence' on the nation . . . can have their rights to
collective action limited or withheld."[36] In essence, as Ogle observes,
"the Yushin Constitution places union action and economic
development in contract to each other, and stresses the need for
limitation on unionism."[37] In fact in 1970, a law covering foreign-
capitalized firms provided for compulsory arbitration. These laws
and the effectiveness of the KCIA assure that labor problems are
minimized and productivity increases.

The picture that has been drawn of South Korea is perhaps a little
less forgiving than that of North Korea because of our expectations of
the Park regime. Even though in a political sense we may fault Park
for disallowing a free society, his achievements in the economic area
have been legion and may, in the long run, create an environment
that will lead to the granting of greater personal political freedoms.
Perhaps Park realizes that the age-old Korean cancer—that of
factionalism—can only be restrained by liberal governmental use of
proclamations and decrees.

KOREA: TINDERBOX OF ASIA

Is There Any Way Out?

Since June 1950, relations between the two Koreas can best be
described as "semiconflict." Rather than trace each turn in the
diplomatic relations of the two states, we will look at some of the
more recent events that may cause the Korean Peninsula to become
the tinderbox of Asia.

In the Blue House raid of 1968 a crack assassination team from
North Korea was given orders to eliminate President Park. Members
of the team were intercepted on the grounds of Park's official
residence. This attack marked the crescendo of a coordinated series of
attempts to place North Korean agents in South Korea to create
organized dissidence and gather information. Great sums of money
and manpower were expended by South Korea in rounding up these
agents. The capture of the USS Pueblo several days after the Blue
House raid was as blatant a move as the raid on the executive

mansion. The seizure of the U.S. intelligence ship in international waters led the U.S. to actively reinforce its Northeast Asian bastion. The affair was perfectly timed to draw U.S. naval and tactical air resources away from North Vietnam, thus helping the beleaguered sister socialist state of North Vietnam. The shooting down of a U.S. EC121 intelligence-gathering aircraft in 1969 was another crisis point. This was followed by the downing of a U.S. Army helicopter in August 1969, and the tragic beating deaths of two U.S. servicemen in the truce village of Panmunjom in 1976. Meanwhile, North Korean tunnels were discovered under the DMZ. In July 1977 a U.S. helicopter was shot down after it "inadvertently" strayed into North Korean territory. There were also countless incidents at sea between North and South Korean naval units and firefights along the DMZ for no apparent reason. Even the "economic miracle" of South Korea is an irritant to the North. The only appropriate phrase for such a situation is "tinderbox."

There have been periods of rational relations between the two states. The most notable thaw began in August 1970 when President Park Chung-hee, responding to the international era of detente diplomacy, spoke about the desirability of reunification. One year later, talks began between representatives of the Red Cross organizations of both nations in order to lessen the hardships of families separated by years of national animosity. Intergovernmental talks reached a high point on July 4, 1972, when the South-North Joint Communique was signed by representatives of both governments. The main points of this joint communique were:

1. The two sides have agreed to the following principles for unification of the fatherland:
   First, unification shall be achieved through independent Korean efforts . . .
   Second, unification shall be achieved through peaceful means . . .
   Third, . . . national unity shall be sought above all, transcending differences in ideas, ideologies, and systems.
2. In order to ease tensions . . . the two sides have agreed not to slander or defame each other, not to undertake armed provocations . . . and to take positive measures to prevent inadvertent military incidents.
3. The two sides . . . have agreed to carry out various exchanges in many fields.
4. The two sides have agreed . . . to seek early success of the South-North Red Cross talks . . .
5. The two sides . . . have agreed to install a direct telephone line between Seoul and P'yongyang.

6. The two sides . . . have agreed to establish and operate a South-North coordinating committee . . .
7. The two sides . . . hereby solemnly pledge before the entire Korean people that they will faithfully carry out these agreed terms.

Unfortunately, these fine objectives—and other reunification ideas such as confederation and peninsula neutralization—have been largely dissipated by recent territorial disputes and the North Korean campaign to have the United Nations terminate the charter of the U.N. Command in South Korea.

Although the immediate future holds little prospect for reunification, there is reason to believe that an era of relative stability has been entered and that such stability will last as long as the current leadership is in power. Kim Il-sung, after the fall of Saigon, reportedly asked Peking for support in "liberating" South Korea. Inasmuch as support has not been forthcoming from either Peking or Moscow, Kim has responded to the changed realities. The level of invective has been lowered, and the U.S. helicopter intrusion into North Korea in July of 1977 was generally treated with an absence of inflammatory language.

South Korea does not openly advocate a "go-north" policy, but some 30,000 U.S. ground troops are to be withdrawn over the course of the next several years, and will probably be interested in measures to assure continued stability. Thus, although it is premature to applaud the coming of reunification, the gradual reduction of big power involvement in the peninsula bodes well for the future. Ideology still plays much too great a role to permit unification to be more than a long-term desire; continued emphasis on the economic well-being of the peoples of the Koreas is a more feasible short-term objective.

Which Model to Follow?

The authoritarian regimes of North Korea and South Korea offer interesting examples of alternative developmental models for other Third World nations to emulate. The North has opted to follow the model offered by Marx and Lenin as interpreted by Kim, and South Korea has chosen a variation on the model successfully developed by Japan during the period of the Meiji oligarchs, encouraging domestic reinvestment of accumulated capital and inducing a massive influx of foreign capital. Both states suffer from approaching or current debt servicing crises and will have difficulty paying the yearly interest on the foreign capital. In 1976-78 North Korea began to default on outstanding debts that ran to as much as one billion dollars. South Korea finds foreign investors increasingly reluctant to advance money under current market conditions. North Korea finds it difficult to meet its planned objectives by depending on Communist states and has turned to the West for technological assistance. South Korea has become the primary recipient of Japanese business acumen and technological competence and has seen its GNP increase to $18.4 billion as compared to North Korea's GNP of $8.9 billion. South Korea, with a population of 34 million and considerable U.S. aid, has been able to make striking economic gains. North Korea with a population of 16 million, has also recovered from the devastation of the Korean War, but may have overextended itself in its bid to introduce western technological support to aid in the six-year development plan initiated in 1971.

Human rights and respect for the dignity of man could be improved in both nations. Under pressure from the United States South Korea began to release some of its political prisoners in July 1977. It was estimated at that time that 263 political prisoners remained incarcerated.[38] Similar facts on North Korea are not readily available, but one would have to say conditions are better in South Korea even though room for improvement exists.

By resorting to one-man, dictatorial rule both states have been able to deal successfully with the ancient and well-documented problem of factionalism. It is possible that this phenomenon can only be dealt with as the current incumbents are dealing with it, in which case Korean politics will differ from that of Japan and the West for some years to come.

Finally, the problem of leadership succession faces both regimes. The South Koreans have had several leaders and the North only one since independence, and the question of leadership after Kim and Park stands immediately across the threshold of the future. Perhaps this issue might provide the common basis for efforts at reunification. In the interest of peace and stability in Northeast Asia, it is a question that should be addressed.

Report of the Economic Deliberation Council

CHAPTER I: CHANGES IN THE INTERNAL AND EXTERNAL
ENVIRONMENTAL CONDITIONS AND THE PROBLEMATICAL POINTS
DURING THE PLAN PERIOD

(Details omitted here.)

CHAPTER II: BASIC DIRECTION FOR THE OPERATION OF POLICIES

Recovering of demand-supply balance and dissolving of difficulty in formulating an outlook for the future. Due to the policy for curbing total demand to cope with the wildly rising commodity prices since the autumn of 1973, commodity prices have begun to calm down. On the other hand, however, the depression has become protracted, and with our country's economy burdened with a big demand-supply gap, the payability of enterprises and the employment situation have worsened. In addition, there is the sense of uneasiness that low growth, as at present, may continue in the future, too, and both enterprises and households have begun to lose confidence. This has given rise to the vicious circle of causing further stagnation in demand.

In order to overcome this situation, it is necessary to narrow the demand-supply gap, and place the economy of our country on the track of proper growth, while paying attention to the stabilization

Reprinted by permission of *Nihon Keizai*, December 23, 1975.

of commodity prices and the maintenance of the international payments balance. In fiscal 1976, it is necessary to make efforts for the steady recovery of business, and against the background of the recovery of the world economy, it is necessary to maintain economic growth slightly higher than the average in the first part of the Plan period, and to improve balance in the economy and to restore confidence among enterprises and households.

Firm Implanting of the Stable Growth Policy Line

However, it is not permissible to regard the recovery of business this time in the same way as in the days of high growth. Internal and external restrictive factors are making high growth as in the past difficult. Furthermore, the world economy is expected to continue in a state of fluidity for some time to come, and there are still many indefinite factors in regard to the enterprises' investment activities, etc., compared with the days of high growth.

For this reason, it is necessary to shift our country's economy to a stable growth policy line smoothly, through the further consolidation of the means for controlling demand, and through the proper coping with the changes in the situation through the flexible and timely operation of these means.

CHAPTER III: GOALS OF THE PLAN AND NEW POLICY STRUCTURE

The goals to be aimed at by the Plan will be: (1) the stabilization of commodity prices and the ensuring of complete employment, (2) the securing of stabilized livelihood and the formation of a comfortable environment to live in, (3) cooperation with and contribution to the development of world economy, and (4) the securing of economic safety and the fostering of the foundation for long-term development. In order to attain these goals harmoniously, the following policies will be promoted:

Stabilization of Commodity Prices and Ensuring of Complete Employment

Through the proper control of total demand, efforts will be made to maintain proper growth and a stable economy, and to ensure the stability of commodity prices and complete employment. On that occasion, the induction of new policy measures, such as the adjustment of business through the effective utilization of taxation measures, will also be studied.

Efforts will also be made for the stabilization of commodity prices through the consolidation of the competition conditions, through the proper operation of the antimonopoly measures, and by giving consideration to structural policies for low productivity sectors and to the amount of currency supply.

As regards public utilities charges, the general principle will be for the users to shoulder proper costs, premised on efficient management. As a result, the goal will be to keep the rate of rise for wholesale commodity prices on the 4 percent level and to hold down the rate of rise in the consumer commodity prices to less than 6 percent in the last year of this Plan.

As for employment, efforts will be made for the improvement of the employment structure and for the securing of complete employment through the correction of demand-supply imbalances by age and sectors, through the improvement of the flow of manpower and the consolidation of the labor market.

Securing of Stabilized Livelihood and Formation of an Environment Comfortable to Live In

From the standpoint of making improvements in the people's daily lives, which are most urgently needed in this difficult time of low growth, measures will be carried out centering on the improvement of social security, the securing of housing, and the formation of a safe and comfortable living environment.

Social security. Improvement of the annuity systems and the consolidation of health and medical care systems will be pushed in response to the changes in the community structure, such as the sharp increase in the number of older-age people in the population. Also, from the standpoint of ensuring social fairness and justice, and the raising of the efficiency of various systems, proper and rational payments and the sharing of the burden will be restudied. For the concrete materialization of these measures, a long-range social security plant will be formulated. The ratio of transfer incomes to the gross national income will be raised from 8.6 percent in fiscal 1975 to little less than 10 percent in fiscal 1980.

Housing. Based on the principle of securing proper housing corresponding to family composition, efforts will be made for securing public rental housing. Also, through the expansion of housing loans, the construction of privately owned houses will be promoted. Also, as the foundation for these measures, the stabilization of land prices, the increasing of the supply of housing lots, and the lowering of housing construction costs will be pushed.

Environmental conservation. Aiming at the goal of the attainment and the maintenance of environmental standards, the development of prevention techniques will be promoted, and discharge restrictions will be strengthened. Also, comprehensive environmental conservation measures will be pushed through the establishment of a system for the assessment of effects on the environment and the proper utilization of national land. A long-range environmental conservation plan will be formulated at an early date.

Social capital. Under the situation of limited resources, priority will be laid on the consolidation of social capital. The establishment of transportation and communications systems, which will require large-scale investments, will be consolidated steadily over a long period of time. During the period of this Plan, a total of about 100 trillion yen (at the value in fiscal 1975) will be invested.

Education and culture. Efforts will be made for the improvement of the contents of education, and academic research, the development of culture, and international exchange will be promoted.

Tax burden. In keeping with the improvement of welfare, the ratio of taxes and nontax burden to the national income will be raised by about 3 percent in the last year under this Plan, compared with the average for the period between fiscal 1973 and 1975. For this purpose, efforts will be made to increase revenue, for the time being within the framework of the taxation system now in force and studies will also be made in regard to new fund sources for the future in keeping with the development of the economic situation.

Accompanying the increase in the social security payments costs, the ratio of the social insurance burden to the national income will also be raised by about 1.5 percent in the final year of this Plan, compared with the average for the 1973-75 period. Also, in order to ensure the proper distribution of financial disbursements and for the securing of fund sources, a long-range financial outlook will be clarified.

Government bond policy. It will be based on the principle of centering on government construction bonds. Special exception measures will have to be taken during the transition period, but finances will be returned to a state where they will not have to depend on special exception government bonds as quickly as possible. The terms for the flotation of the bonds will be strengthened, and efforts will also be made to broaden the strata for the digestion of the bonds. At the same time, the public bonds and debenture market will be consolidated, and the basic principle for general city digestion will be firmly maintained. Also, from a long-range standpoint, public bonds control policies will be established.

Utilization of interest. In order to utilize effectively the business adjustment functions and resources allocation functions of financing, the increasing of the flexibility of money interest will continue to be pushed, and the raising of the efficiency of financing will be promoted.

Rationalization of administration and finances. The raising of the efficiency of administration and finances, including the reform of the state and local administrative structure, will be promoted. Efforts will also be made for the securing and the stabilization of local financial sources. Also, the allocation of administrative work and the allocation of funds between the state and local entities will be studied from a long-range standpoint.

Cooperation with and Contribution to the Development of the World Economy

External economic policies will be carried out in the direction of harmony with the world economy and the reconstruction of a stable economic structure. Also, paying attention to the possibility of the fluctuations in world business appearing simultaneously, policy cooperation among the main nations of the world will be tackled.

International trade. Standing on the basis of a free trade structure, efforts will be made for the promotion of the New International Round and for the establishment of international rules for the prevention of export restriction measures. For the developing nations, general preferential tariffs will be expanded. In regard to primary products, an international system for the compensation of incomes and measures for the stabilization of demand and supply will be studied.

Economic cooperation. Effective and priority aid will be carried out according to the stages of the economic development of the developing nations and according to sectors. Efforts will be made for the attainment of the international goal for the Government's development aid (ratio of 0.7 percent to the GNP), but for the time being, efforts will be made to raise this to the level of other advanced nations. Also, by making communications and coordination between the government and private circles closer, efforts will be made for the smooth promotion of overseas investments.

International payments situation. For the time being, deficits in the current accounts balance will continue, but as a medium-range goal, efforts will be made to balance basic payments.

Ensuring of Economic Safety and Fostering of the Foundation for Long-term Development

Attention will be paid to the safety of the economy concerning energy, resources, and food. At the same time, structural consolidation will be carried out for the securing of the proper growth of the economy on a long-term basis.

Economic security. Efforts will be made for multi-faceted international cooperation, and the economy will be operated with attention given to security. Also, in regard to oil and agricultural and food products, efforts will be made for the securing of reserve stockpiles and for the stabilization of imports.

Energy countermeasures. The development of alternative energies, such as atomic energy, will be promoted. At the same time, various measures for the stable securing of oil will be carried out. While utilizing the economization effects produced through the price mechanism, resources economization and energy economization measures will be promoted.

Agricultural-forestry-fisheries industries. Through the consolidation of the production structure, efforts will be made to increase the self-supply capacity, especially in regard to basic foodstuffs.

Industrial structure. Shift to a resources-saving, energy-saving, technical know-how concentration-type industrial structure will be pushed. To correspond with this, efforts will also be made to upgrade the export structure to a more advanced level. At the same time, the smooth development of industries utilizing the most advanced technology will be promoted.

Local policies. In order to promote the dispersion of industries and population to local districts, the improvement of city functions, the consolidation of livelihood environment, and the development of new locations for industries in local district blocs will be promoted. Also, the consolidation of key transportation and communications systems and the development of water resources, which will provide the basis for these measures, will be promoted.

Science and technology. For the fostering of the vitality of the economic society, on a long-term basis, efforts will be made for the promotion of science and technology.

CHAPTER IV: WAY FOR THE DEVELOPMENT OF THE ECONOMIC SOCIETY

As regards the world economy, the growth of world trade will slow down to a little less than 6 percent, accompanying the slowing down of the growth rate of the world economy. Furthermore, there still remains strongly the cost inflation factor among the advanced nations, and it is hypothesized that the prices of primary products will also continue to increase. Based on these premises, it was hypothesized that the maintaining of a real growth rate of a little over 6 percent will be the proper level for our country's economy for the next five years.

As for the stages of growth during the period covered by this Plan, efforts will be made for the steady recovery of business in fiscal 1976, so that it will become linked with the upswing of business after then. And in this Plan, the course for realizing a long-term stable growth policy line, at a moderate rate, during the second half of this Plan was hypothesized.

TABLE A.1
Framework for Our Country's Economy in Fiscal 1980

Item	Actual Records for FY 1975 (estimate)	Prediction for FY 1980	1975-80 Annual Average Growth Rate
Labor population	52,800,000	55,400,000	Less than 1%
World trade (real)	--	---	Less than 6%
Gross national product (real)	¥150 trillion	About ¥200 trillion	Slightly over 6%
Gross national product (at current prices)	¥ 150 trillion	About ¥280 trillion	Slightly over 13%
Composition of the government's fixed assets (real)	¥14.6 trillion	(Cumulative public investments for 1975-80 about ¥100)	About 7%
Transfer from government to individuals	¥10.5 trillion (ratio of 8.6% to the national income)	About ¥23 trillion (a little less than 10% of national income)	About 17%
Ratio of tax and nontax burden (ratio to national income)	20.7% (1973-75 average of 22.7%)	(Rise of about 3% in ratio to the national income during the Plan period, compared with the 1973-75 average)	

Ratio of social insurance burden (to the national income)	6.1% (1973–75 average of 5.5%)	(Rise of about 1.5% in ratio to the national income during the Plan period compared with the 1973–75 average)
Consumer commodity prices (average annual rise rate)	10.5%	Below 6%, by the final year of the Plan	On the 6% level
Wholesale commodity prices (average annual rise rate)	2.8%	On the 4% level by the final year of the Plan	About 5%
Current accounts balance	Deficit of about $1.2 billion	Surplus balance of $4 billion	
Unemployment rate	1.9% (October 1975)	On the 1.3% level	

Notes:
1. The real value of the gross national product and the composition of the government's fixed assets are at the current prices in fiscal 1975.
2. The cumulative amount of public investments for the fiscal 1975–80 period includes the costs of land (at 1975 prices).
3. The estimated actual records for fiscal 1975 are based on the government's revised economic outlook.

Keidanren's Opinion of the Future Course of Japanese Industries under a Decelerated Economy

Iron and Steel. The position of this industry as a supply base in the world will probably continue for the time being. There are problematical points, such as the rising prices of iron ore, coking coal, etc., restrictions as to the environment, and moves for restricting imports. However, it will also probably be necessary to promote cooperation, including exports of technology to developing countries.

Automobiles. The international competitive power of this industry in the field of quality is strong, but in the field of price is weakening gradually. However, it will probably continue to occupy an important position in the industrial structure of our country. It is also necessary to contribute toward the developing of the world economy by pushing overseas investments.

Oil. This industry is facing such problems as the increasing of stockpiles and the sharply rising crude oil price. Autonomous development is also necessary, and the role to be fulfilled by the government is big. In order to strengthen the autonomy of industrial circles concerned, it is necessary to restudy the Oil Enterprise Law.

Aluminum. This industry is losing its international competitive power due to rising electric power costs. However, domestic production must be secured to some extent. Appropriate government measures are desired, such as the establishment of special electric power prices. It is also necessary to promote the establishment of

Reprinted by permission of *Asahi*, March 9, 1977.

enterprises concerned overseas.

Soda. The change in the manufacturing method was based on a political decision, and it has left behind problems. There is the fear that management may go bankrupt due to rising costs. This will also probably have effects on soda-consumer industry circles. It is also necessary to study the problem of having the government buy up the mercury-method facilities.

Chemical Fertilizer. In the importer countries concerned, self-sufficiency has progressed; therefore, the excess of facilities is coming to the fore. Chemical fertilizer is necessary for securing foodstuffs. Therefore, in order to secure the continuation of the fertilizer industry, the government ought to consider extending economic aid to developing countries for fertilizer.

Textiles. It is impossible to restrict imports from the developing countries. Push technological improvement, as did U.S. textiles which were driven by Japan into a difficult position in the past, and which have recovered through their high level of development. Efforts should be made to give positive guidance in the field of policy. At the same time, industrial circles concerned ought to consider the readjustment and integration thereof.

Shipping. From the standpoint of the nontrade accounts, and also from the viewpoint of economic security, it is necessary for Japanese ships to secure a certain fixed percentage of cargoes. Efforts should be made to strengthen the enterprises concerned. However, in view of the fact that in Europe and America, such enterprises are being protected warmly, it is necessary to restudy the fostering of the shipping industry.

Shipbuilding. This industry is falling into a very serious crisis because there are no new orders for tankers. Enterprises concerned should endeavor to develop LNG (liquified natural gas) carriers and other new ships using highly advanced technology, while striving to establish side business. The government ought to make efforts to increase opportunities for accepting orders, for example, through the extending of loans to developing countries.

Petrochemicals. The international competitive power of this industry is weakening. The problem of how to secure naphtha as raw material is also connected with energy policy, and talks should be held with related industrial circles. It is necessary to consider a new way for operating the Government-Private Cooperation Discussion Council.

Machine Tools. They are important as machines for manufacturing machinery. The problem of conventional types of machines should be entrusted to the developing countries, and exports should be expanded through the development of technology which will be acceptable to the world. The government also ought to realize the planned deduction from the taxable amount of investments, thus backing up this industry.

Keizai Doyukai Declaration of Seven Principles for Management Renovation

Management Which Is Sufficient in Humanity and Sociality: It goes without saying that enterprises must not become the main causes of social tension, friction, and dissatisfaction, which are apt to arise under a low-growth-rate economy. Efforts must also be made to establish a vital welfare society and realize social justice, as promoters of renovation based on sociality.

Management for Fulfilling Self-Responsibility Thoroughgoingly: (Enterprise operators) should return to the starting point of a liberal economy, and should change their attitude of relying on others in an easy-going way. Standing on their sense of duty as enterprisers, they should secure management for fulfilling their own responsibilities thoroughgoingly, while taking the mental attitude of settling various problems by their own efforts.

Management for Constant Renovation and Creation: On the basis of the frontier spirit, enterprise operators should make efforts to ascertain their personality, to make the most of their power accumulated through the use of their wisdom, to develop the basis for pushing technical renovation, and to secure self-improvement constantly in conformity with the change of the times and social changes.

Qualitative and Efficient Management: Efforts should be made to emerge from the trend toward easy-going quantitative expansion; to recognize the value of human power, commodities, and money; and

Reprinted by permission of *Nihon Keizai*, June 24,

to shift to the direction of qualitative improvement for attaching importance to efficiency in order to make the best use thereof.

Management Steered by Top Leaders: The top leaders should definitely base their intentions on positive dialogues within and outside the enterprises, while displaying their creative leadership and responsibility.

Management Seeking Establishment of Competition Order: From the stand that the creative and renovationist nature of free competition will contribute toward social development and social welfare, efforts should be made to push fair competition and to increase the efficiency of industrial society as a whole, thus pursuing higher-level economic rationality.

Management Which Can Be Accepted by International Society: Efforts should be made to expand the community-bound-together-by-common-fate-type sense of solidarity, which is a special characteristic of Japanese management, to a sense of all mankind, to induct the principles of management which will be integrated into the customary practice and culture of other countries, and to carry out operations which can be accepted by the world.

Nissho General Meeting Resolutions

General Outline of the "Economic Plan for the Second Half of the 1970s"

1. The ruling and opposition parties should unitedly exert all-out efforts for the early passage of the fiscal 1976 budget, whose role as the fifth round of the depression counter-policies is being marked with expectations. Adverse effects upon business, due to the prolonged compilation of a provisional budget and the delay in the carrying out of public projects, should be confined to the minimum.

2. It is requested that in carrying out public projects, consideration be given to regional allocation and to securing of order-receiving opportunities for medium, small, and petty enterprises and that, at the same time, local revenue sources be improved and strengthened so that the local entities can smoothly carry out public projects on their own.

3. The lower official discount rate has hitherto been about half the level before (the adoption of) the stringency policy. For further lowering of the interest level, we desire further lowering. Efforts should be made to correct binding deposits.

4. In order to overcome the stagnation of private consumption and buoy up business steadily, it is necessary to carry out income tax reduction.

5. In the spring wage hike, the raise should be confined to the payability of enterprises, so as not to worsen the employment and unemployment situations. Even in case a wage hike exceeding a one-digit rate should be possible, it is desirable that the raise be confined

Reprinted by permission of *Nihon Keizai*, March 18,

to one digit from the standpoint of stabilizing the people's economy.

6. In order to dispel uneasiness arising from the current employment and unemployment situations, it is requested that the employment adjustment benefit system be further expanded and improved, including the raising of the limit in the number of days (75 days) for the receiving of the benefit.

7. Illegal strikes by the National Railways Workers' Union, which have become a schedule, will throw cold water upon the efforts of the Government and the people to buoy up business and will cause immeasurable losses to various strata of people. Therefore, the plan should be canceled immediately.

Notes

CHAPTER ONE

1. Mao Tse-tung, "Report on an Investigation of the Peasant Movement in Hunan," (March 1927), *Selected Works,* vol. I, (Peking: Foreign Languages Press, 1977), p. 28.

2. Chalmers Johnson, *Revolutionary Change* (Boston: Little, Brown and Co., 1966).

3. A good example of this is to be found in Mao's personal experience. See Edgar Snow, *Red Star over China* (New York: Grove Press, 1961), pp. 121-36.

4. Franklin W. Houn, *A Short History of Chinese Communism* (Englewood Cliffs, N.J.: Prentice-Hall, 1967), pp. 6-7.

5. John K. Fairbank, *The United States and China,* 3d. ed. (Cambridge, Mass.: Harvard University Press, 1972), pp. 147-49.

6. Robert J. Lifton, *Revolutionary Immortality* (New York: Vintage Books, 1968); Richard Solomon, *Mao's Revolution and the Chinese Political Culture* (Berkeley: University of California Press, 1971). Also see Richard Solomon, "From Commitment to Cant: The Evolving Functions of Ideology in the Revolutionary Process," *Ideology and Politics in Contemporary China,* ed. Chalmers Johnson (Seattle: University of Washington Press, 1973), pp. 47-77. For a critique of studies on ideology and politics see Frederic Wakeman, Jr., "The Use and Abuse of Ideology in the Study of Contemporary China," *China Quarterly* no. 61 (March 1975), pp. 127-52.

7. Benjamin I. Schwartz, *Communism and China: Ideology in Flux* (Cambridge, Mass: Harvard University Press, 1968); Stuart R. Schram, *The Political Thought of Mao Tse-tung* (London: Pall Mall Press, 1964); Frederic Wakeman, Jr., *History and Will, Philosophical Perspectives of Mao Tse-tung's Thought* (Berkeley: University of California Press, 1973). More recently the issue has been debated in *Modern China.* See Richard M. Pfeffer,

"Mao and Marx in the Marxist-Leninist Tradition: A Critique of 'The China Field' and a Preliminary Reappraisal," *Modern China* 2:4 (October 1976): 421-60. Benjamin Schwartz replies to Pfeffer in the same issue, pp. 461-72. Part II of this symposium includes Andrew G. Walder, "Marxism, Maoism, and Social Change," *Modern China*, Part A, 3:1 (January 1977): pp. 101-18; Part B, 3:2 (April 1977):125-60. Frederic Wakeman's response is in the April issue, pp. 161-68. Stuart Schram's response is in the same issue, pp. 169-84.

8. Chalmers Johnson, *Peasant Nationalism and Communist Power* (Stanford, Calif.: Stanford University Press, 1962).

9. Mark Selden, *The Yenan Way in Revolutionary China* (Cambridge, Mass.: Harvard University Press, 1971). For a critique of both Selden and Johnson and an alternative hypothesis see Carl E. Dorris, "Peasant Mobilization in North China and the Origins of Yenan Communism,"*China Quarterly* no. 68 (December 1976), pp. 697-719.

10. For example, Richard C. Thornton, *China: The Struggle for Power, 1917-1972,* (Bloomington, Ind.: Indiana University Press, 1975).

11. For an example of the Soviet position see "Hitler and Mao—Two of a Kind," *Literaturnaya gazeta*, August 7, 1974, translated in *Current Digest of The Soviet Press* 26:32 (September 4, 1974), pp. 1-4.

12. Anthony Kubek, *The Amerasia Papers: A Clue to the Catastrophe of China*, 2 vols. (Washington, D.C.: U.S. Government Printing Office, 1970). This document was prepared under the auspices of the Senate Internal Security Subcommittee.

13. John S. Service, *The Amerasia Papers: Some Problems in the History of US-China Relations*, China Research Monographs #7 (Berkeley: University of California, Center for Chinese Studies, May 1971).

14. For example see Barbara W. Tuchman, *Stilwell and the American Experience in China 1911-45,* (New York: Macmillan, 1971). Also see Joseph W. Esherick, ed., *Lost Chance in China: The World War II Dispatches of John S. Service* (New York: Vintage Books, 1975).

15. Franz Schurmann, *Ideology and Organization in Communist China*, 2d ed. (Berkeley: University of California Press, 1968), pp. 17-57.

16. Ho Ping-ti, "Salient Aspects of China's Heritage," *China in Crisis*, ed. Tang Tsou, 2 vols. (Chicago: University of Chicago Press, 1968). Also see Tang Tsou, "The Values of the Chinese Revolution," *China's Developmental Experience*, ed. Michel Oksenberg (New York: Praeger Publishers, 1973), pp. 27-41.

17. L. La Dany, "Mao's China: The Decline of a Dynasty," *Foreign Affairs* 45:4 (July 1967), pp. 610-23.

18. John B. Starr, *Ideology and Culture* (New York: Harper & Row, 1973), pp. 31-43.

19. G. William Skinner, "Marketing and Social Structure in Rural China," *Journal of Asian Studies* 24:1 (November 1964), pp. 2-43; 24:2 (February 1965), pp. 195-228; 24:3 (May 1965), pp. 363-99. Part III deals with the People's Republic of China.

20. This point is particularly made by Ho Ping-ti, "China's Heritage."

21. See Chao Kuo-chun, *Agrarian Policies of Mainland China: A Documentary Study (1949-56)*, (Cambridge, Mass.: Harvard University Press, 1963).

22. Allen S. Whiting, *China Crosses the Yalu: The Decision to Enter the Korean War* (New York: Macmillan, 1960); Robert R. Simmons, *The Strained Alliance* (New York: Free Press, 1975).

23. For a diagram of this development please see Starr, *Ideology and Culture*, pp. 66-67.

24. Mu Fu-sheng, *The Wilting of the Hundred Flowers* (New York: Praeger Publishers, 1963). Mu experienced the movement and gives a vivid account of its progress.

25. Peter Van Ness, *Revolution and Chinese Foreign Policy* (Berkeley: University of California Press, 1970).

26. William W. Whitson, *Chinese Military and Political Leaders and the Distribution of Power in China 1956-1971*, Rand R-1091-DOS/ARPA (Santa Monica, Calif.: Rand Corporation, 1973).

CHAPTER TWO

1. "Introducing a Cooperative," April 15, 1958.

2. Schurmann, *Ideology and Organization*, p. 30.

3. Wakemann, *History and Will*.

4. Mao, "Build Stable Base Areas in the Northeast," *Selected Works*, vol. IV, p. 84.

5. Mao, "The Foolish Old Man Who Removed the Mountains," *Selected Works*, vol. III, p. 322.

6. "Chairman Hua Inspects Three Northeastern Provinces," *Peking Review* no. 20 (May 13,1977), pp. 10-15.

7. Mao, "Some Questions Concerning Methods of Leadership," *Selected Works*, vol. III, p. 120.

8. See Schurmann's chapter on ideology, *Ideology and Organization*, pp. 17-104.

9. For a comprehensive discussion of the mass campaign see James Townsend, *Political Participation in Communist China* (Berkeley: University of California Press, 1967). Townsend also has a good discussion of the mass organizations in China.

10. Whiting, *China Croses the Yalu*.

11. Mu Fu-sheng, *The Wilting of the Hundred Flowers*. This account gives good insight into the development of the Hundred Flowers campaign.

12. Skinner, "Marketing and Social Structure in Rural China."

13. For an account of the Socialist Education Campaign see Richard Baum and Frederick C. Teiwes, *Ssu-ch'ing: The Socialist Education Movement of 1962-66*, (Berkeley: University of California Press, 1968).

Also see Richard Baum, *Prelude to Revolution: Mao, the Party, and The Peasant Question, 1962-66*, (New York: Columbia University Press, 1975).

14. A number of books which deal with the Cultural Revolution are noted in the bibliography. A good treatment of developments can be found in Jacques Guillermaz, *The Chinese Communist Party in Power 1949-1976,* (Boulder, Colo.: Westview Press, 1976); see especially pp. 359-451.

15. For an evaluation of Lin Piao's career see Michael Y. M. Kau, ed., *The Lin Piao Affair,* (White Plains, N.Y.: International Arts and Sciences Press, 1975).

16. Feng Yu-lan, "Changes in My Understanding of Confucius," *China Reconstructs* 23:8 (August 1974), pp. 8-11.

17. For some of the current criticisms of the "Gang of Four" see "Articles Exposing the 'Gang of Four,' " *China Reconstructs* 26:2 and 3 (February and March 1977).

18. See Hua Kuo-feng, "Mobilize the Whole Party, Make Greater Efforts to Develop Agriculture and Strive to Build Tachai-Type Counties throughout the Country," *Peking Review* 18:44 (October 31, 1975), pp. 7-10, 18. The same theme was continued after the second conference held in December 1976. Several provincial radio broadcasts have mentioned coverups and distortions caused by henchmen of the "Gang of Four" which have resulted in inflated agricultural production statistics.

19. "Chairman Hua in Taching," *China Reconstructs* 26:8 (August 1977), pp. 2-5.

20. Quotations in this section are taken from translations made by the Foreign Broadcast Information Service (hereafter FBIS), *Daily Reports* (People's Republic of China). For further information on the campaign against Teng see articles by John Starr, John Gittings, Edward Rice, and Michel Oksenberg in *China Quarterly* no. 67 (September 1976), pp. 457-518. Also see William Heaton, "The Dismissal of Teng Hsiao-p'ing" (unpublished paper prepared for the Western Conference of the Association for Asian Studies in October 1976).

21. G. William Skinner and Edwin A. Winckler, "Compliance Succession in Rural Communist China: A Cyclical Theory," *A Sociological Reader on Complex Organizations,* ed. Amitai Etzioni (New York: Holt, Rinehart and Winston, 1969), pp. 410-38.

22. A good discussion of political culture and the socialization of the Chinese people is to be found in James R. Townsend, *Politics in China* (Boston: Little, Brown, and Co., 1974), pp. 179-224.

23. Martin King Whyte, *Small Groups and Political Rituals in China* (Berkeley: University of California Press, 1974).

24. William L. Parish, "China—Team, Brigade, or Commune?" *Problems of Communism* 25:2 (March-April, 1976), p. 51.

25. Martin King Whyte, "Inequality and Stratification in China," *China Quarterly* no. 64 (December 1975), pp. 684-711. Also see Richard Curt Kraus, "The Limits of Maoist Egalitarianism," *Asian Survey* 16:11 (November 1976), pp. 1081-96. There is some disagreement between scholars as to how family size affects peasant income. Regional diversity accounts for much of this disparity.

26. See William L. Parish, "Socialism and the Chinese Peasant Family," *Journal of Asian Studies* 34:3 (May 1975), pp. 613-30 for an excellent examination of the sociology of a commune. This article should be read in conjunction with his article in *Problems of Communism* cited above and the article by Whyte on inequality and stratification in *China Quarterly*. Also see Byung-Joon Ahn, "The Political Economy of the People's Commune in China: Changes and Continuities," *Journal of Asian Studies* 34:3 (May 1975), pp. 631-58.

27. An example given of typical family income is that of Yang Yu-chuan and his wife Tang Ken-ti. Yang is a cadre at the Shanghai No. 5 Steel Mill and his wife works at the Shanghai No. 2 Cotton Mill. They have three children. They live in a modest two bedroom second floor apartment in Shanghai's Puto district. Yang earns 76 Jenmin Pai ($1 US = 1.85 JMP) and his wife earns 70 JMP monthly. Their combined income is 146 JMP, or about $79. Their monthly expenses are as follows:

Item	Amount JMP	% of income
Food	60.0	41
Clothing	10.0	7
Rent, water, gas, electricity	12.0	8
Tuition, day care, newspapers, stationery	4.0	3
Miscellaneous	5.0	3.5
Money sent to Yang's mother for support	10.0	7
Extras and entertainment	25.0	17
Savings	20.0	13.5
Total	146.0	100.0

Source: "Two Family Accounts," *China Reconstructs* 24:4 (April 1975), pp. 14, 34.

28. Whyte, "Inequality and Stratification," pp. 704-05.

29. Ibid., p. 694.

30. Yung Hung, "Education in China Today," *China Reconstructs* 24:5 (May 1975), pp. 2-6. Also see articles in the same issue related to the *hsia fang* of students.

31. "The Road for China's School Graduates," *China Reconstructs* 24:7 (July 1975), pp. 2-8; also see related articles pp. 9-13. More recently some talented students have been able to go directly into higher education without participating in agriculture or industry. Still others have been assigned to areas very near their homes. In view of Hua Kuo-feng's commitment to achieve economic modernization in China, it is likely that further changes in the education system will be made in order to encourage the development of technical experts.

32. Reports in July 1977 indicated that underground literature was circulating in China. Some publications were by former Red Guards, who expressed dissatisfaction with the present situation. See "Hong Kong Magazine Reports 'Underground' Literature in PRC," FBIS (citing Agency-France Press), June 23, 1977.

33. For the impact of the New Marriage Law see C.K. Yang, *Chinese Communist Society: The Family and the Village* (Cambridge, Mass.: M.I.T. Press, 1959).

34. For the official Chinese Communist view of women see the series entitled "Women of New China" in the June 1975 issue of *China Reconstructs*. A somewhat different view is taken by Shelah G. Leader, "The Emancipation of Chinese Women," *World Politics* 26:1 (October 1973), pp. 55-79. For a more extensive view of women in China see Margery Wolf and Roxane Witke, eds., *Women in Chinese Society* (Stanford, Calif.: Stanford University Press, 1975).

35. The best treatment on Chinese minorities is June Dreyer, *China's Forty Millions: Minority Nationalities and National Integration in the People's Republic of China* (Cambridge, Mass.: Harvard University Press, 1976).

36. On the issue of human rights in China see the series of articles by Ross Munro in the *New York Times*, October 9-12, 1977.

CHAPTER THREE

1. This editorial appeared on October 10, 1976. An English translation is given in *Peking Review* 19:42 (October 15, 1976), p. 7.

2. For an analysis of leadership changes through the 10th CCP Congress see A. Doak Barnett, *Uncertain Passage* (Washington, D.C.: Brookings Institution, 1974), pp. 202-42.

3. For a discussion of Hua's career see Michel Oksenberg and Sai-cheung Yeung, "Hua Kuo-feng's Pre–Cultural Revolution Hunan Years, 1949-66: The Making of a Political Generalist," *China Quarterly* no. 69 (March 1977), pp. 3-52.

4. Barnett, *Uncertain Passage*, pp. 36-7.

5. Robert A. Scalapino, "The CCP's Provincial Secretaries," *Problems of Communism* 25:4 (July-August 1976), pp. 18-35.

6. See David Bonavia, "Teng Back in Driving Seat," *Far Eastern Economic Review* 97:31 (August 5, 1977), pp. 8-9, 11.

7. Starr, *Ideology and Culture*, pp. 184-5.

8. For a good discussion of the development of the Communist Youth League see Townsend, *China*, pp. 253-58.

9. An account of a young person who was sent to a rural area and subsequently became a member of the Party is Ho Li-chun, "How I Feel at Home in the Forest," *China Reconstructs* 24:7 (July 1975), pp. 11-13.

10. The ministries and commissions of the PRC are given as follows: Foreign Affairs, National Defense, State Planning Commission, State Capital Construction Commission, Public Security, Foreign Trade, Economic Relations with Foreign Countries, Agriculture and Forestry, Metallurgical Industry, First Ministry of Machine Building, Second Ministry of Machine Building, Third Ministry of Machine Building, Fourth Ministry of Machine Building, Fifth Ministry of Machine Building, Sixth Ministry of

Machine Building, Seventh Ministry of Machine Building, Coal Industry, Petroleum and Chemical Industries, Water Conservancy and Power, Light Industry, Railways, Communications, Posts and Telecommunications, Finance, Commerce, Culture, Education, Public Health, Physical Culture, and Sports Commission.

11. Hua Kuo-feng, *Report on the Work of the Government*, February 26, 1978, in FBIS, March 7, 1968.

12. For a discussion of methods used by the Party to control the state bureaucracy during the pre–Cultural Revolution period see A. Doak Barnett, *Cadres, Bureaucracy and Political Power in Communist China* (New York: Columbia University Press, 1967). Also see Barnett's work *Chinese Communist Politics in Action* (Seattle: University of Washington Press, 1969).

13. For some observations about a May 7 Cadre School see Alexander Casella, "The Nanniwan May 7th Cadre School," *China Quarterly* no. 53 (January-March 1973), pp. 153-7. Also see the series of translated articles in *Current Background* no. 899 (January 19, 1970).

14. An example is the discussion with the leader of a factory revolutionary committee in the film *Shanghai: The New China* (CBS, 1974).

15. Mark Gayn, "A View From the Village," *Problems of Communism* 23:5 (September-October 1974), pp. 10-15.

16. For an account of the corrective labor system see Martin K. Whyte, "Corrective Labor Camps in China," *Asian Survey* 13:3 (March 1973), pp. 253-69.

17. Article 15, PRC National Constitution, 1975.

18. All figures used in this section are taken from *The Military Balance 1976-77* (London: Institute for Strategic Studies, 1977), pp. 50-51. The ISS figures on China are highly regarded as authoritative. Also see Angus M. Fraser, *The People's Liberation Army* (New York: Crane, Russak and Co., 1973).

19. For recent developments in China's military preparations see a series of three articles by Drew Middleton in the *New York Times*, December 1976. These were reprinted in the *Denver Post*, December 9, 1976. Also see Russell Spurr, "China's Defense: Men Against Machines," *Far Eastern Economic Review* 95:4 (January 28, 1977), pp. 24-30. Also see the report made by correspondent Tadokoro on his visit to PLA units in Tientsin, *Asahi Shimbun*, July 10, 1977.

20. Among Whitson's contributions are "The Field Army in Chinese Communist Military Politics," *China Quarterly* no. 37 (January-March, 1969), pp. 1-29; "Organizational Perspectives and Decision-Making in the Chinese Communist High Command," *Elites in the People's Republic of China*, ed. Robert A. Scalapino (Seattle: University of Washington Press, 1972), pp. 381-415; *The Military and Political Power in China in the 1970s* (New York: Praeger Publishers, 1972); with C. Huang, *The Chinese High Command—A History of Communist Military Politics 1927-71* (New York: Praeger Publishers, 1973); *Chinese Military and Political Leaders and The*

Calif.: Rand Corporation, 1973). Whitson is by no means the only contributor to our knowledge of the Chinese military. Others include Parris Chang, Ralph L. Powell, Thomas Robinson, Harvey Nelson, Jonathan Pollack, Michael Pillsbury, and of course many others.

21. Whitson, "The Field Army."

22. *Radio Peking*, Feb. 2, 1977, in FBIS, Feb. 3, 1977.

23. For an excellent review of literature on the PLA and some of the outstanding issues see Jonathan D. Pollack, "The Study of Chinese Military Politics: Toward A Framework for Analysis," *Political Military Systems: Comparative Perspectives*, ed. Catherine M. Kellcher, vol. 4, Sage Research Progress Series on War, Revolution, and Peacekeeping (Beverly Hills, Calif.: Sage Publications, 1974), pp. 239-70.

24. See William Heaton, "The Minorities and the Military in China," *Armed Forces and Society* 3:2 (February 1977), pp. 325-42.

25. Lei Feng was a PLA soldier killed in the line of duty in 1962. On how the PLA emulates Lei Feng and other socialization activities see "Men With Tough Bones," *China Reconstructs* 26:8 (August 1977), pp. 34-38.

26. Neville Maxwell, *India's China War* (New York: Pantheon Books, 1971).

27. Thomas W. Robinson, "The Sino-Soviet Border Dispute: Background, Development, and the March 1969 Clashes," *American Political Science Review* 66:4 (December 1972), pp. 1175-1202.

28. William Heaton, "Chinese Military Power and Foreign Policy: The Case of the Paracel Islands" (Unpublished paper, U.S. Air Force Academy, Colorado Springs, Colo.).

29. See Michael P. Pillsbury, *SALT on the Dragon: Chinese Views of the Soviet-American Strategic Balance* RAND P-5457 (Santa Monica, Calif.: Rand Corporation, 1975).

30. Andrew Nathan, "A Factionalism Model for CCP Politics," *China Quarterly* no. 53 (January-March 1973), pp. 34-66. The debate is continued by Tang Tsou, "Prolegomenon to the Study of Informal Groups in CCP Politics," *China Quarterly* no. 65 (March 1976), pp. 98-114. Nathan's response is in the same issue, pp. 114-16.

31. An example of the two-type approach in the press may be seen in Fox Butterfield, "China: Unraveling the New Mysteries," *New York Times Magazine*, June 19, 1977.

32. Barnett, *Uncertain Passage*, pp. 8-19.

33. Michel Oksenberg and Steven Goldstein, "The Chinese Political Spectrum," *Problems of Communism* 23:2 (March-April 1974), pp. 1-13.

34. Michael Pillsbury, "How 'Useful' A Model?" *Problems of Communism* 24:1 (January-February 1975), pp. 72-73. Other criticisms and the response of Oksenberg and Goldstein are in the same issue.

35. Kenneth Lieberthal, "China in 1975: The Internal Political Scene," *Problems of Communism* 24:3 (May-June 1975), pp. 1-19.

36. The passing of the "Gang of Four" will result in some changes in the composition of factions made in the models cited. It is presently too early to

suggest what the composition of new groups will be.

37. Roxanne Witke, *Comrade Chiang Ch'ing* (Boston: Little, Brown and Co., 1977).

38. These categories are taken from the systems approach outlined by Gabriel Almond and G. Bingham Powell, Jr., *Comparative Politics: A Developmental Approach* (Boston: Little, Brown and Co., 1966). The terms are not identical, but the concepts stem from this approach.

39. Parris H. Chang, "Mao's Last Stand?" *Problems of Communism* 25:4 (July-August 1976), pp. 1-17, see especially pp. 3-4.

40. These are my inferences from the various reports on Tangshan in the Chinese media. The alternatives have not been clearly specified by the Chinese themselves.

41. This is the central thesis of Chang's book *Power and Policy in China* (University Park: Pennsylvania State University Press, 1975).

42. For examples of these dialogues see Kau, *The Lin Piao Affair*.

43. Michel Oksenberg, "Methods of Communication within the Chinese Bureaucracy," *China Quarterly* no. 57 (January-March, 1974), pp. 1-39.

44. Ibid., pp. 36-38.

45. "Tangshan Industrial Capacity Recovers Since Quake," *New China News Agency* July 29, 1977; FBIS, July 29, 1977.

46. "The Railroads—From Order to Disorder," *China Reconstructs* 26:8 (August 1977), pp. 6-9; Also see Liu Tung-chou, "I Fought for the Truth" in the same issue, pp. 10-11.

47. For an evaluation of Mao as a decision maker see Michel Oksenberg, "Mao's Policy Commitments, 1921-1976," *Problems of Communism* 25:6 (November-December 1976), pp. 1-26.

48. Andrew J. Nathan, "Policy Oscillations in the People's Republic of China: A Critique," *China Quarterly* no. 68 (December 1976), pp. 720-33.

49. Edwin A. Winckler, "Policy Oscillations in the People's Republic of China: A Reply," *China Quarterly* no. 68 (December 1976), pp. 734-50.

CHAPTER FOUR

1. Hua Kuo-feng, *Political Report to the 11th National Party Congress,* August 12, 1977 in FBIS Supplement, September 1, 1977.

2. Much of the information on China's economy cited in this chapter comes from Robert F. Dernberger's section on the Chinese economy in Allen S. Whiting and Robert F. Dernberger, *China's Future: Foreign Policy and Economic Development in the Post-Mao Era* (New York: McGraw-Hill Book Co. for the Council on Foreign Relations, 1977), pp. 80-188.

3. Ibid., pp. 90-91. Dernberger notes that some analysts, notably Audrey Donnithorne, have posited the possibility of a cellular economy in China, that is, regional economic autonomy, cf. pp. 92-93. Derberger rejects the cellular economy hypothesis. Events since the 11th CCP Congress would seem to bear out the increased importance being given to central planning.

4. Ibid., p. 126. Also see Alexander Eckstein, *China's Economic*

Resolution (New York: Cambridge University Press, 1977), pp. 206-13.

5. Dernberger, *China's Future*, pp. 152-54.

6. On China's petroleum capabilities see Selig S. Harrison, "Time Bomb in East Asia," *Foreign Policy* no. 20 (Fall 1975), pp. 3-27. Also see the article in the same issue by Choon-ho Park and Jerome Alan Cohen, "The Politics of China's Oil Weapon," pp. 28-49. Another view is taken by Vachlav Smil, "Energy in China: Achievements and Prospects," *China Quarterly* no. 65 (January 1976), pp. 54-82.

7. Eckstein, *China's Economic Revolution*, pp. 260-261.

8. Dernberger, *China's Future*, pp. 172-73.

9. *People's Daily*, August 28, 1977.

10. See Harry Harding and Melvin Gurtov, *The Purge of Lo Jui-ch'ing: The Politics of Chinese Strategic Planning* RAND R-548-PR (Santa Monica, Calif.: Rand Corporation, 1972).

11. This was emphasized in public statements by Chinese leaders just before the Vance visit. See the interview of Li Hsien-nien by Swedish journalist Stefan Lindgren published in *Svenska Dagbladet*, August 14, 1977, translated in FBIS, August 18, 1977. After the Vance visit Teng Hsiao-p'ing claimed that there had been a step backward in U.S. relations since President Ford had pledged to normalize relations with China if reelected; Vance only offered to normalize relations if the U.S. could open a "liaison office" in Taipei. Ford denied Teng's claim.

12. For a lucid analysis of China's three-way conception of international relations see Robert A. Scalapino, *Asia and the Road Ahead: Issues for the Major Powers* (Berkeley: University of California Press, 1975); see the section on China. Scalapino observes that the Chinese often distinguish between state-to-state and people-to-people diplomacy.

13. The Chinese position is outlined in the December 1974 issue of *Lishih Yenchiu* [Historical Research]. See translations in FBIS, January 6, 1975.

14. The various statements on the differing positions of the two sides are frequent and too numerous to cite here. However, there are two useful articles which outline the development of Mao's feelings toward the USSR and foreign policy in general. See John Gittings, "New Light on Mao: His View of the World," *China Quarterly* no. 60 (October-December 1974), pp. 750-66. Also see Richard Levy, "New Light on Mao: His Views on the Soviet Union's Political Economy," *China Quarterly* no. 61 (March 1975), pp. 95-117.

15. Gene T. Hsiao, "Prospects for A New Sino-Japanese Relationship," *China Quarterly* no. 60 (October-December 1974), pp. 720-49.

16. There are a number of good books on China's relations with Southeast Asia. For example see Jay Taylor, *China and Southeast Asia: Peking's Relations with Revolutionary Movements*, 2d ed. (New York: Praeger Publishers, 1976). Also see Melvin Gurtov, *China and Southeast Asia—The Politics of Survival* (Lexington, Mass.: D. C. Heath & Co., 1971). For an examination of China's relations with the overseas Chinese see Stephen

Fitzgerald, *China and the Overseas Chinese* (New York: Cambridge University Press, 1972).

17. Van Ness, *Revolution and Chinese Foreign Policy.*

18. S. P. Seth, "Sino-Indian Relations: Changing Perspectives," *Problems of Communism* 23:2 (March-April 1974), pp. 14-26.

19. For insights into China's Africa Policy see Bruce Larkin, *China in Africa, 1949-1970* (Berkeley: University of California Press, 1971). Also see Alaba Ogunsanwo, *China's Policy in Africa, 1958-71* (New York: Cambridge University Press, 1974). Also see Warren Weinstein, *Chinese and Soviet Aid to Africa* (New York: Praeger Publishers, 1976).

20. Samuel S. Kim, "The People's Republic of China in the United Nations: A Preliminary Analysis," *World Politics* 26:3 (April 1974), pp. 299-330.

21. On China and its international position see Scalapino, *Asia and the Road Ahead.* Also see Harold Hinton, *Three and a Half Powers: The New Balance In Asia* (Bloomington: Indiana University Press, 1975). On the impact of detente on China see Walter C. Clemens, Jr. "The Impact of Detente on Chinese and Soviet Communism," *Journal of International Affairs* 28:2 (1974), pp. 133-157.

CHAPTER FIVE

---

1. Peter Duus, *Party Rivalry and Political Change in Taisho Japan* (Cambridge, Mass.: Harvard University Press, 1968), p. 251.

2. Ibid., pp. 6-7.

3. John K. Fairbank, Edwin O. Reischauer, and Albert M. Craig, *East Asia, The Modern Transformation* (Boston: Houghton Mifflin Co., 1965), p. 569.

4. Hugh Borton, *Japan's Modern Century*, 2d ed., (New York: Ronald Press Corp., 1970), pp. 320-21.

5. Robert A. Scalapino, "Elections in Prewar Japan" in Robert E. Ward, ed., *Political Development in Modern Japan* (Princeton, N.J.: Princeton University Press, 1968), p. 270.

6. Scalapino in Ward, *Political Development*, p. 271.

7. Duus, *Party Rivalry*, p. 83.

8. Ibid., p. 272.

9. Duus, *Party Rivalry*, p. 117.

10. Ibid., p. 137.

11. Borton, *Japan's Modern Century*, p. 340.

12. Ibid., p. 341.

13. Fairbank, *East Asia*, p. 572.

14. Duus, *Party Rivalry*, p. 146.

15. Ibid., p. 225.

16. Scalapino in Ward, *Political Development*, p. 274.

17. Fairbank, *East Asia*, p. 573.

18. Duus, *Party Rivalry*, p. 183.

19. Borton, *Japan's Modern Century*, p. 349.

20. Scalapino in Ward, *Political Development*, p. 276.

21. Borton, *Japan's Modern Century*, p. 351.

22. Duus, *Party Rivalry*, p. 203.

23. Borton, *Japan's Modern Century*, p. 351.

24. Ibid.

25. Ibid., pp. 351-52.

26. Duus, *Party Rivalry*, pp. 214-15.

27. Ibid., pp. 234-35.

28. Borton, *Japan's Modern Century*, pp. 355-56.

29. Ibid., p. 355.

30. Edwin O. Reischauer, *Japan, The Story of a Nation* (New York: Alfred A. Knopf, 1970), p. 181.

31. Fairbank, *East Asia*, p. 578.

32. Reischauer, *Story of a Nation*, pp. 184-88.

33. Ibid., p. 189.

34. Scalapino in Ward, *Political Development*, p. 278.

35. Borton, *Japan's Modern Century*, pp. 360-61.

36. Ibid., p. 362.

37. Reischauer, *Story of a Nation*, p. 192.

38. Borton, *Japan's Modern Century*, p. 377.

39. Ibid., p. 378.

40. Fairbank, *East Asia*, p. 580.

41. Ibid., p. 594.

42. Kurt Steiner, "Popular Political Participation and Political Development in Japan: The Rural Level," in Ward, *Political Development*, p. 239.

43. Leonard Mosley, *Hirohito, Emperor of Japan* (Englewood Cliffs, N.J.: Prentice-Hall, 1966), p. 337.

44. Ibid., p. 341.

45. Ibid., p. 347-48.

46. Mark Gayn, "Drafting the Japanese Constitution," in Jon Livingston et al., eds., *Postwar Japan, 1945 to the Present* (New York: Pantheon Books, 1973), p. 20.

47. John M. Maki, *Court and Constitution in Japan* (Seattle: University of Washington Press, 1964), pp. 411-24.

48. Walt Sheldon, *The Honorable Conquerors, The Occupation of Japan, 1945-1952* (New York: Macmillan, 1965), p. 109.

49. Ibid., p. 112.

50. Hans H. Baerwald, *The Purge of Japanese Leaders under the Occupation* (Berkeley: University of California Press, 1959), pp. 78-80.

51. Borton, *Japan's Modern Century*, p. 477.

52. Fairbank, *East Asia*, pp. 816-17.

53. Ibid., p. 817.

54. Borton, *Japan's Modern Century*, p. 473.

55. Robert E. Ward, "Reflections on the Allied Occupation and Planned Political Change in Japan," in Ward, *Political Development*, p. 502.

56. Borton, p. 479.
57. Ibid., p. 480.
50. Ibid., p. 482.

CHAPTER SIX

1. *Japan Echo* 4:2, 1977, p. 56.
2. Government of Japan, *The Japan of Today* (Tokyo: Ministry of Foreign Affairs, 1976), p. 73.
3. Edwin O. Reischauer, *The Japanese* (Cambridge, Mass.: Harvard University Press, 1977), p. 294.
4. Scalapino in Ward, *Political Development*, p. 285.
5. *Mainichi*, March 23, 1975, and *Asahi*, June 14, 1977.
6. Bradley M. Richardson, *The Political Culture of Japan* (Berkeley: University of California Press, 1974), pp. 8-9.
7. Ibid., pp. 31-33.
8. Ibid., p. 42.
9. Ibid., p. 52.
10. Ibid., p. 56.
11. Ibid., p. 67, 71-73.
12. *Sankei*, February 24, 1975.
13. *Yomiuri*, March 20, 1977.
14. Richardson, *Political Culture*, p. 98.
15. Taketsugu Tsurutani, *Political Change in Japan* (New York: David McKay Co., 1977), pp. 32-58.
16. Richardson, *Political Culture*, pp. 110-12.
17. *Sankei*, November 25, 1975. However, that figure had declined to 24.8 percent in April, 1977 (*Tokyo Shimbun*, April 24, 1977).
18. Richardson, *Political Culture*, p. 156.
19. Ibid., p. 168, 175.
20. Ibid., p. 183.
21. Ibid., pp. 196, 205.
22. Ibid., p. 219.
23. *Asahi*, December 2, 1975.
24. Richardson, *Political Culture*, pp. 230-31, 234.
25. I am heavily dependent on the excellent account written by Gerald Curtis dealing with the details of elections in Japan, *Election Campaigning Japanese Style* (New York: Columbia University Press, 1971).
26. Ibid., pp. 22-23.
27. Reischauer, *The Japanese*, p. 274.

CHAPTER SEVEN

1. Theodore McNelly, "The Constitutionality of Japan's Defense Establishment," in James H. Buck, ed., *The Modern Japanese Military*

System (Beverly Hills, Calif.: Sage Publications, 1975), p. 102.

2. Ibid., p. 104.

3. Ibid., p. 106.

4. *Nihon Keizai,* November 18, 1975.

5. *Tokyo Shimbun,* May 14, 1975.

6. *Sankei,* March 5, 1975 and September 30, 1975.

7. *Asahi,* evening ed., October 14, 1975.

8. *Asahi,* November 3, 1975.

9. *Yomiuri,* November 2, 1975.

10. *Yomiuri,* evening ed., September 23, 1975.

11. Tsurutani, *Political Change,* p. 216.

12. Koichi Kishimoto, *Politics in Modern Japan* (Tokyo: Japan Echo, Inc., 1977), p. 61.

13. Hans H. Baerwald, *Japan's Parliament* (Cambridge: Cambridge University Press, 1974), p. 76.

14. Ibid.

15. Kishimoto, *Politics in Modern Japan,* p. 52.

16. Baerwald, *Japan's Parliament,* p. 86.

17. Ibid., pp. 81-84.

18. Ibid., p. 85.

19. Ibid., p. 109.

20. Baerwald, *Japan's Parliament,* pp. 108-10.

21. *Tokyo Shimbun,* evening ed., January 23, 1976.

22. Baerwald, *Japan's Parliament,* p. 93.

23. Ibid., p. 101.

24. Ibid., pp. 90-91.

25. Article 66, Constitution of Japan, 1947.

26. Nathaniel B. Thayer, *How the Conservatives Rule Japan* (Princeton, N.J.: Princeton University Press, 1969), p. 188.

27. Government of Japan, *The Japan of Today* (Tokyo: Ministry of Foreign Affairs, 1976), p. 27.

28. *Asahi Evening News,* July 7, 1972.

29. Thayer, *How the Conservatives Rule Japan,* p. 191.

30. One member had been elected fourteen times; two, twelve times; two, ten times; three, nine times; three, seven times; one, six times; four, five times; and one, three times. Two were from the upper house; both had been elected three times, and one was not a Diet member.

31. Thayer, *How the Conservatives Rule Japan,* p. 198.

32. Ibid., p. 203.

33. Article 81, Constitution of Japan, 1947.

34. The following description of the Japanese judicial system is from John M. Maki, *Court and Constitution in Japan* (Seattle: University of Washington Press, 1964), pp. xxiii-xxxii.

35. Underlining added. Articles 92 and 93 of the Constitution of Japan, 1947.

36. McNelly in Buck, *The Modern Japanese Military System,* p. 159.

37. Alvin L. Hanks, "A Comparative Study of Municipal Administration in Japanese and American Cities," (unpublished manuscript, 1972), p. 12.

38. Ministry of Foreign Affairs, *The Japan of Today*, pp. 15-16.

39. McNelly in Buck, *The Modern Japanese Military System*, p. 161.

40. Frank Langdon, *Politics in Japan* (Boston: Little, Brown and Co., 1967), p. 187.

CHAPTER EIGHT

1. Nathaniel B. Thayer, "Elections, Coalitions, and Prime Ministers," in Lewis Austin, ed., *Japan: The Paradox of Progress* (New Haven, Conn.: Yale University Press, 1976), p. 13.

2. Robert A. Scalapino, *The Japanese Communist Movement: 1920-1965* (Santa Monica, Calif: Rand Corporation, R-447-PR, 1966), pp. 79-80.

3. Ibid., pp. 80-81.

4. Ibid., p. 94.

5. Ibid., p. 137.

6. Scalapino, *Japanese Communist Movement*, p. 138.

7. Allan B. Cole, George O. Totten, and Cecil Uyehara, *Socialist Parties in Postwar Japan* (New Haven, Conn.: Yale University Press, 1966), p. 4.

8. Ibid., p. 23.

9. Robert A. Scalapino and Junnosuke Masumi, *Parties and Politics in Contemporary Japan* (Berkeley: University of California Press, 1967), pp. 28-31.

10. Ibid., p. 39-40.

11. Thayer, *How the Conservatives Rule Japan*, p. 159.

12. Ibid., p. 17.

13. Kishimoto, *Politics in Modern Japan*, p. 74.

14. Ibid.

15. *Asahi*, April 26, 1977.

16. Thayer, *How the Conservatives Rule Japan*, p. 210, 217-28.

17. Foreign Broadcast Information Service (hereafter FBIS), Oct. 26, 1976, p. c9.

18. A series of exposés appeared in the Japanese magazine *Bungei Shunju*, which went into the organization of businesses to which Tanaka was connected. The article included allegations of substantial improprieties to which Tanaka replied in defense. He was eventually forced from office in December 1974.

19. The Lockheed scandal broke when in congressional hearings in the U.S. it was asserted that millions of dollars had changed hands in the form of "commissions" in the process of selling Lockheed products in Japan. The trading company Marubeni, the rightist Kodama Yukio, Tanaka Kakuei, and others were implicated in what eventually involved a $12 million scandal.

20. *Sankei*, November 17, 1976.

21. FBIS, April 26, 1977, pp. c6-c7.

22. *Nihon Keizai*, February 10, 1977.

23. *Asahi,* July 28, 1976.

24. Chie Nakane, *Japanese Society* (Berkeley: University of California Press, 1970), pp. 78-79.

25. *Asahi,* evening ed., April 27, 1977.

26. *Tokyo Shimbun,* August 5, 1977.

27. Ibid., August 15, 1977.

28. Ibid.

29. Ibid.

30. *Sankei,* October 20, 1977.

31. Ibid., January 18, 1976 and January 15, 1977.

32. *Shakaito,* February 1977.

33. Tsurutani, *Political Change,* p. 130.

34. *Sekai,* September 1975, as found in *Japan Echo* 2:4, p. 71.

35. Ibid.

36. I am indebted to Kenji Hattori for his in-depth presentation on this subject at the 1977 Annual Meeting of the Western Conference of the Association for Asian Studies, USAF Academy, Colorado, October 7-8, 1977.

37. *Nihon Keizai,* May 17, 1977.

38. FBIS, January 1, 1977, p. c9.

39. *Asahi,* January 18, 1976.

40. FBIS, August 25, 1976, p. c3.

41. *Japan Times,* December 4 and 5, 1977.

42. *Tokyo Shimbun,* March 25, 1977.

43. *Shakaito,* February 1977.

44. *Asahi,* March 25, 1977.

45. FBIS, May 12, 1977, p. c6.

46. *Tokyo Shimbun,* July 28, 1975.

47. *Shakaito,* February 1977.

48. *Asahi,* August 24, 1975.

49. *Manichi,* August 24, 1975.

50. Ibid.

51. *Nihon Keizai,* July 13, 1975.

52. *Shakaito,* February 1977.

53. *Japan Echo,* 3:4 (1976), pp. 81-95.

54. Ibid., pp. 91-92.

55. FBIS, April 20, 1977, p. c2.

56. Kishimoto, *Politics in Modern Japan,* p. 127.

57. *Asahi,* June 15, 1976.

58. *Shakaito,* February 1977.

59. Ibid.

60. *Mainichi,* March 28, 1977.

61. Ibid.

CHAPTER NINE

---

1. Tsurutani, *Political Change,* p. 27.

2. Akira Kubota, *Higher Civil Servants in Postwar Japan* (Princeton, N.J.: Princeton University Press, 1969), p. 71.

3. *Japan Report*, August 16, 1977.

4. *Japan Echo*, 3:4 (1976), p. 63.

5. Ibid., p. 65.

6. Ibid., p. 66.

7. Thayer, *How the Conservatives Rule Japan*, pp. 61-62.

8. Chitoshi Yanaga, *Big Business in Japanese Politics* (New Haven, Conn.: Yale University Press, 1968), p. 42.

9. Reischauer, *The Japanese*, p. 193.

10. Yanaga, *Big Business*, pp. 46-49.

11. Ibid., pp. 49-50.

12. Donald P. Whitaker, et al., *Area Handbook for Japan*, 3d ed. (Washington, D.C.: United States Government Printing Office, 1974), p. 391.

13. Government of Japan *Defense of Japan, 1976* (Tokyo: Defense Agency, 1976), p. 160.

14. Ibid., p. 132.

15. *Mainichi*, May 25, 1976.

16. *Kanagawa Shimbun*, March 31, 1976.

17. *Nikkan Kogyo*, August 23, 1977.

18. Paul F. Langer, *Japanese National Security Policy—Domestic Determinants* (Santa Monica, Calif.: Rand Corporation, 1972), p. 72.

19. *Nihon Keizai*, December 5, 1975.

20. Langer, *Japanese Security Policy*, p. 73 (footnote).

21. Ibid., p. 66.

22. Ibid., p. 67.

23. *Mainichi*, February 3, 1976.

24. *Mainichi*, evening ed., April 5, 1977.

25. *Japan Echo*, 4:2 (1977), p. 96.

26. *Japan Quarterly*, April/June 1976, pp. 116-120.

27. *Asahi*, evening ed., July 14, 1976.

28. *Japan Echo*, 4:2 (1977), p. 96.

29. *Japan Quarterly*, April/June 1976, p. 118.

30. *Nihon Keizai*, January 28, 1977.

31. Government of Japan, Ministry of Foreign Affairs, *Information Bulletin, 1974* (Tokyo: Public Information Bureau, 1973), p. 122.

32. *Nihon Keizai*, evening ed., January 29, 1977.

33. *Tokyo Shimbun*, March 3, 1977.

34. *Yomiuri*, June 29, 1977.

35. *Yomiuri*, March 29, 1976.

CHAPTER TEN

1. *Yomiuri*, March 20, 1977.

2. Reischauer, *The Japanese*, p. 270.

3. Ibid., p. 271.

4. *Nihon Keizai,* October 6, 1976.

5. Ibid., May 17, 1977.

6. *Tokyo Shimbun,* March 15, 1977.

7. John E. Endicott, *Japan's Nuclear Option: Political, Technical, and Strategic Factors* (New York: Praeger Publishers, 1975), p. 123.

8. *Nihon Keizai,* May 17, 1977.

9. *Yomiuri,* June 25, 1977.

10. *Asahi,* May 21, 1977.

11. Defense Agency, *Defense of Japan,* p. 53.

12. Government of Japan, *Defense of Japan, 1976, Summary* (Tokyo: Defense Agency, 1976), p. 12.

13. Ibid., p. 13.

14. *Survival,* November/December 1972.

CHAPTER ELEVEN

1. Kyung Cho Chung, *Korea, The Third Republic* (New York: Macmillan, 1971), p. 74.

2. Nena Vreeland and Rinn-Sup Shinn, et al., *Area Handbook for North Korea* (Washington, D.C.: United States Government Printing Office, 1976). p. 31. The author highlights the significant contribution of this book to this current effort. It was an invaluable source.

3. Koon Woo Nam, *The North Korean Communist Leadership, 1945-1965: A Study of Factionalism and Political Consolidation* (University, Ala.: University of Alabama Press, 1974), p. 15.

4. Ibid., p. 141.

5. Ibid., pp. 144-49.

6. Lawrence E. Grinter, "South Korea, Military Aid, and U.S. Policy Options," *The National Security Affairs Forum,* Spring/Summer 1975, p. 37.

7. Vreeland and Shinn, *Handbook for North Korea,* p. 159.

8. Ibid., p. 169.

9. Ibid., p. 160.

10. Ibid., p. 162.

11. Ibid., pp. 166-67.

12. Ibid., p. 158.

13. Ibid., p. 184.

14. Ibid., p. 155.

15. Grinter, "South Korea, Military Aid," p. 39.

16. Vreeland and Shinn, *Handbook for North Korea,* p. 312.

17. Ibid., p. 238.

18. Ibid., p. 239.

19. Arthur S. Banks, ed., *Political Handbook of the World: 1975* (New York: McGraw-Hill Book Co., 1975), p. 188.

20. Chung, *Third Republic,* p. 30.

21. Gregory Henderson, *Korea, the Politics of the Vortex* (Cambridge,

Mass.: Harvard University Press, 1968), pp. 304-305.

22. The following events of the coup are from Se-Jin Kim, *The Politics of Military Revolution in Korea* (Chapel Hill: University of North Carolina Press, 1971).

23. Ibid., p. 35.

24. Ibid., p. 91.

25. *Washington Star*, December 12, 1975.

26. FBIS, October 17, 1972.

27. *Washington Post*, May 14, 1975.

28. Ibid.

29. Ibid., June 29, 1975.

30. *Asian Survey*, 14:1 (1974), p. 45.

31. *Japan Times*, June 6, 1974.

32. *Haptong*, August 13, 1977.

33. John L. Frisbee, "Korea," *Air Force Magazine*, 58:12 December 1975.

34. Ibid.

35. George Ogle, "Changing Character of Labor-Government Management Relations in the Republic of Korea," Unpublished paper, p. 3.

36. Ibid.

37. Ibid.

38. *Far Eastern Economic Review*, vol. 98, July 29, 1977, p. 22.

Selected Bibliography

CHINA

For the undergraduate student there are a number of English language publications with valuable information on China. Among publications from China are *Peking Review* and *China Reconstructs*. Translations of broadcast materials may be obtained from the Foreign Broadcast Information Service (FBIS) *Daily Reports* (green cover for the People's Republic of China). Another good primary source is *Survey of the People's Republic of China Press*, published by the U.S. Consulate General in Hong Kong, which contains dispatches from the New China News Agency and translations from the Chinese Press.

The reader will readily recognize that many of our notes refer to articles in *China Quarterly* and *Asian Survey*. Besides those periodicals there are valuable materials in *Pacific Affairs, Modern China, The Journal of Asian Studies, Problems of Communism,* and a host of other journals both on Asia and in the scholarly disciplines. We suggest that these sources be used to supplement materials in this text.

We also wish to list a few books which we have found to be especially useful in our preparation of this text. This list is by no means exhaustive; however, we are selecting those that we believe undergraduate students could readily utilize to obtain a greater depth of information.

Barnett, A. Doak. *Cadres, Bureaucracy, and Political Power in Communist China.* New York: Columbia University Press, 1967.
____. *China in Transition.* Washington, D.C.: Brookings Institution, 1976.

_____. *Chinese Communist Politics in Action*. Seattle: University of Washington Press, 1969.

Baum, Richard, ed. *China in Ferment: Perspectives on the Cultural Revolution*. Englewood Cliffs, N.J.: Prentice-Hall, 1971.

Belden, Jack. *China Shakes the World*. New York: Harper & Row, 1949.

Ch'en, Jerome. *Mao and the Chinese Revolution*. London: Oxford University Press, 1966.

Clough, Ralph N., et al. *The United States, China, and Arms Control*. Washington, D.C.: Brookings Institution, 1975.

Dreyer, June T. *China's Forty Millions*. Cambridge, Mass.: Harvard University Press, 1976.

Durdin, Tillman, et al. *The New York Times Report from Red China*. New York: Avon Books, 1972.

Eckstein, Alexander. *China's Economic Revolution*. New York: Cambridge University Press, 1977.

Fairbank, John K. *The United States and China*. 3d ed. Cambridge, Mass.: Harvard University Press, 1972.

Guillermaz, Jacques. *The Chinese Communist Party in Power 1949-1976*. Boulder, Colo.: Westview Press, 1976.

Hinton, Harold. *China's Turbulent Quest*. New York: Macmillan, 1970.

Hinton, William. *Fanshen: A Documentary of Revolution in a Chinese Village*. New York: Monthly Review Press, 1966.

Ho Ping-ti and Tsou Tang. *China in Crisis*. 2 vols. Chicago: University of Chicago Press, 1968.

Houn, Franklin W. *A Short History of Chinese Communism*. Englewood Cliffs, N.J.: Prentice-Hall, 1967.

Johnson, Chalmers, ed. *Ideology and Politics in Contemporary China*. Seattle: University of Washington Press, 1973.

_____. *Peasant Nationalism and Communist Power*. Stanford: Stanford University Press, 1962.

Kau, Michael Y. M., ed. *The Lin Piao Affair*. White Plains, N.Y.: International Arts and Sciences Press, 1975.

Levenson, Joseph R. *Confucian China and Its Modern Fate*. Berkeley: University of California Press, 1964.

Lewis, John Wilson. *Party Leadership and Revolutionary Power in China*. New York: Cambridge University Press, 1970.

Lieberthal, Kenneth. *A Research Guide to Central Party and Government Meetings in China, 1949-1975*. White Plains, N.Y.: International Arts and Sciences Press, 1976.

Lindbeck, John M. H., ed. *China, Management of a Revolutionary Society*. Seattle: University of Washington Press, 1971.

Mao Tse-tung, *Selected Works*. 5 vols. Peking: Foreign Languages Press, 1977.

Maxwell, Neville. *India's China War*. New York: Pantheon Books, 1971.

Mehnert, Klaus. *China Returns*. New York: E. P. Dutton & Co., 1972.

Mu Fu-sheng. *The Wilting of the Hundred Flowers*. New York: Praeger Publishers, 1963.

Myrdal, Jan. *Report from a Chinese Village.* New York: Random House, 1965.

_____, and Kessle, Gun. *China: The Revolution Continued.* New York: Pantheon Books, 1971.

North, Robert C. *Chinese Communism.* New York: McGraw-Hill Book Co., 1966.

Oksenberg, Michel, ed. *China's Developmental Experience.* New York: Praeger Publishers, 1973.

Peck, Graham. *Two Kinds of Time.* Boston: Houghton Mifflin Co., 1950.

Reischauer, Edwin O., and Fairbank, John K. *East Asia: The Great Tradition.* Boston: Houghton Mifflin Co., 1960-65.

_____, and Craig, Albert M. *East Asia: The Modern Transformation.* Boston: Houghton Mifflin Co., 1960-65.

Robinson, Thomas W. *The Cultural Revolution in China.* Berkeley: University of California Press, 1971.

Scalapino, Robert A. *Asia and the Road Ahead.* Berkeley: University of California Press, 1976.

_____, ed. *Elites in the People's Republic of China.* Seattle: University of Washington Press, 1972.

_____, ed. *The Communist Revolution in Asia,* 2nd ed. Englewood Cliffs, N.J.: Prentice-Hall, 1969.

Schram, Stuart R. *Mao Tse-tung.* Baltimore, Md.: Penguin Books, 1968.

_____, ed. *Authority, Participation, and Cultural Change in China: Essays by a European Study Group.* New York: Cambridge University Press, 1973.

Schurmann, Franz. *Ideology and Organization in Communist China,* 2nd ed. Berkeley: University of California Press, 1968.

_____, and Schell, Orville. *The China Reader,* 4 vols. (vol. 1, *Imperial China;* vol. 2, *Republican China;* vol. 3, *Communist China;* vol. 4, *People's China,* (this volume also prepared by David Milton and Nancy Milton) New York: Random House, 1967, 1974.

Schwartz, Benjamin. *Chinese Communism and the Rise of Mao.* Cambridge, Mass.: Harvard University Press, 1961.

_____. *Communism and China: Ideology in Flux.* Cambridge, Mass.: Harvard University Press, 1968.

Selden, Mark. *The Yenan Way in Revolutionary China.* Cambridge, Mass.: Harvard University Press, 1971.

Service, John S. *The Amerasia Papers: Some Problems in the History of US-China Relations.* Berkeley: University of California, Center for Chinese Studies, 1971.

Snow, Edgar. *Red Star Over China.* 1938 Reprint. New York: Grove Press, 1961.

Solomon, Richard H. *Mao's Revolution and the Chinese Political Culture.* Berkeley: University of California Press, 1971.

Starr, John Bryan. *Ideology and Culture.* New York: Harper & Row, 1973.

Taylor, Jay. *China and Southeast Asia.* New York: Praeger Publishers, 1974.

Terrill, Ross. *800,000,000: The Real China.* New York: Dell Publishing Co., 1971.

Townsend, James. *Political Participation in Communist China*. Berkeley: University of California Press, 1968.

_____. *Politics in China*. Boston: Little, Brown and Co., 1974.

Treadgold, Donald W., ed. *Soviet and Chinese Communism: Similarities and Differences*. Seattle: University of Washington Press, 1967.

Tuchman, Barbara W. *Stilwell and the American Experience in China, 1911-45*. New York: Macmillan, 1971.

Van Ness, Peter. *Revolution and Chinese Foreign Policy*. Berkeley: University of California Press, 1970.

Van Slyke, Lyman P. *Enemies and Friends: The United Front in Chinese Communist History*. Stanford: Stanford University Press, 1967.

Wakeman, Frederic. *History and Will*. Berkeley: University of California Press, 1973.

Whiting, Allen S. *China Crosses the Yalu*. New York: Macmillan, 1960.

_____, with Dernberger, Robert F. *China's Future*. New York: McGraw-Hill Book Co., 1976.

Whitson, William. *The Military and Political Power in China in the 1970s*. New York: Praeger Publishers, 1972.

_____, with Huang, C. *The Chinese High Command*. New York: Praeger Publishers, 1973.

Whyte, Martin K. *Small Groups and Political Rituals in China*. Berkeley: University of California Press, 1974.

Wilson, Dick. *Anatomy of China: An Introduction to One Quarter of Mankind*. New York: Weybright and Talley, 1968.

_____, ed. *Mao Tse-tung in the Scales of History*. New York: Cambridge University Press, 1977.

Witke, Roxanne. *Comrade Chiang Ching*. Boston: Little, Brown, and Co., 1977.

Yang, C. K. *Chinese Communist Society: The Family and the Village*. Cambridge, Mass.: M.I.T. Press, 1969.

JAPAN/KOREA

Austin, Lewis, ed., *Japan: The Paradox of Progress*. New Haven, Conn.: Yale University Press, 1976.

Baerwald, Hans H. *Japan's Parliament*. Cambridge, Mass.: Cambridge University Press, 1974.

_____. *The Purge of Japanese Leaders under the Occupation*. Berkeley: University of California Press, 1959.

Borton, Hugh. *Japan's Modern Century*. 2d ed. New York: Ronald Press Company, 1970.

Buck, James H., ed. *The Modern Japanese Military System*. Beverly Hills, Calif.: Sage Publications, 1975.

Brzezinski, Zbigniew K. *The Fragile Blossom: Crisis and Change in Japan*. New York: Harper & Row, 1972.

Cole, Allan B.; Totten, George O.; and Uyehara, Cecil. *Socialist Parties in*

Postwar Japan. New Haven, Conn.: Yale University Press, 1966.

Cole, Robert E., *Japanese Blue Collar: The Changing Tradition.* Berkeley: University of California Press, 1971.

Chung, Kyung Cho. *Korea, The Third Republic.* New York: Macmillan, 1971.

Curtis, Gerald L. *Election Campaigning Japanese Style.* New York: Columbia University Press, 1971.

Dimock, Marshall E. *The Japanese Technocracy.* New York: Walker/ Weatherhill, 1968.

Duus, Peter. *Party Rivalry and Political Change in Taisho Japan.* Cambridge, Mass.: Harvard University Press, 1968.

Emmerson, John K. *Arms, Yen, and Power.* New York: Dunellen Publishing Co., 1971.

Endicott, John E. *Japan's Nuclear Option: Political, Technical, and Strategic Factors.* New York: Praeger Publishers, 1975.

Fairbank, John K.; Reischauer, Edwin O.; and Craig, Albert M. *East Asia, the Modern Transformation.* Boston: Houghton Mifflin Co., 1965.

Fukui, Haruhiro. *Party in Power: The Japanese Liberal Democrats and Policy-Making.* Berkeley: University of California Press, 1970.

Hanks, Alvin L. "A Comparative Study of Municipal Administration in Japanese and American Cities." Unpublished manuscript, 1972.

Henderson, Gregory. *Korea: The Politics of the Vortex.* Cambridge, Mass.: Harvard University Press, 1968.

Ike, Nobutaka. *Japanese Politics: Patron-Client Democracy.* 2d ed. New York: Alfred A. Knopf, 1972.

Japan, Government of. *The Defense of Japan, 1976.* Tokyo: The Defense Agency, 1976.

_____. *The Defense of Japan, 1977.* Tokyo: The Defense Agency, 1977.

_____. *Information Bulletin, 1973.* Tokyo: Ministry of Foreign Affairs, 1973.

_____ *The Japan of Today.* Tokyo: Ministry of Foreign Affairs, 1976.

Kim, Se-Jin. *The Politics of Military Revolution in Korea.* Chapel Hill: University of North Carolina Press, 1971.

Kishimoto, Koichi. *Politics in Modern Japan.* Tokyo: The Japan Echo, Inc., 1977.

Kubota, Akira. *Higher Civil Servants in Postwar Japan.* Princeton, N.J.: Princeton University Press, 1969.

Langdon, Frank E. *Politics in Japan.* Boston: Little, Brown and Co., 1967.

Langer, Paul F. *Japanese National Security Policy: Domestic Determinants.* Santa Monica, Calif.: Rand Corporation, 1972.

Livingston, Jon; Moore, Joe; and Oldfather, Felicia, eds. *Postwar Japan, 1945 to the Present.* New York: Pantheon Books, 1973.

Maki, John M. *Court and Constitution in Japan.* Seattle: University of Washington Press, 1964.

_____. *Government and Politics in Japan.* New York: Praeger Publishers, 1962.

Mosley, Leonard. *Hirohito, Emperor of Japan.* Englewood Cliffs, N.J.:

Prentice-Hall, 1966.

Nakane, Chie. *Japanese Society*. Berkeley: University of California Press, 1970.

Nam, Koon Woo. *The North Korean Communist Leadership, 1945-1965: A Study of Factionalism and Political Consolidation*. University, Ala.: University of Alabama Press, 1974.

Reischauer, Edwin O. *Japan, The Story of a Nation*. New York: Alfred A. Knopf, 1970.

——. *The Japanese*. Cambridge, Mass.: Harvard University Press, 1977.

Richardson, Bradley M. *The Political Culture of Japan*. Berkeley: University of California Press, 1974.

Scalapino, Robert A. and Masumi, Junnosuke. *Parties and Politics in Contemporary Japan*. Berkeley: University of California Press, 1967.

——. *The Japanese Communist Movement: 1920-1965*. Santa Monica, Calif.: Rand Corporation, 1966.

Sebald, William J., with Brines, Russell. *With MacArthur in Japan*. New York: W. W. Norton & Co., 1965.

Sheldon, Walt. *The Honorable Conquerors*. New York: Macmillan, 1965.

Thayer, Nathaniel B. *How the Conservatives Rule Japan*. Princeton, N.J.: Princeton University Press, 1969.

Tsurutani, Taketsugu. *Political Change in Japan*. New York: David McKay Co., 1977.

Vreeland, Nena and Shinn, Rinn-Sup, et al. *Area Handbook for North Korea*. Washington, D.C.: United States Government Printing Office, 1976.

Ward, Robert E., ed. *Political Development in Modern Japan*. Princeton, N.J.: Princeton University Press, 1968.

Whitaker, Donald P., et al. *Area Handbook for Japan*. Washington, D.C.: United States Government Printing Office, 1974.

Yanaga, Chtoshi. *Big Business in Japanese Politics*. New Haven, Conn.: Yale University Press, 1968.

——. *Japanese People and Politics*. New York: John Wiley & Sons, 1956.

Index